My Soul's Embrace

Rev. Cathi Burke

authorHOUSE®

AuthorHouse™
1663 Liberty Drive
Bloomington, IN 47403
www.authorhouse.com
Phone: 1 (800) 839-8640

Published by AuthorHouse 03/02/2018

ISBN: 978-1-5462-2991-9 (sc)
ISBN: 978-1-5462-2992-6 (hc)
ISBN: 978-1-5462-2993-3 (e)

Library of Congress Control Number: 2018902416

Print information available on the last page.

Table of Contents

Divine Dedication

I dedicate this book to my dear Mother, Susan Maria Giannino, who taught me the richest of lessons, helping my Soul to grow and transform.

*Also to my beloved husband, Walter, who brought me
Cristina, our beautiful daughter, and to my students, clients,
spiritual teachers and all of my Soul family who taught me
the greatest lessons and how to love unconditionally.
A Special thank you to Susan Taylor for her
part in editing my Souls Embrace*

Preface

My purposes for writing this book is to have you the reader become aware and re-connect with the beauty and the light of your Soul. Throughout this book you will hear true stories that will help you to process your own history. You will begin to connect with your deepest Soul yearnings, and re-connect with a part of you that may have gone to sleep. As my Soul reaches out to yours, we will partner together, filled with intention and light, as you rediscover just how cherished and loved you truly are, and how Divine Spirit delights in connecting with your true Soul essence and purpose.

At the beginning of each chapter you will see the Lotus flower – This sacred flower grows in muddy water and rises above the surface to bloom with remarkable beauty. Untouched by the impurity, the Lotus symbolizes purity of heart and mind, and the expansion of the Soul. Like the Lotus may your Soul grow into its perfection and may you live a prosperous and abundant life here on Earth and beyond.

I suggest while reading this book that you keep a journal by your side. There will be many opportunities for you to go within and connect deeply with your Soul.

Each chapter begins with a special channeled affirming statement that will connect you to the writings in each chapter.

Special Prayers of Soul Expansion will be at the end of each chapter, as well *My Soul's Embrace Review*. This will keep you focused and moving forward, bringing you clarity and guidance towards your Soul Mission and Purpose.

Remember to honor your feelings and emotions as you read each chapter knowing that your Angels and Soul Guides are right by your side and that you are supported and cherished by them all.

Be assured that your Soul loves you completely, supporting the lessons that you brought in this lifetime to learn and grow from. Your Higher Self also helps you to stand outside of ourselves and observe what is going on. So express your emotions in a healthy way - write, chant, and talk about how you feel, and remember that your Soul is so much bigger and stronger than all of your emotions put together.

The Lightness of my Soul

My Soul much like a feather
So light and filled with life
So ready to expand and fly
And put aside all strife
For deep inside my Soul is filled
With gifts for all to see
And like the little feather
So light, so fine, so free
I know its time for me to fly
Above what I now see
So like the feather I will float
In pure and trusting faith
My path is open and I can see
There is no time to waste
My Soul is ready, the time is right
I spread my wings and Fly
I have arrived, I celebrate
My Soul's true beauty and light

Many Blessings, Cathi

A special channeling from the Angel of Grace Anachel

"I expand my Soul through the power of Grace"

"I am here to place you on your Soul's Path of Grace, a path that will always be available to you in each and every moment of everyday. As your Soul's path expands you will begin to see that life can be simple, and that your day can flow with ease. I only ask that you be willing to leave the old behind to welcome the new. Stop for a moment now and breathe, quiet your mind, and allow God's loving energy to flow from the heavens above as you are joined with the essence of Source. Together you will celebrate in this quiet time, and your Soul will take you exactly where you desire to go. No struggle or effort is needed, just a pure light and loving heart that is ready and willing to receive.

The light from Divine Source shines down upon you now as you give me permission to open the pathways to grace and to God. You will begin to feel lighter, and more confident as faith will be anchored deep within your heart and Soul. Your intuition will expand and your Soul will listen as it acts upon each wondrous clue that presents itself to you. Great movement will take place, and your Soul will flow along the path of grace as it expands out into a world filled with wonder and delight.

As you relax and breathe, your Path of Grace will be placed before you and with each step you take you will become closer and closer to that which is your true perfection. The path of grace is now open for you, so take my hand, and together we will step onto this golden path of light knowing that you are being divinely guided for your highest and best each moment of everyday.

Much Love,
Anachel

Introduction

"I am one with God and worthy of all good things"

I feel blessed to have had all the many experiences that have made me who I am today. Many of course, were not easy and the changes were constant, but as I know now, a bigger and more divine plan was unfolding as my Soul was ready to experience each day as a transformation and new beginning. My goal in writing My Soul's Embrace is to share a wealth of deep spiritual knowledge from my perspective as an Interfaith Angel Minister, Creative Life Coach, Spiritual Teacher and Healer acknowledging the spark of divinity in me, and in you.

Over the years, the many spirit filled classes, workshops, seminars and degree programs that I undertook, guided me and helped me to connect deeply with my heart and my Soul. My physical body had also taught me many lessons. From the age of twenty when I took my first Transcendental Meditation classes to help alleviate back pain and stress, my journey has been a pure and enlightening adventure of the Soul. If I were to look back upon my childhood, I would have never imagined just how far I could grow, but as they say, the proof is in the pudding, and my Earth journey has been richly filled with experiences, adventures and Soul expansion.

My greatest hope is that you can connect with the many stories and lessons that I have learned over the years, knowing that your Soul is filled with a similar kaleidoscope of experiences that provide the most profound lessons, leading to glorious spiritual growth.

While reading this book you will be invited to venture deep inside and to use the resources that resonate with your Soul. I ask that you be willing to expand your body, mind and Soul and join me, as together we embrace this beautiful journey. My Soul is happy to share and lead you to understand and appreciate the profound and wonderful being that you truly are.

And so it is!

Chapter One

My Soul's Entry into Earth School

"My Soul embraces all of life"

I joined the world on December 27th 1953 in a small southern town in Wilmington, Delaware at 4:04 in the afternoon. The weather had been threatening to rain, but had held off as the wind blew gently through the trees outside of the delivery room. Clouds seemed to be parting swiftly and the skies began to brighten as patches of blue sky began to peak through. It was then that my Soul looked down from the Heavens knowing it was time for me to rejoin the Earth plane. My birth had not been an easy one. My mother had been sedated and had a very hard time releasing me from the womb. The doctors used forceps to bring me into the world and there was a great struggle to separate. At that point my tiny Soul looked around and made the assumption that life was important and worth the struggle! My mother fell off to sleep now exhausted, no longer able to keep her eyes open.

Out in the waiting room my father waited to hear the news. Finally he could see the doctor walking towards him. The doctor reached out for my dad's hand and said "Congratulations Mr. Giannino, you have a beautiful baby girl" and with a grin that spread from ear to ear he asked;" How is my wife?" The doctor replied "She's very tired, but otherwise fine. Come with me, I will have the nurse take you to see her." The nursery was full of babies both male and female, cries of all types were permeating through the walls, but all Mr. Giannino was looking for was his baby girl. As they turned the corner they gazed through the glass where all the babies lay. So many of them, he thought, which one could she be? His eyes roamed each corner of the room and then finally in the center of the second row, he saw her. I was told that I had light golden wisps of hair around my head, and to dad I was the most beautiful baby in the world. The doctors told him of my ordeal. "She sure put up a good fight. A few times we almost lost her, but she never gave up." "She will be strong willed and full of life," my father replied and the doctor nodded. For as I pushed my little body from my mother's womb into the world I knew on some level that I was a survivor and would always find my way.

Embracing my Soul Family

Growing up in a large New England Italian Family was quite an experience. Emotions ran high and love was strong. I can remember my grandparents always finding something to argue about, but you knew under it all they truly loved one another. My grandmother was the first love of my life. She was the one who truly knew how to take care of me, and I loved her with all of my heart. Little did I know that this small built Sagittarian woman, who was filled with knowledge and wisdom, would be such a driving force in my life. She loved and cared for me like no other.

My mother was there as well, but Nana had the strength, Nana had the power, and Nana had the wisdom. Even as a small child I remember feeling her presence and feeling safe. I wanted to be just like her, and I wanted her to be with me always, and so the lessons began to unfold. Gift after gift would appear throughout my life, many that were harsh and traumatic, some were truly divine. Oh and the lessons, so many lessons. When I look back over the years I often think "Wow if only I knew what I know now, how different it would have all been" and the gifts continued to flow as the lessons began to unfold, one by one, one after the other.

By the age of two, I had grown accustomed to being pampered and loved. One of the first of many grandchildren to be born, I was one of the favorites and my aunts and uncles adored me. My mother was one of nine, and I was receiving special attention from each one. I know that in my two year old mind, I felt as if I were the luckiest girl in the whole wide world. I felt as if I had hit the jackpot, as my life was filled with a kaleidoscope of loving experiences. Most weekends were spent at my grandparents where the whole family would gather to eat, talk, cavort, and share. It was a grand party and I was in the center of it all. I loved the excitement and the feeling of security. I loved feeling so loved. I adored my family and they adored me. What more could anyone ever need or want. My Soul was confident, as I fully embraced the love and the joy that surrounded me.

The lessons begin

Shortly after my third birthday, my father received word that he was being transferred to Hartford, Connecticut. The day we moved was one of the most traumatic days of my life. Why was this happening? And where would my aunts and uncles be? And what about Nana? Was she coming with us? I felt so lost and so out of control. Deep within my heart I felt great sadness and pain. I remember thinking why did it hurt so much? And why was nobody paying any attention to me? Sure they had given me breakfast and lunch and someone was keeping an eye on me, but for the most part, my parents were only concerned about one thing, getting settled in their new home. That day was a turning point for my young Soul, as beliefs began to build and my once perfect life began to feel more like a nightmare.

It felt as if I were being punished. I felt sad and abandoned. All I knew was that I was being taken away from my beloved grandmother and everything and everyone I held dear. It was my first sense of loss in this lifetime and it hurt down to my very core. Once we had moved into our new home I remember crying and asking for Nana. It was at those times that my mother would feel sorry for me and pick up the phone to call her. I just needed to hear her voice. This would soothe the both of us, but that didn't last very long, for the telephone bill grew and dad wasn't happy. Perhaps it was then that my Soul was being given the opportunity to learn patience and trust.

The days turned into months and I have to admit it was a lovely little red house, with a nice yard and a swing set out back, and it was there where I meet my first spirit friend Patti. Till this day I can remember her long red hair and freckles and how she used to call my name. "Cathi Ann, Cathi Ann" come and find me. "She was a welcome surprise as I began to become more comfortable with my new surroundings. I can remember my mother telling me when I got older, that I would sit for hours and play with my imaginary friend, and would say her name. Mom thought it was cute and began to talk to dad about having a sister or a brother for me. "Cathi is lonely and needs a sibling," and dad would say "All in good time."

When I look back and think about my spirit friend even at the tender age of three, I know that she was a guide and a spirit who was there to help me and show me that I was truly never alone. As the days passed by, the tears grew less and less, and Patti occupied my time with fun and great conversation. Of course looking back I truly can't tell you everything that she said, but she continues to be a guide for me today. The gifts of mediumship were unfolding, and it would take many years before I actually began to put them to good use.

My grandparents and my aunts and uncles began to visit most weekends and a great deal of the pain began to subside. I had overcome my first true loss, and had made a new and lasting friend in the meantime. Looking back it's funny because no one really believed that I could see Patti. She was a figment of my imagination they would all say, and many would tell my parents that I was a very creative and artistic child. The truth of the matter was that I could see Patti and my Soul could feel her as the gifts from this first encounter would follow me throughout my entire life.

~~~~~~~~~~~~~~~

For many who are reading this book, you will find that your greatest gifts began at a time in your life when you were going through challenges. Great lessons are an opportunity and eventually you will see that there is a time and a purpose for everything. The timing of these gifts was orchestrated by your Soul, and as you embrace each one of these gifts, your Soul stirs with delight, for it knows you are "Growing" in the right direction. The Soul holds great hope for each of us, and never gives up. Through the many lessons, emotions, and traumas that we experience throughout our life, it is our Soul that becomes the compass for our existence and with great conviction and wisdom tries to guide us towards the path of wholeness and wellbeing.

So join me now on this special Journey of the Soul, remembering that your Soul is our most precious gift on Earth and beyond. It is your vehicle of light that travels with you lifetime after lifetime, and it knows you better than anyone. Throughout this journey you will receive Twelve Soul Keys, which if used daily can bring forth greater understanding, healing and enlightenment.

A channeled message from Spirit

As the Soul is born it is filled with potential, like a flower whose seed has been planted deep within the fertile soil, it begins to experience the warmth of the sun, the cooling rain, and the nourishment of the Earth, and so the Soul begins to experience life. It is fed and nourished by all of life, each and every experience is food for the Soul, and as it begins to blossom it yearns for acceptance and authenticity. The Soul holds the wisdom of the ages and will take you on a magnificent and joy filled journey if it is allowed to be what it was meant to be. Cherish your Soul, allow it to guide you, as you embrace all of its many gifts, knowing that the Father/Mother God, and all of the divine walk with you both day and night.

Great gratitude fills my heart and Soul, each time that I am given special messages from my Angels and Guides. My Soul feels honored and blessed to be a vehicle for their light and love.

You are a Shining Star!

From the beginning of time, stars have filled the universe with their life giving qualities. They twinkle and shimmer through the night sky and are filled with potential and life. As they expand and eventually explode, a process known as a supernova, they fill the universe with stardust which to me is God's way of spreading life force energy into the universe. Each particle of that star becomes shaped into what we call the human body, and when the universe was formed this very star dust became the building blocks for your physical body and your form. The Soul gently enters this magnificent creation which is you, for at your birth you begin to vibrate to the energies of the stars, waiting to explode, waiting to share your sparkle, and shine with the world.

Your Soul is alive

Your Soul is the part of you that never dies. It is the part that knows all that is, and has lived with you many times. It is the part that never disconnects from the God source. It is wise and all knowing. Your Soul is the part of you that is omniscient, omnipresent, and omnipotent. Your Soul is the part of you that is God.

Your Soul is waiting

Stop for a moment or two now, and bring your attention to your heart center. It is said that the Soul pulsates deep within the heart, so take a gentle breath into your heart space and relax. Take another gentle breath in as you begin to feel the pulsating energies that lay deep within your heart. Rub your hands together briskly now and place them beneath your left breast in a place I like to call deep heart and Soul. Now with each breath in go a little deeper. What colors do you see? How does your heart space feel? Invite your Soul to come forward as you begin to feel its shimmering light and energy. Be with your Soul, allowing its energy to permeate throughout your body. Continue to breathe and receive. Feel your Soul expanding, as it comes alive. Now let's take it one step further and ask your Soul its name. See what comes forth and write it down in your notebook. Now from this day forward you can call upon your Soul with ease, calling it by name, and feeling it come alive. You have just experienced your Souls essence! Congratulations. Practice this daily, as you begin to ask your Soul questions and receive answers from this deep and loving place within your heart.

The Soul lessons of My Youth

As far back as I can remember I was always asking why? Why are we here? And what are we supposed to be doing? I knew I could see and feel energy, and I knew that there was so much more going on than I could ever imagine. Born an Empath, I guess I just wanted to know the true meaning of my life. For years I questioned my existence, knowing that somewhere there was a divine universal plan. Many didn't have answers for me, and told me that I was such a deep thinker, and to just take life day by day and go with the flow. I was a true baby boomer, living in the Beaver Cleaver generation where it was better to be seen, and not heard. In my teens I was neither a hippie nor a jock, and thought of myself as a normal kid with good values, a kind heart, and lots of determination. I remember in the late sixties and early seventies looking forward to traveling the world and searching for answers.

Born under the sign of Capricorn, it was natural for me to want to climb the ladder of success, and it wasn't until later in life that I realized that my Soul had other plans, and that my success would be more in the humanitarian field. I had never really considered marriage or children, and had studied business all through high school. Graduating from business school, and planning a career in corporate America, I began working in offices, applying what I had learned, but for some reason never felt happy or satisfied at the end of the day. There was just something missing. So I started asking more questions, and began to see that there was so much more to my Soul's mission and purpose.

At age twenty, I decided to study Transcendental Meditation to relax and connect deeper with my spiritual guides. It was an amazing training and taught me how to tune out the world for a period of time, and venture deep within, allowing myself to just be. Since meditation is a huge part of what I offer at my spiritual center, I believe I was being set-up by my Soul in more than one way, as I would later become a teacher of meditation and journey work.

Puppy love and the Soul

At age fifteen, I met Walter Burke, who was destined to become my husband. I remember how much we loved each other as teenagers, and how much fun we had. We had so much in common at the time and he adored me. I felt as if I was on top of the world. We were Soul mates, feeling that we would be together forever. By the end of my senior year in high school however Walter wanted us to get married. Marriage always scared me, maybe because of all I saw as a child. Marriage to me meant responsibility and a time to grow up. I was still trying to figure out who I was and what I wanted to do with my life and marriage just didn't seem like an option. I began to feel pressured by Walter and the resentment started to build. At one point I remember taking off the friendship ring he had given me and handing it back to him. "Walter, I don't want to get married right now." He smiled and placed the ring back on my finger. This went on for almost a year and several times I had told him that I wanted to take a break but he never listened.

Then on Christmas day in the mid seventies Walter brought a huge gift box into the house. Inside was another box, and yet another until finally I found a small red velvet box and opened it. My heart pounded, a bit of this was excitement and a whole lot of fear. I wasn't ready to get married, I was barely twenty years old, and I was still trying to figure out what I wanted to do with my life. I swear on that day, my Soul stood still. I felt a deep foreboding in the center of my gut, and my Soul was screaming as if it were trying to jump out of my chest. I didn't know what to do. All of my high school friends were getting married. A few had already tied the knot and it felt like it was my obligation to be next. So I opened the box and there was a beautiful pear shaped diamond staring back at me. It was so delicate and pretty. It shimmered and shined and I could feel the love emanating from its tiny facets, like a crystal ball, ready to predict my future. What could I do but say "Yes." Walter was so happy. His dream had come true, and yet something inside of me felt sad and very alone.

From that day forward it was all about planning the wedding. It was to be on September twentieth in Randolph, Massachusetts at the Lantana. We had gone and made all the plans. I picked out everything I wanted and was able to find a beautiful sample gown in Boston that fit me to a tee. Part of me was getting excited, but another part of me was still screaming "No"!

I had adopted a set a beliefs over the years that just wouldn't allow me to listen to myself. I didn't trust what was going on inside of me, and thought that everyone else knew what was best. I mean Walter was a great guy, a good catch and he adored me. What else could a girl want? I had been deeply hurt in the past by several boy friends that had professed their love and cheated on me, so in light of that, Walter was my Prince Charming. I truly believed it was the right thing to do. So the days passed and the wedding got closer. I had my two closest friends as bride's maids, my soon to be sister in law Marge and my sister Suzy as the maid of honor. Everything was all set down to the color of the napkins. It would be a beautiful and elegant wedding. We had one hundred and fifty people coming and my dad was thrilled and of course footed the bill. My mother and father loved Walter as did everyone.

The Clock was ticking

The summer before the wedding I began to get really cold feet. I had met a friend at work who was single, and we began to go to night clubs on Friday nights. I went because I loved to dance and mingle, and she was there looking for Mr. right and it was on those special Friday nights that I felt free and would have a few drinks and dance the night away. I remember one night I was asked to dance, and said "Yes". It was all in fun so what the heck. We began to dance fast, and then a slow song came on and he was all over me. I told him I was engaged and he laughed, and said "What's this a final fling?" I tried to pull away from him and he kissed me. His hands were all over my body. I pulled away and left the dance floor. Shortly after that we left, and when I got home I went to bed and cried. I was so confused, and it seemed as if my Soul was nowhere to be found.

Was I doing the right thing? Should I get married and begin a whole new life as a wife and possibly a mother? I was only twenty years old and hadn't even had the chance to live on my own. Once again I felt a huge sinking feeling in the center of my stomach. I attributed it to fear and remember finally falling asleep and having a dream that I was married and in a long house dress doing all the chores, carrying kids around on my hip feeling really miserable. In the dream it seemed like I was in Europe in the 1700's, in a house with a dirt floor, with a husband who was more like a dictator. Looking back I believe it was a past life that my Soul was showing me. Perhaps it's why I didn't want to get married.

I woke in a sweat, thinking Walter isn't like that. He would never treat me like that and I cried even more. I didn't know where to turn, all I knew was that for some reason it just didn't feel right. It was Sunday and I was supposed to go out with some friends, but I was feeling very blue so I called and cancelled. I just wanted to be alone. I talked to my mom, who said she understood, and told me that I was just getting cold feet. "Every bride and groom goes through this. Walter is a great guy and I know the two of you will be very happy." I smiled and went back to my room even more confused and unable to process what was going on. I fell asleep and didn't wake up until dinner.

I remember my dad saying that he was looking forward to the wedding, and my sister was all excited because she was going to be my maid of honor. I got up and left the table, and decided it was all in my head, and that I was getting married and that was that.

Body, Mind and Soul Rebellion

As the summer began to come to an end, I went out one final time with my friend from work. This time we were going on a boat with a new guy that she had just met. He was from France and spoke with an accent. He was older than the both of us and very charming. I remember thinking that night that I had never really even traveled very much and would love to see Paris. He was so romantic and lit candles and made us both wine coolers. It was a balmy summer evening, and I was feeling relaxed and happy to be on the boat. We cruised around the harbor and laughed and flirted, all in good fun of course. I felt like there was so much more for me to discover. I felt light and free. This was living, and I wanted more. My friend from work was really smitten by this new guy and took me aside and said "Isn't he amazing? Can I take him to the wedding"? I gasped at the thought and after thinking about it for a moment or two, I said "Yes".

She was all excited and told him. He looked at me and said "You're getting married?" I nodded yes, to which he replied "Why? You are so young and beautiful; you have your whole life ahead of you". My heart sank deep into my chest and I didn't know how to answer him. I said to my friend, "It's time to go, I have a busy day tomorrow" and since we were close to the dock and I was driving, we did just that. The fun was over, it was time to bite the bullet and just do it! I remember climbing up the ladder and stepping over the edge of the boat and heading home. I went to bed with the question why am I doing this? And for some reason couldn't really come up with one good answer. I wanted to learn and grow and travel the world, and getting married was something I would do when I got older, when I truly felt it was the right time.

I fell off to sleep, hoping it would all be gone in the morning, but when I woke up I couldn't move. My back had locked up, and I was in a great deal of pain. 'Why is this happening to me? I didn't do anything to hurt my back. I hadn't been to the gym in over a week, and hadn't fallen or done anything that I could think of that would do this to my back. I crawled out of bed and went into the kitchen in great pain looking for some aspirin. My mother was at the table having her morning coffee and asked me what was wrong. I told her about my back and she frowned. "Well that's not good. You will be getting married in less than a month. You can't go on a honeymoon like that!" The words pierced my ears and at that moment they actually hurt. "Honeymoon? Is that all you can say"? Communication was not one of my family's greatest attributes. So here I was with another complication. Why are you doing this to me God? Did I do something wrong? Did I make you mad? I felt as if I was being punished. So the days went by and my back pain continued. Never once did I think that my Soul was trying to tell me to slow down and listen.

Day after day the pain got worse, until one day a friend of the family told my mom about a chiropractor that her husband had gone to with great success, and so I made the appointment to see him. He took x-rays and told me that I had a birth abnormality and had an extra disc at the bottom of my spine, and that it was herniated. He asked me if I had done anything to have this happen and I told him "No. I haven't done anything; I just went to bed and woke up this way". He smiled and said, "Maybe your body is trying to tell you something"! It's funny because looking back now I can see that he was trying to get me to listen and tune into my body and my feelings. Dr. Joe was my first experience with holistic medicine and the mind body connection. I remember he taught me so much, and as I headed home I wondered how do you tune into your body? What does that mean?

I will never forget the day of my wedding, my throat was sore and my back hurt and I was about to get my monthly friend! Wow what more could a girl want? It was times like these that I felt cursed or just plain unlucky! And the wedding was at six p.m. I called the doctor who gave me a prescription for penicillin. I took it along with my aspirin for pain and cramps and dressed for the wedding. The bride's maids showed up at the house and pictures were taken. I have to say I was a beautiful bride, and everyone looked spectacular. I remember us all standing on the front porch of my parents' house, lined up perfectly as pictures were taken.

My dad got down on one knee and placed a shiny new penny inside of my shoe for good luck and then he hugged me and told me that I looked beautiful and that I would be happy. "Just be happy Cathi" and I smiled. I was going through the motions but seemed frozen inside. Looking back, I know my Soul was screaming at me to stop and think about what I was about to do, and I ignored it and took some more aspirin. Right about then the car was ready and we took off for the church. It's funny because I was late! I am never late, always on time, but that day I was late for my own wedding! Walter on the other hand was always late, but not that day.

There he stood at the front of the altar with a huge smile on his face. He looked so young and so handsome. The wedding march began and I stepped forward in pain with my dad by my side. I was nervous and felt sick to my stomach yet forged onward. I will never forget the huge smile I had plastered on my face. It felt like it was stuck in place, as my heart pounded.

What am I doing? Why am I doing this? And the wedding march played on. "I know pronounce you husband and wife, you may kiss the bride". I felt Walters lips on mine and felt nothing. Is this what it's going to be like? I thought. All I felt was numb as I walked down the aisle with my new husband. I was going through the motions and was now Walter's wife.

We got into the car and headed for the reception. It was a beautiful wedding and everything was going as planned. I remember drinking a lot of wine that night and I smoked cigarette after cigarette until I almost got sick. I actually quit smoking the next day. The wedding itself was perfect and we ate and we kissed over and over again, and I was still numb! By the end of the wedding I was exhausted. It was time to go, and everyone stood around us wishing us well, my mom, my dad, my sister, my friends and family.

As I gazed at them all, my friend from work and her boyfriend were the very last ones to say "Goodbye. Good luck Mona me" he said, "May all your dreams come true". His comment made me sad, but I smiled and gave him a hug. I felt as if it was all over for me, and then my mom came over and said "Its time for you and Walter to leave for your honeymoon. I love you Cathi, have a wonderful time. You will get used to being married, just like I did." So we headed toward the Hilton in Boston for the evening and then left for Disney World, Florida in the morning. The week of our honeymoon flew by, and my body continued to act up. I continued to pop aspirin, but somehow through it all we did manage to have a good time. We were greeted upon our return by two friends from the wedding and it was back to opening presents at Walter's parents' house. My life as Walter's wife had begun.

Soul Contracts = Soul Growth

As we arrive on the earth plane as spirits in a human body, I believe that we sit with the Father/Mother God, in heaven before descending into our chosen host, having chosen our mother, our father, our siblings and all whom we meet as a Soul Family on earth. This special family has traveled together from the beginning of time, and continues to help us to grow through each incarnation, until we truly understand the meaning of unconditional love. I also believe that those who bring the greatest challenges also bring the greatest lessons and rewards, as the Soul learns to listen, make choices and to embrace each lesson as a gift.

Looking back, I can see how my Soul was preparing me for many new and exciting adventures. From my issues as a child, feeling lonely and abandoned in my marriage to Walter and the birth of my daughter, to developing my skills and Soul gifts and then opening the Angels of Light Healing & Intuitive Center, my Soul was at the helm showing me the way. Once I began to realize that I could tune into my deepest stirrings, I began to see that I had a confidant and a true friend and partnership with my Soul, as well as with God, Jesus, my Angels and the many Soul guides that have presented themselves to me over the years. I had learned to embrace my Soul's teaching and the gifts that followed.

Through the many classes, courses, seminars and degree programs I took to owning my own business and the partnership my husband sealed when we brought our daughter Cristina into the world, I could see a beautiful story unfolding. The walk down the aisle had meaning, and Walter's Soul understood that his mission was to marry me so together we could bring our daughter Cristina into the world. I now know that we are all united for many reasons. It was extremely healing to understand that my connection with my husband had a true purpose and meaning, and as I grew into the woman I am today, my life path continues to unfold and surprise me.

Each Soul contract is Heaven made before we arrive on Earth. Our Soul family is here to help us to grow and flourish. I've learned over the years to listen and follow the guidance of my Soul, as I've noticed the many synchronicities that manifest. Many times I looked back and thought how did I get here? I had never thought about owning my own business. My dream was to work for a fast paced, successful company in the city, but as my path began to unfold more and more, I could see that there was certainly an agenda of sorts forming. I was in training, just as we all are from the minute of our birth to our death and beyond. I began to think back to my early twenties, when I began to have an array of health issues, visiting doctor after doctor, trying to find out why I didn't feel well. I remember having test after test, just to find out I was o.k. I remember losing sixty pounds in my late teens, which had been a dream of mine for many years, and how it made me feel like a whole new person. I can see know how I was on the path of healing and renewal and how my body had played a huge role in my transformation.

Through all of this, my husband Walter stuck with me, and together we began to grow as a couple. I was told at one point that I would never have children because of severe endometriosis, and it was then that I began to see that I did want children. I was beginning to enjoy my married life. Perhaps my mother was right after all.

The Determined Soul

After being told I could never have children, I was determined to at least try. Walter and I had bought an adorable ranch in a local town, and we began talking about having kids. On a vacation to the Pocono's, relaxed and ready we did just that, and lo and behold I got pregnant. I knew I wasn't imagining my many symptoms and it was only when I found out it was real that I searched high and lo for answers. I had learned that when you ask you do receive, and so the more I searched the more the doors began to open. I began to see that my path and my health were very connected, and that many lessons were unfolding.

My Soul contract brought me to a Naturopathic doctor in New Hampshire, who for the past thirty six years has been my doctor and friend. Oh yes, my Soul knew just where to take me as I began working on my entire being, body, mind and Soul. This new avenue was something that the doctors I had gone to never really addressed. My whole life was turning around and my Soul was guiding me all the way. I knew that the little baby I was carrying within me had a chance now to be healthy and whole. I was on a path of true self discovery.

Nine months went by and on June 2, 1979 our daughter Cristina Michelle was born, healthy and full of life. What was even better is that she was born on my dad's birthday. It was such an amazing time in my life, and when I look back, I can see how all the pieces of the puzzle fell into place. I know deep down inside that Dr. Snow is part of my Soul family as well, and will be there with me always. Through her love and devotion, my own Soul began to grow in a whole new direction and way of life. It was then that I began sharing my new knowledge in health and nutrition with everyone.

Embracing my Soul Prayer

I no longer ignore the stirrings of my Soul, as I embrace its guidance and
gifts. I put aside all fear as I know that I will be pleasantly surprised
at the beauty and the light that begins to emanate from this place deep
within my heart. I invite a pure beam of brilliance to accompany all of
my experiences. I feel all darkness is cleared as pure grace shines through.
I open the door to my Soul's beauty and light, I open the door.
And so it is! Amen

My Soul's Embrace Review

What was the tone of your childhood?
How does it connect with your Soul lessons today?
Who were the key people in your life from the
age of birth through your teen years?
How did they play a role in your lessons and Soul growth?
What issues did you have with your physical body growing up?
How do you feel they served you? And what lessons did they teach you?

Chapter Two

A time of Soul Growth and Expansion

"My life is in perfect order at all times"

After being married for seven years to my husband Walter and bringing our daughter Cristina into the world, everything began to change. It all happened very quickly and directed Cristina and I into a whole new way of life. It all began in March of 1982 when my husband Walter began to act rather peculiar and was having some bouts of depression. As you read previously in earlier chapters of this book, Walter was a kind and generous man with a heart of gold. He loved both Cristina and I unconditionally and would have done anything for anyone as he was a good Soul who was here to make others laugh and bring joy.

For awhile it seemed as if our life together was getting better and better. We had a lovely home, a good marriage and a healthy happy three year old daughter. Life was good! Then in March several things happened which began to shift all that. Walter had been working long hours and was getting severe headaches. He wasn't much of a complainer, but I could see that he was in distress. He didn't smile much anymore and would often snap at me for no reason. He had several head traumas the year before. Both events seemed to make things worse, and I began to have visions of him leaving us. It was a tumultuous time and great fear was building within me. I tried my best to erase what I was feeling, but my psychic abilities were strong and relentless. I knew in my heart and in my Soul that a huge change was on the horizon.

I was twenty eight years old and just beginning my first Saturn return, which for most people brings forth great change and a time of growing up. I could feel my Soul was expanding for I was being pulled more and more into the holistic and spiritual field. Books, classes, seminars and more kept appearing, and I couldn't seem to get enough. Walter on the other hand was not open to any of this and was having a hard time with my enthusiasm. I remember going to him and saying, "Walter, I have a feeling that something bad is about to happen" He would always laugh and say "You worry too much." But I knew on a Soul level that this was furthest from the truth.

As the days went by I continued to have spurts of uneasiness about Walter and our life. He continued to work long hours as he became more and more unhappy. I tried to talk to him about this, but he assured me that nothing was wrong. I finally got him to agree to see a therapist friend of mine, but when we got there he simply sat down and replied "I don't know why I'm here, there's nothing wrong." It was then that I started to remember how I resisted getting married and how something inside of me was filled with fear. Maybe all that resistance was for a reason and perhaps I should have listened and trusted my inner wisdom. All I knew was that something big was happening. We were now in the therapist's office getting nowhere.

Then out of the clear blue Walter began to speak. "I shouldn't have pushed so hard to get married. Maybe we weren't ready. Maybe I should have let Cathi experience life, and maybe I was selfish, and wanted her all to myself." I looked at Walter in awe and I couldn't believe what I was hearing. He had apparently been thinking about this for quite some time. It was funny because at that point in our relationship I felt content and wanted us to be a family. I told Walter that wasn't the case and that we had a whole life together ahead of us.

We left the therapists office and drove home with little to say. Walter promised to go back the following week and to begin therapy. In that moment I began to feel some hope, that it would all turn out o.k., but something deep within me continued to tell me otherwise.

Soul transformation

In the spring of 1982, on May 5th my dear husband and Soul mate made the choice to leave the planet. He went to work and kissed me saying "I love you and Cristina" and I never saw him alive again. He had made the choice to leave, and on that sunny afternoon in May, he went to one of our favorite spots and ended his life. I actually know exactly what time it all happened because at 4:15 pm as I was making deliveries for work, I got back into the car and began to experience a feeling of release.

It was a rather strange yet freeing feeling which ran from the bottom of my feet to the top of my head. It was a sensation like no other and for a brief moment I felt as if my Soul had made a transition of some sort. I continued to finish my deliveries and headed home. When I got there my mother and father - in- law greeted me and for or a split second all seemed well with the world. I had started cooking dinner and felt good about their visit. We didn't see them very often and they adored Cristina. Time seemed to fly by and as I looked up at the clock I realized that Walter should have been home by now. We didn't have cell phones at the time and so we waited. Two more hours passed by and I started to worry.

I remember calling John, the co-worker that drove to work with Walter. When he answered the phone and I asked him if Walter was working late, his words cut through me like a knife. "Walter never came back to work after going out for coffee this morning. We just assumed he wasn't feeling well and went home and then we never heard from him" My heart started to pound and I began to have the vision of six months prior when I knew that something awful was about to happen. I began to feel sick to my stomach and then realized that Walter was gone and not coming back. The feeling I got at 4:15 that afternoon was our separation and release from each other as his Soul had made the journey home.

I didn't want to believe this but somehow deep in my heart I knew that life was about to change drastically, and it did. I turned to my in-laws and told them what Walter's co-worker had told me and we sat and waited. The hours seemed like days, and then at midnight I heard a car pull up in front of the house. It was the police, and as they came to the door I held Cristina in my arms, praying that they had good news. "Mrs. Burke, we found your husband and his car at College Pond in Plymouth." I remember letting out a scream as my mother and father in-law came running from the den. "Sorry Mrs. Burke, he did not survive the gunshot wound to the head. We believe it was self-inflicted, and we are holding the rifle as evidence." This isn't happening I thought Walter would never do this. He wouldn't leave Cristina and me. I sobbed uncontrollably and then I remembered Cristina was in my arms. She was about to turn three years old and didn't understand what was happening. I held her and said "Daddy had to go with the Angels and that God needed him in heaven." She smiled and put her head on my shoulders. I do believe in some way her Soul knew exactly what had happened. She was brave and loving and comforted me. Our whole life changed that very night, and it was then that my Soul began its magnificent journey into wholeness.

On Mother's Day 1982 we honored Walter's life. He was buried the next day. I remember feeling numb, but at the same time began to receive messages from him. He had left a note behind in the car, saying that his death had nothing to do with Cristina and I and that he loved us very much. He went on to say that it was something he just had to do, and that we should go on with our lives. He said that the time we had spent together was precious to him, and that he would always be there to watch over us. It was that letter that I kept over the years, and read over and over again knowing that what Walter had done would someday serve a purpose.

When Cristina was old enough to understand what had happened I shared the letter with her and till this day she connects with Walter as he presents himself to her in the form a Red Tailed Hawk. We feel him by our side, and know that he is in the arms of God. I began to think back to the time before my marriage and how confused I had been, not knowing why I had such a bad feeling about getting married, and now it all started to make sense. I believe our Souls did create that special contract in Heaven before getting here to bring Cristina into the world. I also believe that part of my apprehension about getting married was that, on some level, I knew what the outcome would be. Despite the shock and loss at the passing of my dear husband I was left with the gift, in the form of the beautiful little girl we brought into the world together. I thank my husband Walter for the many gifts he has afforded us both. Today as Mediums we have compassion and understanding for all who come to us, looking for guidance and completions from their loved ones in spirit.

Would I ever marry again? The answer is "Yes" for I do believe marriage can be an amazing journey of two Souls, bringing in the gifts of love, healing, and joy.

A whole new life

The Days began to turn into months and as time went by I felt very drawn to greater personal growth and my spiritual path. At the age of twenty-eight, my life mission and journey had begun to unfold. Books lined the shelves in our home and I had connected deeply with such people as Deepak Chopra, Wayne Dyer, Robert Fritz, Gary Zukov and a host of others in their field. I couldn't seem to get enough, hungry for more. It wasn't easy, but I was certain it was the perfect path for both Cristina and I. Both of us would go through many challenges over the years to come, until we began to understand why Walter had left, learning that it was a Soul contract made in Heaven, and that he had brought us as far as he could. Both Cristina and I will always cherish the time we had with him.

I soon began to connect with like minded groups and take more and more seminars, certifications, and degree programs. Life changed very quickly and I was learning all about myself, my Soul and my purpose here on earth. I could feel that although Walter's passing was painful and unexpected, that there were many gifts unfolding. My Soul had begun a whole new chapter, and although there were many times when I was filled with sadness and grief, something deep inside of me kept me going. My Angels, Guides and my Soul were showing me the way.

As I look back at that time in my life, I can see that everything that had taken place from the time I met Walter until his passing was a journey that I had agreed to take on and a pass to explore who I truly was. Walter continues to be with Cristina and me as we feel his presence and dream of him often. It has been over thirty four years since his passing, but I know that he watches over us, and loves us from beyond. The lessons that my dear husband left, although painful and challenging, opened a door of opportunity that presented lessons for both Cristina and I. As we moved forward into a whole new way of life, we were able to allow our Souls to grow and learn, and today we are two compassionate women who understand and know how to reach out to others in similar circumstances.

Together we opened the Angels of Light Healing and Intuitive Center and reach out to people daily, bringing forth guidance and healing for those who cross our path. It's amazing to know that each and every lesson our Soul goes through will bring about a shift and a change that will mold our future. Each challenge that we overcome makes us stronger and gives us the opportunity to be filled with courage and faith, moving forward into our perfection and our joy.

When we arrive on Earth, I believe we bring our Soul family back with us over and over again. With each Earth incarnation we have the opportunity once more to learn how to work and grow with these special Souls. Think about your life right now and the people that are in it. Immediate family is a huge part of our Soul circle and although at times the ones closest to us can be the biggest challenge, they also offer us the biggest Soul rewards. Throughout my Soul's Embrace I will continue to share this concept through many of my own experiences with family. Below you will find a wonderful process that will help you to understand why your loved ones, friends and even foes, are here with you at this time, and how they help you to grow and expand on your Soul Journey.

Special Soul Family

Who do you consider your Soul family here on earth? I suggest you take your Soul Journal out and title this page "My Soul Family." Now begin to write them down one by one. Stop for a moment and think of each person and the situations that surrounds you and them.

What have you learned? How has your Soul family members helped you to grow? What gifts have come from your connection with them? There is no right or wrong answers. Just keep writing as you feel your Soul come alive. Now place your hands over your heart and thank them for all that they have taught you. Begin to send pure light from your heart to theirs. If thoughts of un-forgiveness appear, bring in the light of St. Germaine and the violet flame. Send this light into each feeling, each thought, and each part of your body. You will begin to see this old stagnant energy being transmuted and your Soul will smile. Don't be surprised if your relationships begin to improve, for you have shifted the energies from victim to student, as you take the lesson and leave the rest behind.

A personal Soul Journey- Keep out your notebook

Begin to think back to a time when you were challenged in your life. Recall when you were a small child in school, when an illness presented itself, a relationship ended, or you felt you were at a crossroads in your life. Write down exactly what happened at that time and begin to see how you overcame and grew stronger through it all.

Now embrace your Soul by rubbing your hands together and getting them nice and warm. Place your hands under your left rib as you did in an earlier chapter going into deep heart and Soul, allowing the warmth to flow through. Feel your Soul stirring as it begins to open, ready and willing to give you the guidance you desire. Now with paper and pen in hand be ready to write.

Ask your Soul "What is it that I needed to learn from this situation?" and listen. Begin to write down whatever comes. No judgment! Just allow your Soul to show you the way! Continue to write until you draw a blank, and know that this is as much information as you need at this time.

Your Soul knows exactly how to guide you and over the coming days and months it will connect you to the right people, places and situations bringing you clarity and confirmation. This is a powerful Soul tool and will help you to connect anytime day or night. Remember your Soul is your very best friend, and here to bring you guidance and understanding.

An old friend from Salem!

It seemed liked an ordinary day as I headed out to the Center. I had several clients that afternoon and was looking forward to meeting one of them for the first time. I entered the center and felt a wonderful sense of peace come over me. The Angels of Light Center has always made me feel as if I had come home. We had just painted the center in the most beautiful soft turquoise and the energy was brilliant and welcoming. I was ready to start my day as a healer and so I took a deep breath in and began to set up for my first client. Shortly after the door opened a very attractive blonde woman in her forties walked in and greeted me.

The minute I saw her my heart began to pound. I thought to myself, "I know this woman from somewhere, but from where?" She smiled, and I asked her if we had met before. "No I don't believe so" she replied, and then she came over to me and gave me a huge hug. Again my heart pounded. Her energy was so familiar and I felt as if I could have sat and talked to her for hours, but we had work to do. She was meeting me to have a twelve month Angel/Soul Forecast and so I directed her over to the table and we began. As she continued to share and pick the cards that accompanied the forecast, I began to relax; she smiled often, and made me feel right at home. As I was channeling messages from her Angels and her Soul guides, I could see that she was very gifted and felt she may even be an Empath. When I asked her if she had ever done readings before she said "No, but I have thought about it many times."

She began to tell me of her re-occurring dreams of living in Salem. She felt that she had lived there offering guidance and healing. She also told me that she had to do most of her work secretly because of the town politics. Apparently these dreams were often cut off and she couldn't understand why. As her own reading continued, I could see that she was a very old Soul, and then it all came flooding back to me. I saw us together in Salem as two sisters who were very gifted in both the healing arts and psychic realms. As I continued to read and share the guidance that was coming to me, all of a sudden I asked her if she would be willing to close her eyes and go on a little journey with me. She agreed and so I made suggestions to her Soul and together we traveled back in time.

She smiled and said, "Is it possible that we were together in the lifetime I am experiencing?" And I said "Yes"! So together we journeyed back in time, and found out many things about our relationship in our Salem past-life. We began to finish each others sentences and laughed each time. We felt so comfortable together. At one point she asked me if we were crazy, and I said "No way" we are Soul family and have been brought back together again. Tears began to flow from the both of us and we hugged. We realized that we were being brought back together after a great deal of time to complete our relationship. It appeared that one of us had died of influenza and the other was burnt at the stake. We had been pulled apart, and we were being brought back together again in this life to heal the wounds of the past.

When we finally came back into the room I looked at the clock. We had been together in this past life for hours. We laughed and decided to reschedule the Forecast and went out to lunch. We have kept in touch and every once in a while meet and share our new relationship. She has moved away and lives in Florida now, but we talk every so often, knowing that our relationship is one of Soul family and never to be broken.

Embracing my Soul Prayer

As I pray for guidance and support I expand my horizons each and everyday allowing the right people, places and situations to come into my life. I begin to heal the wounds of the past, as my Soul connects to the most perfect scenarios, being open and honest with those who cross my path. I embrace my Soul family and I am willing to share my feelings, thoughts, hopes and dreams with each of them, for as I do, great karma and Soul healing will be the outcome. I open the door to this healing and joy.
And so it is! Amen

My Soul's Embrace Review

What major challenges have you experienced in your life?
Who were the key players in these challenges?
How do you feel your Soul family has helped you?
At what ages do you feel you were at a crossroads which
lead to a Soul awakening, and where did it lead to?

Chapter Three

Nourishing the Desires of your Soul

"I am one with Spirit, light, joyful and free"

The Nourished Soul

Your body is the vehicle for your Soul! Treat it with loving care! Listen to the signals from your body. Stop and ask, sit down and feel, go deep and write all about what comes to mind. Your body is your Soul's barometer and a vehicle for movement and growth. It needs to be fed with kind words, acknowledgement, and nourishing food, hydrated with plenty of clear, clean water for it to flourish.

I remember learning in one of the many classes and workshops that I had taken, that we can go right into our ache or pain and ask, "What are you trying to tell me?" "What do I need to change or do to feel better?" So I suggest right now as you're reading this book to stop for a moment and think of an area of your body, or an emotion that keeps bugging you. Bring your attention directly to the area, and ask "What do I need to know?" "What do you want to say?" Have your notebook ready to receive and don't stop writing until it all comes out.

Now look back at what your body is telling you and listen a little bit more. As you begin to listen and take advice you will see that ache, pain or emotion easily and effortlessly drift away. This is another powerful way to enhance your body, mind and Soul connection. Now you're on the way to enhancing your connection with self. Remember to ask your body for what it needs, listen, and receive, as together you support your Soul's means of growth and transformation.

Remember that your Angels and Guides know your limits! Even when you don't, they always remember that taking care of your Earthly body is a must. Then and only then will your special mission be carried out. I have to laugh because every so often when I get too busy and feel burnt out, I notice that the phone stops ringing and my meditations, classes and workshops are smaller. The minute I take care of my needs, my Angels and Guides give the go ahead and the energies begin to flow once more, bringing me more people and more growth.

Think about it, how can you be a healer, when you are the one that needs the healing? How can you give advice when you don't know what you truly want or need? So take care of your body, feed your Soul, and embrace who you are with love and compassion and you will begin to attract clients and people who are ready and willing to learn from your example.

Soul Delights

Practice daily joy, love, peace, harmony and gratitude and you will experience immediate Soul union. Sending pure white light to every situation through your heart center and bathing everything you no longer need or want in the Violet Flame will empower and nurture your Soul. Through your heart space your Soul is filled with love.

Make it fun and see the beauty that surrounds you, and remember to embrace your own beauty and light. Allow your star qualities to emerge and shine. In your notebook begin a list of some of the many things that make you happy and refer to it often during your week. Make a plan to expand your Soul delights each week. Your Soul will appreciate the adventure as pure gratitude fills your heart.

Music and dancing are the Soul's inner playmates. So sway to the music you love and watch your Soul come alive, as it expresses itself through music and movement, filling you with pure joy. As you listen to and move in the direction of your Soul, it expands and connects to your highest and most divine self. Your Angels celebrate and dance with you, and your Guides delight in the dance of your Soul.

The Rhythm of the Soul

As a teenager I can still remember yearning to come home from school so that I could go out in the back yard and dance! I would run into the house, drop my books wherever and grab my record player and my Beatles albums and dance the rest of the afternoon away. I would swing and sway and twist and shout and delight in the movement of my body. I'm sure at the time that my Soul was smiling filled with joy, movement and light. All I knew then was that it felt good and helped me to express my inner desires for movement. I remember thinking that I would dance every day for the rest of my life, or until I could no longer move! As time went by however things changed and my time wasn't as free.

As I was writing this book, it dawned on me that I don't really take much time to move to music. I love my work, and I walk most days, practice Chi Gong and love to stretch, but I really hadn't stopped to express myself through dance for a long time. At one point in my life, I had thought about becoming a professional dancer and had taken lessons. I loved watching dancers and how they moved to the rhythm, expanding their energies out from the stage into the world. Music and dance always made me feel alive and free. I can see that I do dance with my Angels, Guides and all of the divine each and every day in my work and that if I just added a bit of music and movement, no matter where I was, I could express the inner desires of my teenage Soul.

We often go about our days with little or no music or dance. I am finding that the older I get, the more important it is for me to just let go and release my energy into movement. You don't have to be a professional dancer to love to move. Recently I began to take lessons in Tai Chi and Chi Gong and love moving with the energy of the universe.

So how does your Soul want to move? What kind of rhythm do you want to create? Stop for a moment now and rub your hands together until they get nice and warm, now place them beneath the left breast in your deep heart and Soul area and begin to feel the warmth from your hands awakening your Soul. Feel your Soul stir and listen. What do you see and feel? This is the rhythm of your Soul. Ask your Soul what form of movement it likes, and see what you get.

Follow the stirring of your Soul and remember as we move our bodies, energetically we move forward in our lives as everything is connected, and body movement will begin to create a shift and a transformation. So find your own rhythm and move to the beat, as you embrace the joy of your true essence and light. Now make an appointment with your Soul and dance, move and enjoy!

Loving your self, body, mind and Soul

As you embrace all that you are, you begin to see that there are many layers that embody your being. From the seed that it planted at conception to the adult that you are now, each growth spurt has one thing in common, and that common thread is Love. When we go within and bring the energies of universal love into your heart and Soul, something very magical begins to happen. We begin to actualize who we really are, as we enhance and strengthen our being one hundred fold.

Below you will find a wonderful process that you can use daily or anytime you need a little more nurturing and self-love.

"Inner Child" Process

Begin to see yourself as a small and beautiful child, and begin to feel appreciation and love for this beautiful baby. Send the heart of your inner child a pure ray of pink and emerald green light as you begin to smile. Feel and see the deep and loving connection you have made and breathe.

Now visualize yourself a little older, perhaps in your teen years and begin to send this pure and loving pink and emerald green unconditional love to the heart and Soul of your teenager. See your heart opening fully to receive. See your Soul smile. Feel and see the deep and loving connection you have made and breathe.

Now begin to visualize yourself all grown-up and in the now. Begin to send yourself a rich beam of pink and emerald green unconditional love. See your heart open wide with gratitude for all that you are and all that you are becoming and breathe. Feel the deep connection as you begin to experience a sense of gratitude for who you are.

Now take all of this amazing love and begin to send it through your body, beginning at the top of your head down to the bottom of your toes. Feel this amazing love flowing now down through your crown, into your mind and gently flowing down upon your face. See it traveling into the center of your body, and expanding out to take in every organ, every cell, every strand of DNA and expanding out into your aura where it returns to the center of your heart fulfilled and whole. Allow yourself to just be for a few moments, allowing every inch of who you are to expand in this pure form of love. You will come back refreshed, nourished and renewed.

Your Soul is connected to the universal life force energy. Your Soul contains the blueprint for your life. This blueprint contains your purpose for coming into your body. It also contains all of the gifts and tools you need to fulfill this purpose. As you look back to the time when you were a child, many clues to your Soul's mission and purpose begin to surface.

Now it's your turn

Have some fun and answer the questions below as your
Soul expands with greater knowledge and insight.
When you were are child, what did you love to do?
What made you happy and brought you joy?

Who were your Soul teachers and how did they inspire you?
What did you yearn to be when you grew up and why?

The Soul's Agenda:

The Soul has a perfect agenda as it travels back and forth to the Earth over and over again and perhaps other galaxies as well. Below you will find some of the things that your Soul has come here to do.

Your Soul is here as a guiding light, it holds the wisdom of the ages, and knows exactly what you need at any given time. You can ask your Soul for guidance knowing that your Angels and Guides are all part of the equation. Ask your Soul to guide you in any way you need, knowing you are never alone and always being supported and loved.

Your Soul is here to empower you so be open and ready to listen. As you connect deeper with your Soul you will become more and more empowered, ego will begin to crumble, and your true self in all of its perfection will begin to emerge. Courage will be available to you at all times, and you will move forward with a sense of joy and empowerment.

Your Soul is here to co-create with you in a pure and divine partnership. It is just waiting to bring you the guidance you desire. Many gifts and great clarity are all part of what your Soul wants to share, and as you embrace your Soul these gifts expand and your authentic self emerges.

The essence of your Soul is love pure and simple. Connecting with the Soul enables divine love to resonate within the personality self. Pure energy from the Soul flourishes as love becomes the driving force in your life. As divine love flows it transforms your inner world, and your outer world reflects this back to you creating a life that is filled with love and joy. Remember what you put out comes back, so if you are embracing and loving who you are, it will come back from others ten fold.

Embracing my Soul Prayer

I pray to Divine Spirit, as my Soul extends its many gifts out into the world each and everyday knowing that a time for acknowledgement feeds its purpose. At the end of each day I will stop and see all the wonderful things I have accomplished, allowing my Soul to expand on its Earth journey, as together I walk hand in hand on a pure path of synchronicity and grace, as my Angels and Soul Guide lead the way. And so it is! Amen

My Soul's Embrace Review

In what ways do you limit your self?
What did you do that you truly enjoyed as a child/
teenager that you no longer do?
Do you give yourself time to have fun and enjoy life?
What holds you back from accomplishing this?
What would you like to begin incorporating
daily into your life to feel pure joy?

Chapter Four

Affirming the destiny of the Soul

"I believe in a future that is filled with joy"

After the passing of my husband, Walter, my Soul's mission began to unfold. In the winter of 1986, I was led to a training course in the power of pure creative thought. It was an amazing training filled with affirmation and intention, that opened my mind and formed many of my beliefs and teachings today. The course showed me through the law of attraction how to create a life that was filled with my deepest heart desires. As a Creative Life Coach, I use every ounce of these teachings on myself and with my clients.

Creating Abundance and Prosperity

After taking the course I put it into action by selling my house. I wanted to create a new home for Cristina and myself, and with intention it all began to fall into place. Then I began to use creative thought in all areas of my life, creating some of the most profound changes in my life including deeper relationships, delightful vacations and the establishment of the Angels of Light Center. Over the years, through my belief that we live in an abundant universe and that there is plenty for everyone, I have adopted a new and prosperous way of thinking. I have learned that if we believe in our goodness and the light within our Soul, all is possible. This allows us to journey together with the Angels, Guides, and all of the divine. When we remember that we are truly loved by the God Source then we partner with all of the Divine, and a form of magic appears. With this focused intention all becomes possible, and we are able to move forward with ease and grace.

As I tune deeper into my Soul, it lets me know that everything is unfolding in the right time and for my highest good. Never holding on too tightly, I continue to affirm my desires, with flexibility knowing that something even bigger and better is available. It's time for you to embrace all of creation, as you allow your Soul to expand with delight. All restrictions are lifted as you give yourself full permission to be all that you are meant to be, remembering that you are being guided to a place of pure Soul perfection.

My own Soul delights in guiding others to look deep within, connecting with that special place of divinity. I love helping each person to identify different areas of their lives where they may have experienced lack and then encourage them to build a greater belief in abundance on all levels. Once we connect deeply with our divine helpers then the right people, the right places and the right situations begin to flow to us with ease and grace. Remember you are a divine being of light and deserve to embrace your Soul and all the abundance of this magnificent universe.

Gratitude holds the key

Looking back through our lives, we see that we were taken care of in different ways. Perhaps we will remember the creature comforts of our childhood, such as food, clothing and shelter or perhaps it was on our birthday when we were given that special gift. We begin to see that we have always been taken care of, even when we thought we needed more.

For many years I have held the belief that the universe will provide, and that when we are in need, the right people and situations always show up. Even the homeless person on the street has the opportunity to go to a shelter, receive food, and hand outs from those around them. It is the power of gratitude that keeps these gifts flowing into our daily lives. When we feel grateful, like seeing the cup half full, our Soul can experience the blessings. When we feel gratitude for the littlest of things we expand our capacity to receive more.

Your Soul's energy will expand with delight when you begin to use the power of gratitude each day. Whether it's getting up in the morning to the warm sunshine or a cleansing rain, the power of gratitude will fill your day with positive, uplifting and light filled energy. Like attracts like, so you have a choice. You can look at your many blessings or concentrate on lack. Either way, you get what you place your attention on. So choose gratitude and embrace the beauty and light of the universe and its multitude of gifts.

Just a reminder that inner goals are just as important as outer goals, so remember to ask yourself the question "What do I want to change internally?" this could be a shift in your self esteem, a desire to connect more deeply with your higher self, or a goal to release your fears and move forward with courage and strength, remembering that what we change inwardly manifests in the outside world – I always say "You can't put the cart before the horse"

This special process brings your deepest hearts desires *Full Circle"* as you begin to look deep within your heart and Soul. Taking time with each area begins to bring clarity, as the wisdom of your Soul comes forth. I have used the Wheel of Life for many years, and find that the energy of the Circle brings things to fruition in the right time and for your highest good.

The Wheel of Life Process

The Wheel of Life can be divided into eight areas like a pie. As you draw a large circle begin to cut it into eight even pieces. Each piece of the pie stands for a part of your life: Family and Friends, Health, Money, Career, Significant other/Romance, Personal growth, Home environment, Fun and recreation.

Take one piece of the pie at a time and begin to think about what you are grateful for. You will begin to see just how much abundance flows throughout your life as you continue to count your blessings each and everyday, and the doors to joy will open fully.

This powerful exercise will lift your vibration and put you on the path of prosperity in all areas of your life.

Now go back to each area on the wheel one at a time, take a gentle breath in and connect with your Soul wisdom by asking your Angels and Guides to bring you into your heart space. Once you feel connected take a piece of the wheel and bring it into your heart and Soul area. Really see this area of your life, and begin to imagine your heart opening. See and feel it opening fully as rich wisdom begins to flow from your Soul into your heart space. Now ask the question;

Where does my heart and Soul want to take me at this time?

Listen, feel and begin to see the doors opening, as a clear vision of where you truly want to go will emerge.

Please don't restrict yourself: see this as a magical process filled with potential.

Next I suggest that you write down each desire/goal in your Soul journal. Label the page "I now have" as you describe each desire as if it were already received.

Here's an example: "I now have this wonderful new home, it is affordable, comfortable, and safe in a nice neighborhood, with great and helpful neighbors, near the school, with plenty of like minded children to play with Cristina."

Fill your piece of the pie up to the brim, and write in each section, holding the space for your goal or something better.

The Power of the New Moon

In many of my Soul Journeys and Soul Goal Workshops I make sure that the planets are aligned for a wonderful and energetic outcome. For the most part I begin these offerings on the New Moon, a time when we can plant the seeds of our desires, and cultivate them with affirming statements and beliefs.

It's as if you just planted a garden filled with exquisite seeds that are filled with your most perfect wishes, goals and dreams. Then your Angels, Guides and the power of your Soul go to work, and the seeds grow into opportunities which attract the right people, places and situations for each goal. I love to use the wheel of life with my clients, as it helps them to look deep within each category making a choice to expand and bring their deepest hearts' desires to fruition.

Creating our new home:

After the passing of my husband, I no longer had the desire to live in the home that we had purchased together. My Soul was urging me to sell the house and so I began to create the perfect home for Cristina and me. Through my training I had the perfect set of tools to accomplish this. I had always wanted to live in Hanover, where many of my fondest childhood memories had occurred. My dear Aunt Mary and Uncle Nick lived close by, and since they were so instrumental in my childhood and an anchor when my husband passed away, I felt compelled to stay in the area.

I began by writing down all the many things that were important to me at that time. Cristina was about to begin kindergarten so one of the main things was to be in a nice, safe neighborhood in Hanover, with a beautiful yard, and kids her own age to play with. I also wanted our new home to feel comfortable and cozy, in a quiet neighborhood, with plenty of trees. A home that was easy to take care of on one floor, close to the school, and close to my Aunt and Uncle so they could pick her up from school when I was at work. I began to create a floor plan on paper of what I felt at the time would benefit us both. The cost of the house was important and had to fit into my budget, and having good neighbors and a safe place to live was on top of the list. Well lo and behold; I received all of this and more.

I wrote it down as if it were already so, and began to visualize daily. I could feel the cozy den, the pretty yard, and seeing Cristina playing with friends on the swing set enjoying her self. I even pictured the realtor taking me to just the right neighborhood and it all showed up! Within six months we moved into our new home. I have been in my house now for close to thirty years, and each time I want to make an improvement or expand my home in some way, I use the same process. To this day it still amazes me and works every time.

So now it's your turn, what do you want to create? Take your notebook and begin to write your deepest hearts desires! Remember to let your Soul guide you, and to not restrict yourself. You are a creative being, and filled with manifestation and movement. Remember to begin your writing with:

I now have, I Am now or I now Claim.

Activating the Wheel of Life each day

After you have filled in all areas of the wheel with your deepest hearts desires you will place the wheel either on a Transformation/Vision Board or on a wall in your home where you can see it daily. Then the fun begins. First and foremost let your goals and dreams develop over time, knowing that all will unfold in perfect timing and for your highest good. Each morning before rising begin to visualize a rich golden beam of light from Source coming down through your crown and landing in the center of your heart chakra. Then expand this Source light from the center of your heart into the deep heart and Soul areas. Next allow the rich golden light to flow gently into your 3rd chakra where it begins to accumulate in the center, and once it's filled up fully begin to see it expanding out in all directions like a warm beautiful sun. I like to say "I am one with God and worthy of all good things" Now begin to direct this same light into the center of your wheel and begin to see it expanding out over all areas, with the energy of all of the Divine. Go about your day, knowing that all will unfold in the right time and for your highest and best. Expect the best and it will be so!

The Transformation Board

If you are ready to take your goals and hearts desires to the next level, then its time to build your transformation board. Simple and easy, this board is all about showing gratitude and as you expand the energies down towards your goals, dreams and hearts desires the energies will explode with possibilities. I love this process that my Angels and Soul guides brought to me, and use it in many of my sessions. Begin by making a list of all the people, places and situations you are grateful for. Once written you can begin to cut out pictures from magazines, or family photo's that fit your gratitude list. At the top of the board in large letters you can write "MY TRANSFORMATION BOARD" and then below that, "All that I am currently grateful for" with this being the beginning of your board, you can begin to fill the top half of the board in. Now right below that is the center of your board, here you will cut out and place your wheel of life. This becomes your intention and focus, harnessing the energies of gratitude to fuel the wheel. Below the wheel you can continue by cutting out pictures and positive phrase that truly expand your Soul's vision, and will remind you of what you have chosen to create. You will activate your wheel daily from above to continue to feed your goals and dreams with expansive energy.

Embracing the Soul as a Guiding Light

There is no separation in the eyes of the Soul. Each one of us is connected to the divine as together we learn and grow on our journey. Our higher self is a deep and rich part of our Soul, bringing forth great knowledge and wisdom into our emotional body, and higher mind. If we remind ourselves that everything we could ever want or need is already within us, then we can begin to expand this awareness out into the world. Once we do this, we began to believe that we are truly whole, and no longer need to be fixed! We are all teachers for one another, and are here on the Earth plane to learn, grow, and pay if forward as we share the knowledge that we have accumulated from this life and all past lives. Remember we are all special in the eyes of the Soul, and it is in sharing these gifts that our true purpose and mission are fulfilled.

We are vehicles for communication from the time we are conceived and stir inside of our mother's womb until the time we take our last breath on Earth. It is important that we listen to our deepest Soul urges and desires. I believe that our DNA is filled with every experience we have ever had, and that our Soul works through this information to bring us certain opportunities in life that we need for growth. Your Soul may urge you to make choices or take actions in areas that are least expected. It could be a desire to make a career change, to move or to end a relationship and so forth.

The ego part of our being often resists these changes out of fear, however as you connect and align to your Soul urges, and begin to trust what you are experiencing, you will find that there is an incredible amount of help available. Your Soul never gives you something you cannot handle, although it can feel overwhelming at the time. Grand and glorious lessons are formulating and as we all know, some of the hardest lessons have led to the greatest rewards. The more you take the time, attention and energy to enhance your Soul awareness and connect to your deepest desires, the clearer and stronger they become. Many times our egos get in the way of what those true Soul desires might be, and if we follow the guidance of the ego we may receive a temporary feeling of satisfaction, however this will be short lived whereas the urges of our Soul are lasting and true.

Soul Desires

As you connect to your desires, your Soul will respond and open more lines of communication within you. I love this and find it very empowering as communicating with this part of self is rewarding beyond measure. The good news is that it is not that difficult to do. Throughout My Soul's Embrace I have included a whole tool box of processes to enhance your connection. Allow each one to guide you as you plan your day. Then, see if you can find the feeling sense of those desires - and follow them. As you follow your Soul's desires, you open the door to full communication with your Soul and its divine guidance.

Respecting each Soul and its Mission

It's important for your Soul to expand and grow as it reaches out to become all that it was meant to be. Competition may often try to creep in as the ego loves to share its opinion. Try to remember that each Soul has its own special gifts and purpose: competition is only a tool for the ego and can cause pain and suffering. You are unique, and by spending time trying to be like someone else, we forgo our own Souls' beautiful gifts. Letting others inspire you however is a wonderful way to connect you to a space within and from there to identify your own hearts' desires. This is the way to truly embrace your Soul and the Souls of others.

Below you will find some wonderful tools for Soul transformation and movement. Use them daily to enhance wellbeing and connections with the Angels, Guides and your Soul.

Cleansing Process for the Soul

1. Take a gentle breath in and begin to see that above you there is a pure beacon of divine light. This light represents the Mahatma energy which is the purest and most divine love of the universe. It is rose/gold in color and it begins to flow softly down through your crown until it lands softly in the center of your heart chakra. See it expand out to embrace your entire heart, all twelve layers and every chamber of your heart until your heart appears to be filled with light. Take a gentle breath in now and anchor this love deep into your heart and Soul, as you begin to see a rich golden flame in the center of your heart.

    Bring your attention once again to the top of your head and begin to see a pure golden liquid stream of light flowing easily through your crown and gently landing on your 3rd eye, take a gentle breath in and see it expand all the way out to your aura (which is five feet out from your body) now envision it coming back and anchoring into your 3rd eye.

You will repeat this with all of your chakras

2. Expand the golden liquid light into your throat chakra, expand out to the edge of your aura and then back as your breath anchors it deep into your throat chakra.

3. Expand the golden liquid light into your heart chakra, expand it out to the edge of your aura and then back as your breath anchors it deep into your heart chakra.

4. Expand the golden liquid light into your 3rd chakra in the center of you stomach, and expand it out to the edge of your aura and then back as your breath anchors it deep into your 3rd chakra.

5. Expand the golden liquid light into your sacral chakra expand out to the edge of your aura and then back as your breath anchors it deep into your sacral chakra.

6. Expand the golden liquid light into your root chakra, expand out to the edge of your aura and then back as your breath anchors it deep into your root chakra.

7. Now expand the golden liquid light into your Earth star chakra below your feet, expanding it out to the edge of your aura and then back as your breath anchors it deep into your earth star chakra.

8. From the Earth star begin to see a pure channel that runs up the middle of your body, until it reaches your third chakra and allow it to accumulate in your center. Now expand it out like a huge ray of sunlight until it fills your entire aura until you are in a pure sphere of golden light above you, below you and around you. Allow yourself a moment or two to experience this light, and see it clearing your energy field completely. Pause.

9. Now bring it back to your center and allow it to flow all the way up to your crown where you see that your crown is open fully ready to receive all the blessing of this abundant Universe. Take

a gentle breath in and see the rich golden liquid light flow down through the channel and through your earthstar chakra and deep into Mother Earth's heart, where it will ground and anchor you.

Take your time coming back, breathe and enjoy.

The Number 8 Vibration and your Soul:

For many years now, I have been using the number eight in many of my workshops and certifications. Start to be aware of the number eight and how it begins to guide you, as it is instrumental in playing a role in your personal transformation. Your Soul is also very connected to this number, for the Soul lives on forever, and the number eight stands for infinity. The number eight is filled with the empowering energies of success and manifestation, and will help you throughout your life to expand and grow.

Feeling Stuck? Draw the figure eight/infinity symbol over and over until you feel a return of clarity. This will connect you with your Souls Wisdom and answers will begin to flow. Remember the Soul and your Angels are working together, so I often like to call upon Archangel Uriel at this time. Uriel loves to work with writers, and anything creative, as he brings forth his amazing light, shining it down upon us, bringing in the light of Source. I see Uriel placing his pure golden cloak on my shoulders, as he gently touches my heart and Soul. My creativity soars, and the blocks to my creative self- expression open wide.

Food for the Soul

Fresh lemon or lime and crisp organic greens and veggies cleanse old stagnant energies from the body and nourish and support the liver and blood. I suggest first thing in the morning that you sip on eight ounces of spring water and half of a lemon or lime.

The body is the vehicle for the Soul and when the body is cleared of stagnant energies we have a much better body, mind and Soul connection. Please use half of one or the other daily to release old layers. You may also consider taking a sea salt bath once or twice a week. This will cleanse and clear the energies within and around you and keep your Soul on its toes! Relax, and pamper yourself. Your Soul will thank you, and your energy will soar. Quiet time soothes the Soul and calms the body inviting our Soul to speak. As we tune in and listen, greater clarity and understanding are the outcome. Once again we have nurtured our Soul.

Intention is everything

Joy is a powerful catalyst to lift your vibration and thus bring forth wonderful manifestation into all areas of your life. When I wake up in the morning I love to claim joy in my day, as it sends out a wave of intention into the world, bringing the right people, places and situations my way.

I choose to have a happy, healthy and joy filled day and so it is!

Your Soul is ready to use the many tools that have been provided through divine spirit. The deeper you connect with this vital and sacred part of yourself, the more progress you will make along your path towards fulfilling the mission of your Soul. Below you will find a wonderful channeled process that my Soul guides gave to me upon awakening one morning. It will set your joy filled day into motion.

Process to Awaken Soul Joy

Begin to relax in a comfortable space and take a deep breath in. Allow this breath to travel through your entire body deep into Mother Earth's heart as you feel grounded and safe. From the top of your head to the bottom of your feet; begin to feel your body melt into the calm and peaceful energy that has been waiting to be part of your life. Feel the energies of the breath as it moves deeper and deeper into the center of Mother Earth, anchoring you in her beauty and light. The palms of your hands await, so take them and put them together. Begin to rub the palms briskly as warm and all knowing chi energy begins to build. Your hands begin to tingle as you create your divine connection. Now place one hand over your heart and the other under your breast on the left side.

Begin to feel the energies now pulsating from your hands awakening your heart and your Soul. Allow the warmth and light to pour into each area and breathe. As the warmth travels deep into heart and Soul you are awakened and your body responds. Allow yourself to remain there for a moment or two, until you feel the stirring of your Soul.

Now bring your attention back to your heart where you feel a soft beam of rose colored light building in a clockwise direction, see and feel this love expand as it begins to create a figure eight. See the rose colored light expand out even further now as the figure eight begins to connect from your heart to your Soul. Feel and see this happening as you connect your heart and Soul in a perfect dance of light and love and smile! Sit for several moments now and allow this connection to strengthen.

You may feel many different sensations and see many shapes and colors as this is taking place. I often see my Soul as a sparkling array of brilliant light, much like electricity, very illuminated and filled with excitement and movement. I like to end by using one of the Soul keys and say:

Today I will take my Soul's hand, and ask it to be fully present in each situation. I will follow my Soul's advice, as I am filled with faith and trust

Empathic Gifts of the Soul

Since the day I was born, I felt a sense of responsibility to others. I was the first born in my family and for some reason always felt as if I had to fix everything and everyone. As a small child I remember being able to feel other peoples feelings and emotions and often had a hard time discerning between their feelings and my own. As I grew older I was labeled an Empathic. Not knowing at the time how to put this gift to good use, often I felt overwhelmed and exhausted. I had to learn to balance and discern all that was flowing my way. At times this was just too much to handle, and as a child I was often caught up in the cross fires of others. I could feel my mother's fear, my dad's anxiety, my sister's sadness and my grandparent's anger. I realize now that my Soul was training me for what was to come.

Gifts from above

Throughout my own inner journey of enlightenment, I have learned and developed many tools and skills for opening the pathways for the Soul. I am a big believer in clearing and protecting one's energy field, and I am grateful for my Angels and Guides who continue to share these gifts on a daily basis. They take me on experimental journeys that have helped me to heal and understand the laws of the universe. I feel elated whenever I am given a new energetic approach to healing and protecting my energy field, and my Soul can't wait to share it with everyone.

Running on empty

From a young age, most of us are led to believe that it is better to give than to receive. Women especially, are drawn to giving too much and often times feel drained, disempowered and resentful. I have adopted the belief over the years that what is truly needed is a balance of giving and receiving. In this way we create a nourishing flow for both ourselves and others.

Over the years I have had my share of being on empty! My many life contracts had given me the opportunity to support my family and many who have crossed my path. My Soul always had a deep urge to give, and to make a difference, leaving me open to fatigue and burnout. Over the years, through my quest for balance, I have channeled many wonderful meditations and energizing techniques to overcome this burnout. Although I continue to give, I have learned to stop and give back to myself, retaining balance in my life and in my work. It has always been exciting for me to share these spiritual tools in my workshops, readings, certifications and classes. Below you will find some examples on how to replenish your physical, emotional and spiritual bodies.

Enhancing your Soul cylinders

Your Soul can be enhanced by taking care of the needs of your body, your mind and your inner spirit. We all know that time is a precious gift and in these shifting and changing times, many feel that there is never enough time to accomplish everything we desire or need to do. We tend to multi-task and sometimes feel just plain burnt out causing overload and exhaustion. Remember that your body is the vehicle for your Soul, so as you embrace this wonderful vehicle your Soul is ready to move forward on its journey. Inside of each of us is a set of what I like to call energy cylinders. These clear tubes of light when depleted can begin to feel cranky, tired, resentful, and overwhelmed.

Each cylinder expands with energy to keep us on the move, and if not replenished like a car, will cause us to stall. I was given this process one evening after coming home completely depleted of energy from a taxing day. Being in the holistic profession and an energy worker, this process made total sense, as I could connect it to the meridian system of the body.

Eight beautiful cylinders process

Begin by visualizing a clear tube of light running from the top of your head down through the center of your body, and landing at your root chakra. This is your central energy cylinder. Begin to examine this clear tube and begin to see if it's empty or full. Begin to ask yourself is my cylinder a quarter full, half full or more? Once you have seen where the light in the tube ends you can get a true sense of whether this cylinder is on empty or full.

The 8 Soul Cylinders are as follows:

Ruby Red/Safety/Security cylinder
Brilliant Orange/Abundance and Prosperity/Passion cylinder
Bright Yellow/Energy/Vitality/Worthiness cylinder
Emerald Green/Love/Appreciation cylinder
Baby Blue/Creativity /Self-expression cylinder
Indigo/Wisdom/Clarity Intuitive cylinder
Lavender/Higher Self/Divine Support cylinder
White/Life Purpose/Karma cylinder

White Light Charka expansion process

Bring your attention to your crown chakra and visualize it open and ready to receive. Imagine a beam of pure golden white light flowing down from the divine. This light is filled with life force energy. I love to picture Jesus with his hands directed over my crown pouring his pure and divine light down from his heart and Soul into mine.

You can visualize your Angels, or the heavens opening wide as the gift of life force energy pours over you. Allow this rich golden white light to flow until it moves down between the soles of your feet. Now feel and see this pure life force energy flowing back up, filling all of your energy cylinders until it reaches the top of your head. Allow it to flow even further as it expands out and around your auric field and then back down into Mother Earth. Repeat this process three times.

Your cylinders begin to fill to the brim as they come alive!

When done daily you will begin to see a pure balance of energy flowing through you to embrace your Soul. You will feel more connected with Source and your path will begin to open in miraculous ways. This simple yet powerful gift from the universe is there to be used freely anytime day or night. So use it often and enjoy.

Enhancing each chakra with the Color of the Breath process

Relax and take a few gentle breaths. Bring your attention down to the soles of your feet as you visualize a group of rich white cords flowing down into Mother Earth. Sit for a moment and feel your self being totally supported.

Now visualize a pure clear cylinder forming and moving up from between your feet through the center of your body all the way to the top of your head. This cylinder is approximately 8 inches wide and flows easily all the way up to your crown as your chakras are being encased. Start with your root chakra and the color ruby red, as you take in a full breath.

Continue to breathe in and release through your nose directing this rich ruby red light into your cylinder. See and feel your root chakra expand with delight as it is nourished and empowered. Remain at your root chakra for a moment or two, and then begin to work your way up.

Next is the brilliant orange light, breathe in and release your breath gently, as you visualize your sacral chakra cylinder being filled to the brim. You have the idea now so work all the way up. Bright yellow in your center, emerald green for your heart, soft baby blue into your throat, rich indigo into your third eye, soft lavender into your crown. One by one all of your chakras will be fed, and your energies cylinders come alive, feeling nourished and rejuvenated.

Embracing my Soul Prayer

Divine Spirit as I expand my horizons by tuning into my deepest Soul's desires, I feel you by my side. These special desires are the ones that make me smile, as my Soul expands with joy. I can feel the pull, as I give myself full permission to ask and receive. You take my hand and show me the way, as I expand my love and release my Soul's true desires out into the world. And so it is! Amen

My Souls Embrace Review

What did you learn about yourself after reading this chapter?
Do you feel you are worthy of positive change?
What seems to be holding you back from moving forward?

Chapter Five

Soul Contracts are made in Heaven

"I choose to bless, forgive and release"

I have a belief that before we enter the Earth Plane, we sit with the Father/ Mother God and plan our return. I know that our Souls have been here many, many times, and that with each incarnation we move and grow towards the perfection that we truly are. Each time we bring our Soul down to Earth we are given another opportunity to get it right, to expand our wisdom and knowledge. I also believe that we choose our parents and all those who are major players in our lives. Each person we come into contact with challenges us to learn and grow.

I would like to share some of my biggest life challenges and gifts with all of you. As you read each section, try to recall situations in your own life where circumstances have led to gifts of learning and growth.

Little Soul Sister

My sister, Susan Beth, was an old Soul who was born in the late 1950's. I was five years old and very excited about her arrival. Her birth was hard and the pain that my mother felt delivering her was so intense that she passed out several times during the birthing process.

Many shifts and changes began to happen for the whole family after the birth of my little sister. My life was about to move in a whole new direction. Shortly after my sister was born, my mother went into a deep depression, so deep that she was hospitalized and given therapies that made her forget who we were. My once happy family vanished and we were separated from one another for the next several years.

I remember the day that I was told I was going to live with my grandparents. My sister would be with my aunt and dad would stay in our home and go to work and visit mom. At first it didn't seem so bad. I was very close to my grandmother and she adored me. From the time I was born she had become my second mother, always nurturing and loving me like no other. So in my five year old mind it was kind of like a vacation. Yes, I would miss mom, my father and my sister, but I got to be with my loving and generous grandparents. As time went on I remember being afraid much of the time, but mostly I remember feeling uncomfortable in my body. I couldn't tell anyone, I just knew they wouldn't understand. It was the 1950's and the word emotion was not in the dictionary! So I stuffed all the emotions, and began to turn into a plump little five year old, holding everything inside and wishing it could all be like it used to be.

At the tender age of five I had deemed myself unlucky somehow as things seemed to get worse and worse. Being very intuitive could be helpful but in some ways was painful. I could feel a fight brewing around my grandparents, the anger my uncle was holding onto and the jealousy of my young aunt who didn't want me in the way. When I look back all I could feel and see were emotions with no place to go.

Growing up in a big Italian family, as I mentioned earlier, was a hoot. They were good people, filled with energy and determination. They came over to this country with nothing and built huge families, established themselves in the community and worked hard, I mean really hard. As I look back now on the stories of their lives and struggle, I can begin to see their possible Soul lessons. We were all interconnected, our Souls growing and learning at all cost.

Days turned into weeks, and the months just seemed to fly by. Mom's depression never seemed to leave no matter what the doctors did, and so I remained with my grandparents in a house filled with anger and upset. Looking back, I ask myself what was my Soul's lesson? What was I being taught? Well, one thing for sure, I learned how I didn't want my life to be. If only I knew what I know now. I remember that food at that point was my only friend and my grandmother was an amazing Italian cook who loved to feed everyone. As my once little body began to grow from the delicious offerings of my grandmother, I was teased and made fun of at school. We call this bullying in current times, and I was bullied constantly.

There were also kids and neighbors who lived on my Grandparents' street who thought I was pampered and spoiled. My grandmother had always dressed me in pretty clothes and for some reason this made one particular neighbor very angry. She would gather the kids in the neighborhood and instructed them to rip my clothes and throw mud on me. Yes, each day was a battle as my little Soul yearned only for peace and love. Yet each lesson, each person and each situation molded me into the person I am today.

Finally my mom began to get better and my dad purchased a new home for us in Braintree. There I would live for many years until I got married. As time passed however, it was evident that my baby sister Susan had taken on the brunt of the dysfunction. She was very sensitive, shy and although she harbored a brilliant mind and a beautiful exterior, it was very hard for her to live in the every day world. From the tender age of twelve until her passing at age of forty three, she would turn to drugs and addictions of all sorts over and over again.

Many times over the years, my family seemed to be on the verge of falling apart. Mom would go through periods when she felt normal and happy only to return suddenly to a state of depression. Dad began to travel a great deal for his work, and I can remember going to school each day wondering what I would find upon returning home. Mom would have physical issues that would put her in the hospital and all of my old feelings of insecurity and fear would reappear.

Life was a roller coaster for me and my little sister growing up, and many lessons were presented to each of us.

Perhaps my deepest lesson was becoming the caretaker. Always the responsible one, it was me who had to make the decisions for my mom, dad and my sister. Hospitals became a second home for me growing up, and whether it was mom getting over pneumonia, or my dad's many surgeries, somehow I was the one who took care of and nurtured them all. This went on for many years, throughout my marriage, after the passing of my husband and into my thirties, forties and fifties. There were times I yearned to be free, silently wishing to just take care of myself. Over and over again I swore to myself that this was the last time. That I deserved to have a life as well, and over and over again I continued to be their care taker. It took many years before I understood that my Soul's contracts were being fulfilled.

Occasionally, I had to have my sister committed for drug abuse. That was the worst of times. I now feel that my sister was teaching me how to set boundaries and I do believe she was in my life to teach me strength, and the courage to make the right choices. It had been a very long road and one evening I just said to myself and my Soul, "I am not going through this again." I could feel a shift taking place and the next morning received a call to inform me that my sister had passed away in her sleep. I was in shock, and couldn't believe what had happened. At her wake, I remember feeling her presence strongly as she communicated that she was finally whole and at peace. I could feel her appreciation for the process and her love beaming down upon me.

My sister Susan had come onto the Earth plane as a major teacher for my family and for me. Her lessons were hard, yet rewarding, and when she had taught all of her lessons her body gave up and her Soul made the journey home.

My sister taught me how to forgive, how to embrace all of life, how to love imperfection, and how to say "No." Each time I had to take responsibility for her, take her under my wing, place her in a rehab situation and use tough love, my Soul was strengthened. I was given the opportunity to stretch my abilities and access the true courage that lay deep within my heart and my Soul. Thank you my little sister. I will always love you and be grateful for your lessons, for they touched my very Soul and will never be forgotten.

Embracing Soul lessons with Mom

After my sister passed away, my mom's health became worse. Mom had suffered with depression on and off for most of her life. I remember inviting her to stay with me while we sold her house, feeling that when she got back on her feet she would get her own place, as I proceeded to place her name on the list of several senior housing establishments nearby.

Although close in many ways, my mother and I were like oil on water. She saw black, I saw white; everything was always a big struggle. I was always trying to find a way to escape from her energy, and found it very difficult to have her in my home both day and night. This of course propelled me to look deeper into my own needs and wants, and to search for holistic methods of healing. I believed in being positive and finding solutions, while mom somehow believed in struggle and drama. My sister's death had been the straw that broke the camels back.

For years, mom had tried to fix my little sister, feeling great guilt over her own illness. She blamed herself for the way my sister turned out. Here grief was overwhelming, and no matter where I took her for relief, nothing seemed to work.

One morning as I was helping her out of bed, she finally broke down and cried. She said she was having dreams of loved ones in spirit and so wanted to be with them. She told me they were waiting for her and promised her a new life. I held mom that morning and we cried together. It had been a very tough road for us both.

During this time I continued to work in the Spiritual/Holistic field, offering healing and guidance to others. For many years I had worked from home and from other centers in the area. At one point, I opened a small center with one of my clients and learned how to manage classes and workshops. Several years later, Cristina and I opened the Angels of Light Center in Norwell. One evening we took mom to see the center and she fell in love with the energy, and didn't want to go home. We sat there for quite some time, and she told me she was so proud of us. She thanked me for all the care I had given her and acknowledged that it wasn't easy. "I love you and Cristina so much, and I want to see you both succeed and be happy." The words will forever be in my heart, for shortly after that mom passed away.

The day of her passing, we all rallied around her hospital bed. She was awake and asked, "When can I go home?" I said, "Soon mom, soon." We prayed over her and Cristina and my friend, Ann, gave her Reiki. She fell off to sleep looking very peaceful. For a split second I remember looking at her and seeing a beautiful young woman appear. My cousin, who was also very psychic, saw it too, and we both gasped. "Did you see that?" "Yes," I replied, "It was mom at age seventeen, all brand new!" It was amazing and I believe she was showing us what she had to look forward to. I believe her Soul came to give us a sneak preview and I had to smile, for I knew my mom would finally be at peace. As we talked and told humorous stories around her bedside, she drifted off again. We all decided to take a break and go down to the cafeteria. No sooner did we get there when my phone rang. It was mom's nurse, telling us she was passing and to come quickly. When we walked into her room, she was gone. Her Soul was free.

Looking back at our life together, I knew that mom had taught me how to be strong and courageous. She was there to show me that I could do anything, and through all of the sicknesses and disappointments, she taught me unconditional love. My mother visits often and loves to be at the center. We feel her with us and we know that she has finally made her way home. Great peace and light surround her, for she was a giving and loving individual who would have given you the shirt off her back. I love you mom and thank you for the many lessons, which have made me who I am today.

Soul Contracts always changing and growing

While writing this book, I began to realize many more of my contracts as the shifting and changing energies of our times began to reveal some of the outdated Soul contracts that I had chosen in many of my Past lives.

It all began to unfold in 2016 when the planet was going through the Universal Nine Cycle. This cycle was all about release and letting go, and it was at the end of this cycle that I began to revisit many of the old ailments I had encountered over the years. My digestion had always been an issue, and although I was lucky to have all the many holistic methods of healing at hand, this time it was different. I could feel the energies in my physical body screaming to be heard, and after seeing the Doctor, I was diagnosed with Colitis. From the moment I heard what was happening inside of me I was convinced that this was very old stuff and a clearing that's time had come. I felt fortunate to have the knowledge in Alternative Medicine that I had studied and used with myself and others for many years, and for my Naturopathic Doctor whose suggestion began to help me to heal. This journey of clearing and healing would bring me to a whole new level of expansion in my work and in my life.

I began to connect and talk to my body, tapping, affirming and visioning myself as healthy and whole, tuning into my angels and Soul guides once again for guidance, and connecting with my higher self in a deep and profound way. I was reading the book, Partnering with God, by Lee Carroll, at the time and began to see more and more that this special clearing and healing was all in perfect timing. The planet was changing and so was my physical body. For many on the planet deep and profound changes were occurring on all levels and for me it was through the physical.

I began to have weekly healing sessions with many of the local light workers, and each one tuned into my issues confirming that a great cleansing was taking place. I had to be patient and allow it to all unfold, as the lessons and growth potential would be great. With intention and vision, natural supplements, and learning how to take care of myself I began to heal. On one occasion I went for a past life reading, and was told that part of my problem was that I had been taking on other peoples ailments for years, processing them through my body for their healing. I had always known on some level I was doing this, but it always felt so natural and second nature to me. I was told that I had been a Shaman and Native American Medicine woman, as well as a Healer of some sort in most of my past lives. This didn't surprise me either, until it came time for the reader to talk about the contract I had agreed to.

This special contract had been made over and over again in each past life, and as a Shaman and Healer, I had taken it very seriously. It had been part of my Soul Mission, and I was here on the planet each time to follow through. With the new energies on the planet however, this contract had become null and void! There was a better way, and for some reason I hadn't moved forward. My body was telling the story, the pain in my lower abdomen, and colitis symptoms that truly made me stop and take notice. Many of you reading this book may know the second and root chakra are great processing plants for emotion, cords, and karma. It all made sense and it was time for a change, and although my mental body hadn't caught up, my physical body had taken control and went ahead to clear the old to welcome the new.

As I continued to listen to what was said throughout the reading, it became crystal clear that I was no longer able to take on other people's stuff, if I wanted to continue my precious work on the planet. So here I was at a cross roads, so use to the status quo. I was a stickler for teaching others how to place protection around them, using these same tools daily to protect and clear, but for some reason I was still taking it on and processing it through my body. It was time for me to release the contract and move forward, and it was time for me to honor my own needs and my well being. This didn't mean I had to give up my work. It meant that there was a better way. So today I stood before the Lords of the Akashic Records and tuned into the Crystal Caves. I held the intention that I was ready to let go of this contract from the past, that said I was a healer that processed other peoples ailments, and that from this day forward I was ready to learn a better way.

I know that many new and exciting avenues of expression will come from this, and I am looking forward to shining my light even brighter than before. It's time to empower others to embrace their own personal healing. It was time for me to let go of the outcome, allowing everyone to be on their own special journey. And so it is!

Gifts of Forgiveness

Over the years I have learned that there are truly no coincidences. I believe that everything that occurs with each person, place or situation is for a reason. Anything that gives us the opportunity to grow and learn can be a catalyst for our Soul's growth and mission. This in turn gives us the opportunity to forgive. As we tune into our Soul lessons, we begin to ask questions and observe. We can ask ourselves, *what is this situation teaching me, and how can I grow from this experience?* The answers lie deep within, and as you embrace these questions your Soul Guides and Angels will bring you clarity and understanding.

If you choose the power of forgiveness, the gifts will multiply ten fold, as the energies begin to move you into a state of pure and lasting joy. Remember that what you surround yourself with, will manifest in your environment. So look for the lesson in each situation. Acknowledge your feelings, but always search a little deeper, for in the farthest reaches of your Soul you will find the truth, and the truth will set you free. Remember to forgive, bless and release each person or situation, as a state of pure freedom fills your heart and Soul.

A contract of release

From this life and all past lives that we may have experienced, our cellular memory holds lower vibrational energies and situations, that have often times keep us feeling stuck, not knowing how to release the old to welcome the new.

As I was developing the Soul Journey, I was guided to create a powerful contract that would help each person with their intentions for healing. As I sat and waited for my Angels and Soul Guides to help me create this for the Journey, I could feel the Lords of the Akashic Records offering their help. They reminded me that lifetime after lifetime our Soul's have come back to experience and heal old wounds from past relationships and situations. At that point I could feel them all supporting me as I began channeling the contract onto the paper.

As each sentenced began to unfold I could feel the power in each word, and began to use it with several situations in my own life. I was reminded that as I let go, and released each one, that I would be helping all concerned. It didn't matter if the person was alive, or had passed, for the energies would work in both the Earthly and Heavenly realms, clearing and opening me to a happier and healthy way of life.

Below you will find the Soul Forgiveness and Release Contract. I ask that you take the time if not now, at some point to read it and place your own situations in the lines provided.

Soul Forgiveness and Release Contract

Dear Higher Self/Soul Consciousness – (By placing your name below you begin to heal and release your Soul Contracts in the right time and for your highest good)

I_____together with my Angels, Soul Guides, the Lords of the Akashic Records and the Divine Four, activate my Higher Self, my Soul, and my Super Conscious Mind, as my DNA and my Cellular Memory are all activated, remembering my Soul Contracts, and holding the intention that I am ready to bless, forgive and release all that no longer serves me in this lifetime.

I_____, choose to forgive myself completely, loving myself unconditionally just the way I am, as I am ready to step into all my power and magnificence.

I _____, thank you, my Soul, for creating the experiences from this life and all past lives that created the un-forgiveness and realize that on some level they have all been my teacher and have offered opportunities for me to learn and to grow. I accept the experiences, without judgment and do hereby release them to the nothingness from which they came.

I _____, choose to

Forgive_____

I release _____for (his or her) highest good as we are now both free. I thank_____for having been willing to by my teacher. I sever all unhealthy attachments to_____ and send (him/her) unconditional love and support.

I_____, do hereby release myself fully from _____ as I embrace and claim a new and expansive life, filled with opportunities for fulfillment, perfect health, joyful love, and a healthy and creative self expression, as prosperity and abundance flows to me with ease.

Signed:_____Date:_____

When complete, I ask that you place it over your heart and repeat the following:

I am ready and willing to release all that is on this paper, as I surrender it up to the highest and most divine power for healing and movement – It is so and so it is! Amen

Now feel free to tear, and perhaps burn this contract as you feel lighter and lighter.

A special Channeling from Divine Spirit:

As you begin to see that the past only serves you when you can take the lessons and leave the rest behind, you begin to see that your freedom lays in just that. As each piece of the past is embraced with a sense of gratitude for what was and what is to come, you will begin to feel a lightness that lifts your heart and expands your Soul.

With great wisdom you begin to see how each person, place and situation has played a role in your life, and how each one taught you a special lesson.

As the Ego slips away and the appreciation awakens, you will smile, as pure wisdom and light has taken over, and you are now in full charge of the progress that begins to unfold. Unlike control, this is a freeing and expansive energy that brings you into a state of wholeness.

So, thank those who have come your way, as some are going and some are coming in. With each new door that opens a fresh array of possibilities appears. The excitement builds, and you take a deep and refreshing breath in, for the adventure known as life continues, and you are at the helm of your ship, sailing into the abundant waters of the Universe, open and ready for what's next.....

Blessings, Divine Spirit.......

Journal

I suggest you take out your Soul Journal and make a list of the people and situations in your life that you are ready to forgive. You know the ones who bring you the greatest challenges. Next to each one write down what you have learned. Tap into deep heart and Soul for the answers, and remember to "bless, forgive and release" each one, taking the lessons and leaving the rest behind.

Forgiveness and Release

As our Soul interacts with others, we experience an array of different feelings; we all have the capacity to get angry, excited, sad, or disappointed. Our first reaction may be to tell someone what he or she did to us, and it's only human to want to sometimes lash out and get it off our chest. In cases like these I always remind myself that lower energies feed on this kind of emotion and as we begin to live in judgment, attack and fear, the ego takes over. Your Soul wants to remind you that you are so much better than that, and encourages you once again to see the bigger picture. Turn to your Soul Guides and Angels for answers. There are an array of wonderful energetic tools and practices to release these lower energies with ease.

When I awoke this morning, I had an enlightening vision of the past and those who had either hurt me, talked badly about me, or were jealous and mean to me. They flashed in front of me like a movie, and a mirage of feelings flooded my body. I was given a message by my Soul to send light and peace to each person and each situation, so I began to send pure rose colored light from my heart to theirs. It felt really good and sending this positive loving energy out to each one helped me see their Soul and mine at peace. When I finally finished, I felt lighter and free. I saw a whole new way to forgive, and felt it was a win-win situation for everyone.

It's important to realize that we can't control the behavior of others, but we can control how we react to them. Remember that inside each person is a small child seeking approval and love. So find a positive outlet for your resentments, fears, and upsets. Most of all embrace and love yourself for all that you are and all that you are becoming.

Below you will find a wonderful life enhancing process to use in all situations where forgiveness is needed.

The Forgiveness and Release process was given to me a number of years ago, after asking my Angels to bring me a way to energetically release the hurt I was feeling. As I sat at the computer my fingers begin to type, and when I was through, this is what I had channeled:

Forgiveness and Release for Others

I lovingly forgive and release all of the past.

I forgive_____for anything I feel (he or she) has done to me.

I release_____and I release myself. We are both free to love and enjoy our lives. The past is over and I am willing to forgive and let go.

My heart and Soul are now free from all resentments, anger, sadness, guilt and fears that have been holding me back. My entire body reflects this freedom and I am able to move forward in my life with ease and grace.

I now take full responsibility for my life. I choose to fill my world with love, peace, joy, happiness, prosperity and vibrant good health. I love and approve of me. My life gets better everyday and all is well. It is so and so it is. Amen

Each time we refuse to think as we did in the past, our vibration lifts and we become connected to who we truly are. Each time you answer the ego instead of getting hooked into its fear your Soul smiles, and each time you forgive and have compassion for those around you, your heart opens wide receiving the grace of the Angels and all of the Divine. We are all on this planet to learn, grow, and become better than we could ever imagine possible. Each person we meet becomes an opportunity for this growth, as karma slips away and we begin to create a life that is truly abundant and filled with joy.

As I looked back on the past, and all of the many hurts that I encountered, I knew in my heart and Soul that what I truly wanted was peace. I wanted to see that everything had been for a purpose and a reason, and I wanted to come to terms with all of it, so that I could move forward in my life with a sense of accomplishment and joy in my heart. I love this process that my Angels and Soul guides gave to me. Each time I use it miracles begin to happen in my life.

Forgiveness and Release for Self

I lovingly forgive and release all of the past, as my heart heals completely filling with the energies of unconditional love and pure joy. I forgive myself knowing that the past is over, and that I've done my very best, giving myself full permission to bring forth the abundance of this amazing universe as I easily release the old to welcome the new. I forgive myself completely as I choose to embrace all of life, releasing that which no longer serves me. Now karma is cleared as I open my Spiritual Bank to all the many blessings that are coming my way. My bright and brilliant life unfolds each day knowing that I am cherished and loved by all of the Divine.

It is so and so it is. Amen

Clearing unwanted negative energies cleanse

There is a rich and cleansing gift that is given to each of us at birth from God through Saint Germaine. His powerful and clearing lavender light is filled with healing, grace and transmutation, and can be used to dissipate and clear the lower energies that often times attach to us during our daily lives. These lower energies flow into our aura and become trapped creating an array of unwanted symptoms for our physical, emotional and spiritual bodies. Some of these experiences include feeling like you're in a fog, spaced out and having a hard time discerning where your energy field begins and ends. Although the Soul remains constant and all knowing, the emotional and physical parts of the body become confused and often begin to go in directions that are not for our highest and best. This could include over eating, sweet addictions, recreational drugs, worry, fear, doubt and more. The cleansing energy known as the violet flame is used to clear away unwanted energy and bring greater clarity, strength, stamina and a sense of wellbeing, connecting body, mind and Soul in pure synchronicity. Your Soul is embraced and together you walk hand in hand creating the bright and brilliant life that you deserve.

There is an amazing number of ways to work with the violet flame and one morning as I was going through my daily meditation with the eight Angel Rays of Light, I was taken through a special process for clearing the energy centers of my body. Just imagine, feeling clear, centered, grounded and filled with light. I am happy to share this wonderful gift with all of you as you embrace your Soul and its many gifts.

The Violet Heart Process

Begin by taking a deep breath in and allowing the breath to gently flow through your body deep into the heart of Mother Earth. Repeat several times until you feel connected to the Earth, relaxed and ready to receive. In your mind's eye begin to visualize a pure white rose with the petals fully open.

The white rose is the highest vibrational flower and will begin to draw to it anything that is stagnant, negative or no longer needed out from each chakra. You will have eight open roses all together.

Now begin to place the white rose on your root chakra, sacral/naval chakra, solar plexus chakra, heart, throat, third eye, crown and the eighth chakra two feet above your head. With each white rose in place take a deep breath in and see them in perfect alignment from the root to the eighth chakra.

Breathe and continue to relax as you begin to visualize a violet shaped heart before you. See this beautiful heart sitting directly in the center of your body. Feel the violet heart filled with amazing love and grace begin to radiate a beam of pure violet light into your root chakra as together with the help of the white rose, it transmutes and clears all stagnant energies from your root, while filling your root with protection and transformation.

Now visualize the violet light moving up and allow the violet heart to embrace each rose all the way up to the 8th chakra. You may feel warmth, a pulling, tingling or cooling energy as each rose with the help of the violet flame is cleared and all negative energies are transmuted.

Take a gentle breath in now and begin to see the violet heart projecting a pure ray, much like a laser beam from your center out to the left side of your body as it moves now over the top of your head to the right and flows to the bottom of your. See it expanding out now as it moves around your body twelve times, gently and easily clearing your aura and restoring your energy field. Cords are cut, stagnant energies released and a stream of pure and vital lavender energy is left around your auric field.

Now take a deep breath in as your Soul smiles. The white roses will remain in place, open and ready to absorb any and all stagnant energies. When full they will close waiting to be cleansed or removed. I suggest that each night before bed and each morning when you wake up that you bring in the violet heart, allowing it to move through each rose and out into your aura, clearing and preparing you to go about your day, whole, happy and ready to receive the gifts of the universe.

Embracing my Soul Prayer

Divine Spirit please guide me as I forgive myself and others today. Like a breath of fresh air, my new heart-filled energies flow from my Soul out into the world, as an array of gifts begin to flow my way. Those around me feel this shift and change in a way that will nourish the heart and Souls of all. And so it is! Amen

My Soul's Embrace Review

Where do you feel you want to apply the tools given in this chapter?
Who do you feel you are ready to forgive?
What did you learn about yourself and Soul forgiveness?
What Soul Contracts are you aware of and ready to release?

Chapter Six

The Soul's Journey back in time

"Fresh and vital energies surround me"

From the time of our birth, life appears to be fresh and new. To a newborn arriving on the planet, it seems as though he or she is seeing things for the very first time. The truth of the matter is that we have all been here before, and have had many incarnations that lay forgotten deep within the recesses of our being. This is the reason we are attracted to certain people and places, loving some and despising others. You know what I mean.

How many times have you met a person and liked them right away? You felt a sense of kinship and love for them, seemingly not knowing anything about them. And then of course there are those you meet and dislike for no apparent reason. You ask yourself, "Why do I feel this way"? And try to figure it all out, but the answers lie very deeply hidden and only with greater knowledge and wisdom do we ever get to answer and heal the habits that shape the way we react to others.

Soul Family members stay together lifetime after lifetime in different capacities. Past lives are here to show us and teach us how we can heal these relationships, and view each one as a pure lesson of love. Karma is accumulated through our past lives, and as we enter the Earth, we are once again given the opportunity to clear and heal this energy.

Past lives can often be a controversial subject, but today many have experienced glimpses of their Soul journey into the past, and have healed, grown and prospered from their adventure.

A Past Life experience

For many years I have believed in the theory of past lives, but I will never forget the first time I experienced one. I was on my honeymoon in Florida, when my husband Walter and I were visiting Cypress Gardens. We were walking through a lush green part of the gardens when I saw a woman dressed in a Scarlet O'Hara ball gown, carrying a parasol. She worked at the gardens and took part in one of the shows. Seeing her stopped me dead in my tracks, and I began to have a flashback of myself. At first I thought I was imagining things, but then it all became crystal clear to me. I had been here before. I shared my thoughts with Walter who laughed and said, "Cathi you have such a wonderful imagination" and then he replied "I suppose I was Red Butler." He truly didn't want to hear about my experience and changed the subject, but from that day forward I knew that past lives were possible.

This same past life surfaced again many years later when I took a trip to the Plantations in Virginia. We had driven up to the first Plantation when all of a sudden a wave of love came over me. I remember feeling that I was home. As we began to walk into one of the homes on the Plantation, I begin to see images, and remember experiencing an array of feelings. A huge picture on the wall triggered a memory of the Civil war and how I had been a soldier. Image after image came forth and by the end of the day, I was in pure amazement. I had taken a journal with me and began to write down all of my experiences, knowing that someday I would share them with others. In fact this particular past life has surfaced for me over and over again in several hypnosis sessions and past life regressions.

I also found it interesting that in my current life I had been born in Wilmington, Delaware which of course is part of the South. It was interesting because in this life, I had always had stomach complaints of one sort or another, and had begun a series of hypnosis sessions to discover the cause. In one of the sessions, I was a soldier in the Civil war, lying on the battle field injured. Standing over me was a union soldier. His sword had penetrated my stomach and I lay there dying. I also remember seeing glimpses of this same soldier in this lifetime: he had come back as a woman. She was someone I was having issues with in this lifetime, and it all made perfect sense. Every time I would think of her I would get a pain in my stomach. I began to work on forgiving her, knowing what I had learned about in that past life. Each time another layer of anger and pain came off from this past life, my stomach issues began to heal.

Lessons from my daughter

It has been written that our Souls often travel together in groups. These Soul groups are here to support one another, to grow, and to heal. Some say that almost all Souls on the planet today were together in the past, and as a result, all of our relationships on the planet are reflections of our past lives with others. A collective consciousness is built from these Soul groups, which seems to influence our lives without our conscious knowledge.

It's interesting to think that we have traveled with a special Soul family from lifetime to lifetime. Great lessons, karma and more are part of our Soul families' mission. We are all on a stage of sorts with a special agenda that we share during our time on the Earth.

Many years ago when my daughter Cristina was small, I remember having visions of her as my mother in a past life. It was a very interesting concept, and one that would eventually be confirmed by a wonderful spiritual woman who was also an intuitive and empathic. I had heard about her and decided to find out why I was always so afraid that Cristina would leave me, or that she would disappear. It seemed like an irrational fear, but internally it felt very real. As we sat and talked she told me that I had been Cristina's daughter in a past life. She went on to say that she saw me at the age of seven bending over a casket and placing a rose on her chest. I couldn't believe what I was hearing. Could this be true? And then it happened. I had a perfect vision of this in my mind. I closed my eyes, and began to have all the feelings from that time in my past life, and they were exactly like the ones I had been experiencing in the now.

She then went on to say that I was abandoned at that early age, and had a very tough life from then on. It all made so much sense. Cristina had always treated me as if she was my elder and I was the child. Now I knew why. As Cristina grew, I began to have visions that she was here now to make up for what had happened in the past, and that she was here for the long haul. Once I understood where the feelings of loss and fear where coming from I could relax. This helped me put many of these feeling and fears into perspective, bringing a greater sense of peace and joy to our relationship.

It's very important that we work through and understand our issues with our family members and others. I believe past life discovery is one of the many ways to release, forgive and let go of the past, moving into the future with greater clarity and peace.

As I gathered more knowledge over the years, I have read that Soul groups cycle in and out of the Earth plane together, and at the same time. Edgar Cayce talked about this in many of his writings, and it was said that Soul groups naturally followed these cycles until their karma and lesson were received.

Healing through Past Life Soul regression

In the early eighties I began working at a Holistic Center in Boston. Here I was to learn not only about many of my past lives, but how to work with others, bringing them through a process that would help them to reveal many of the things that were holding them back in this life. Session after session was held at the Center and with each one I began to see my past lives unfolding. The first regression I went through was with a group, and brought great healing to my Soul. I had been having severe headaches and had gone to the doctor with no results. In the past life circle I was told to breathe in a certain manner as I thought about my headaches, giving my Soul full permission to help me to understand what was taking place. With each breath in I became more and more relaxed, and then begin to fade in and out of the room. Then the pictures began.

First I saw myself in the times of Jesus. I was being held captive in a dungeon of sorts, and was given the information that I was being persecuted for following Jesus and his teachings. I remember that I was wearing a brown sack like piece of clothing tied at the waist with a rope. I was a man with a long beard and felt very tired and forlorn. Then I began to see my surroundings. I was in a place that was very dark, damp and smelly. Before I knew it I began to see a male figure next to me. He was hitting me with what looked like a thick piece of wood in the shape of a pipe. He spoke in a foreign language, as he hit me over and over again in the upper body and head. It was very painful, but I just kept breathing. When it was time for all of us to come back into the room, they brought us back gently, and we all shared our experience. It's funny because even today I am very close to Jesus, feeling a camaraderie and appreciation for his love and teachings. A few days passed and I began to realize that the headaches were gone. I have never experienced them again, and truly believe that by reliving the experience it helped me release the pain and sadness and allowed my body to heal.

Susan's story

Over the years I have both experienced and shared past lives with others. One of my clients had been married several times, and wanted to understand the pattern of betrayal in her love relationships. She shared several of her past life experiences that seemed to be contributing to issues in her current lifetime.

She always had difficulty speaking up for herself, and there was infidelity in her love relationships: She goes on to share her past life experience.

In one of my past lives I was in France where I was married to an aristocrat. Life was all about him, and he had several mistresses living in the household. I remember that I would swallow my feelings, and obey all that was asked of me. We had children, but what I mostly remember is that I always felt beneath my husband. I felt as if I didn't have the right to voice my opinion.

In another of my past lives, I was a young maiden in England. There was a Viking raid and I remembered being kidnapped and taken to live in Scotland where I was forced to marry. Once again I covered up my feelings, and allowed myself to be in complete denial. I do believe this pattern followed me into this lifetime, as I continued to attract love relationships with dominating, unfaithful spouses. Since my last divorce however, I have come to learn that my voice is worthy of attention, and that standing up for myself has been my lesson. I have also learned that care giving had become a compulsion that brought me to co-dependency. I had habitually ignored red flags and had very weak boundaries. I understand now that total compromise to another feels like suffocation, and I am not willing to do this to myself again. I am learning how to set better boundaries in all of my relationships, and give myself permission to share my feelings.

Perfect Timing

Our Souls know exactly when to bring certain people into our lives, and if we stop and listen we can take the lesson and leave the rest behind. I would suggest that if you have trouble with a certain person or situation that you venture to ask your Angels and Guides to connect you with the right situation to help you explore your past lives. Great healing will be the outcome.

The Divine Four Process of Transformation

While writing this book I continued to channel messages and healing processes from my Angels and Guides. One morning during my meditation I was given this amazing process. I find it to be simple and very effective as this team of Archangels and Masters use their divine tools to heal any and all situations. I began to use it daily with many situations, including past lives helping me to release and clear lower thoughts and energies from my life.

An Introduction to the Divine Four

St. Germaine Chohan of the Violet Flame is here to transmute lower energies with his rich violet light.

Archangel Michael is here to clip and cut all cords from this life and all past lives as his spiritual vacuum removes each one.

Archangel Raphael is here to fill the space from all that's been released with his rich cooling emerald green healing flame.

Master Teacher/Healer Jesus here with his rich golden universal Christ consciousness light to bathe us and refill us with pure unconditional love and joy.

Before beginning this expansive process
Please create an intention of what you are ready to release

Dear St. Germaine, Archangel Michael, Master Jesus, and Archangel Raphael, I open my physical, emotional, and spiritual bodies to your many healing gifts.

Dear St. Germaine please bathe and transmute all lower energies from this (situation)_____ As your rich violet flame scans and clears from this life and in all past lives.

Archangel Michael please lift your mighty silver sword and spiritual vacuum to cut all cords and suction any remaining lower energies from this life and all past lives. I ask that you do this with ease and grace.

Archangel Raphael, I feel and embrace your rich emerald green cooling flame —please pour it over me into and through all cords and back to me healing and rejuvenate my body, mind and Soul. I allow this rejuvenating flame to flow into all twelve layers of my aura, as it is then anchored into Mother Earth for grounding.

Master Healer Jesus, thank you for your rich universal white joy filled light that fills me now from the top of me head to the bottom of my feet as it expands out into my aura and surrounds me completely with you unconditional love and joy.

I am free, I am free, I am free

More healing gifts from the Archangel Raphael

Take a gentle breath in and begin to relax deeply in your chair, as you give Archangel Raphael full permission to work throughout your body, mind and Soul. Take another gentle breath in and allow the energies to flow down through each chakra deep into Mother Earth. Feel your energies now connecting with Mother Earth as a rich emerald green light begins to flow up through the soles of your feet. See and feel this emerald green light filled with pure balance and harmony as it begins to run throughout the lower part of your body now, balancing and clearing all that is no longer needed in your life.

Visualize the rich emerald green light flowing gently up through your torso front and back as it begins to bathe each organ of your body. Feel and see your lower abdomen being bathed in pure healing emerald green light, take a gentle breath in now and anchor the light deep within your abdomen and all surrounding organs, glands and cells, as it continues to bring in balance and the courage to move forward.

Gently the emerald green light begins to flow up into your chest front and back as your heart and Soul fill with rich emerald green light, opening the pathways for pure heart healing. Allow your breath to anchor this pure healing light in the center of your heart expanding into your lungs and all surrounding organs, glands and cells. Feel and see this rich emerald green light once again bringing in the balance and courage to move forward into your fullest potential for perfect health and wellbeing.

Generous emerald green light continues to flow now up into your neck and head front and back as emotional healing begins to take place, take a gentle breath in and anchor the rich emerald green light into all areas of your neck, face, and head as it flows softly into your mind with ease and grace. Generous rays of emerald green light begin to flow down from your head into your spine and expanding into your central nervous system where they bring in perfect balance and healing, your chakras expand to receive, and your entire body, mind and soul are bathed in the rich emerald green light of healing.

Take a gentle breath in and allow the light to be anchored within as it surrounds you completely. Begin to visualize the Archangel Raphael as he places his huge emerald green wings around you. Feel and see the love that begins to emanate from his wings, as generous beams of emerald green light activate the light from Mother Earth, and a pure flow of grace follows, bringing balance and healing throughout your entire body, mind and spirit. One more gentle breath in as it flows back into Mother Earth anchoring and grounding you for the rest of the day.

Embracing my Soul Prayer

Thank you Celestial Beings of light as you surround my Soul with your love. You help me to slow down, as you begin to bring me the signs that fill my heart and Soul with joy. I feel my Soul expand with awareness as doors of pure clarity open wide, and I listen and follow the Path of my Soul which is one of pure love and transformation. And so it is! Amen

My Soul's Embrace Review

How do you feel about Past Lives?
When reading this chapter what did you experience?
Did you apply the Divine Four to a person or situation in your life?
How did you feel after using the Healing
Process with Archangel Raphael?

Chapter Seven

Synchronicity of the Soul

"I see my life in a whole new light"

The Universe is filled with possibilities. What a delight to think that there are so many options for your Soul to grow and expand. Throughout our lives we come upon situations that we often call a coincidence. Let me tell you now, there are none! These so called coincidences are pure synchronicities that have been carefully orchestrated by our Soul Guides and Angels.

Synchronicity - a definition: The unexpected merging of two separate events that are emotionally and/or vibrationally connected with each other that comes together in outer or inner reality. These events are brought about by affinity, not through one's own will.

The Path of Synchronicity – On Heavens Wings

For many years I have toyed with the idea of teaching a Mediumship class. I had been offering one-on-one Mediumship sessions for years, and occasionally would do a party or a Mediumship tea. My daughter, Cristina, had many of the same gifts as I did, and was offerings sessions as well. It was the winter of 2014, and I had just woken from a lovely sleep. As I began my daily yoga stretches followed by meditation, my Angels and Soul Guides began to come through loud and clear.

They were very excited and as I listened they told me it was time for Cristina and me to spread our gifts, and teach a ten week Mediumship Certification. We had labeled our Mediumship teas and sessions "On Heavens Wings." It was such a pleasure to help our clients connect with their loved ones in spirit, as great healing often took place. I remember jumping out of bed after receiving the message, preparing to give the news to Cristina. No sooner had I made it through the living room and there she was standing in the kitchen all excited. She said, "I was just coming to see you," and I replied "Let me guess. We're going to teach a Mediumship Certification together?"

"Yes, yes that's exactly what I was told in a dream I had this morning," she replied. I shook my head, for it always amazes me to this day, how that all works. Pure synchronicity, divine timing, Soul mission, call it what you like, for there are truly no coincidences only the purest form of grace from the universe. And so the "On Heavens Wings" ten week Mediumship Certification was born, with a group of 20, who would open their hearts to the many gifts from spirit that was about to come their way.

Following the Path of Synchronicity

The energies to experience synchronicity are at an all time high. To James Redfield, author of The 12th Insight, this path of synchronicity can help us feel our way through anything that comes our way. As we listen to our intuition, we see the path of pure synchronicity from the moment of our birth until we leave the planet.

Knowing that we are on the right path brings an ease and grace to our daily lives. Each hunch, each intuitive stirring is connected to our Soul's deepest knowing, and keeps us on this amazing path, free from worry or fear. Miracles flow along the path of synchronicity, and open us to our true mission and Soul contracts on the Earth. Remember to celebrate when you notice them, and they will continue to unfold. Acknowledge them and smile, and the energies will keep you on your path of self discovery. Allowing doubt to creep in only takes you off the path, so tune in and allow each synchronicity to unfold. Begin to see that there is a divine reason behind each one, and look deeply into the lessons as they are unfolding. Synchronicity is always a reminder that everything is unfolding perfectly, at the right time and for your highest good.

Observe Synchronicity

Pick a day and begin this process when you wake up. Have the intention that you are going to be the observer and watch for all synchronicities that might appear that day. You may want to take a notebook with you, and write down everything that you feel applies. This is an amazing way to stay connected with the power of intention and to notice the many synchronicities of life.

Inviting more Synchronicity into your Life

What if you could tap into life's magical flow more often? Would you be open and willing? Your Soul knows all about the power of synchronicity. What appears as coincidence is the flowering of a seed that you planted with your intentions. It seems like a completely random event but synchronicity manifests from a conscious or subconscious intention that you initially put out there. Believe it or not, you have a hand in making your own magic!

Below you will find 8 keys for opening the pathways of synchronicity in your daily life:

1) Be willing to let go of control as you open the space for amazing energies to flow through you and around you. Step onto the path of grace each day.
2) Be open minded, acknowledging the many possibilities. Synchronicity operates in possibilities so being open is important. Share this with others.
3) Just Be! Allow yourself to be in the moment. Awareness is a huge step towards harnessing the power of synchronicity. The signs are everywhere. An example of this is the same number showing up over and over again or a particular person showing up.

4) Listen with your heart and Soul. Choosing from your heart (versus your head) amplifies the power of synchronicity and movement.

5) Believe in miracles, and magic, knowing you have the right to miracles, as this is an abundant and light filled universe.

6) Invite all parts of your being to share, begin to use your childlike wonder and ask lots of questions. The answers will begin to appear and gratitude will keep the ball rolling.

7) Be open and honest about your goals, dreams and true heart's desires. Be an individual and go with what feels right in your heart and Soul.

8) Intention is everything, so if you have an intention that you are in a pure flow of synchronicity it will be so!

Taking a Soul Journey – Opening the Pathway for Synchronicity

Where do you want your Journey to Go?

Close your eyes and take in an amazing breath of pure spirit filled air. See and feel your lungs expand with this light, as you are supported and nurtured along the way. Relax, bringing your attention to your heart and begin to see it opening fully, as your Soul expands to receive.

A rich and positive energy filled with possibilities begins to fill you now as you affirm; it is time for me to place my body, mind and soul on the path of pure synchronicity and joy. You are energetically placing yourself on this amazing path and feel confident, supported and loved. This path opens fully as you begin to think of something in your life that needs clarification. This could be something that may be confusing to you at this time. Give yourself a moment or two to connect.

Now begin to see yourself holding the issue in the palms of your hands as you begin to step onto a path of possibilities. Breathe and see yourself in a wondrous land filled with bright blue skies, butterflies, and shimmering waterfalls that seem to call your name. See this path of synchronicity as a rich golden brick pathway that shimmers and shines as you step onto it.

Much like Dorothy in the Wizard of Oz you are stepping onto a path that is divinely guided, and ready to take you where you want to go.

Like twinkling stars in the night sky miracles begin to formulate on your journey, and you begin to feel the light of the Holy Spirit shining down upon you. Parts of your life begin to flash before you and you begin to see that you have been taken care of all along, as your Angels and Soul Guides walk by your side. You are surrendering now and allowing room for synchronicity to flow with ease and grace.

Your mind is open and you begin to except the people, places and situations that surround you for their unique gifts. See yourself now being present in the moment and feel the energy around you as you breathe in the sweet air. Feel your body connected to the chair that you are sitting in, and bring your attention to your heart where you begin to accept pure unconditional love for who you truly are. Begin to see a pure white shimming light gently fall over you now, as the power of miracles are gently gifted to you from this day forward.

Begin to believe that synchronicity and miracles are part of every breath that you take, and feel the love and comfort from your Angels and all of the divine universal energies. Bring your attention even deeper into your heart and Soul as you begin to see a small beautiful child before you. This child is you! Now give your inner child full permission right now to walk with you, guiding you each and everyday. Your inner child will bring you towards your deepest heart's desires with the many creative talents that he or she has been given, including a belief in magic and miracles.

Your path is fully open now and together you walk hand in hand with the energy of synchronicity by your side. Continue on the path and feel the light filled energies that surround you. Your Soul Guides and Angels walk with you, and you are given a gift at this time. You are handed a pure ball of light that glows in the center. It is in the shape of a sphere and it is now in the palms of your hands. Take it gently and place it in the center of your 3rd chakra, as it vibrates perfectly to the power of synchronicity and grace. Take a gentle breath in and begin to see your path coming back into the room into your chair and bring your attention to the soles of your feet, where two rich white roots begin to flow from your feet deep into Mother Earth's heart.

Feel the nourishing energies of Mother Earth now pouring up and around you as a pure sphere of light. Breathe and receive. Now see this same light moving back into the Earth where you are now grounded and ready to receive all the gifts of this abundant universe. Gently begin to stretch and wiggle your fingers and toes as you come back into the room, refreshed, revitalized and renewed. When you are ready you can open your eyes and feel your body, mind and Soul smile!

Staying on the Path of Grace and Synchronicity everyday

Begin by bringing your attention to your root chakra and seeing a pure path of light beginning to open from the root onto the Earth below your feet. See and feel a rich golden path of light before you. See yourself stepping on this path and say:

Dear Anachel, Angel of grace, I invite you to walk with me in this new day, as my path of grace and synchronicity continues to guide me to the right people, places and situations. I see and feel the path of grace before me, and I walk onto this enlightened path, as I am guided by all of the divine. It is so and so it is!

Now go about your day in pure synchronicity and light

As Synchronicity on your personal Soul Journey unfolds we often find out that there is a beautiful part of ourselves that is waiting for our attention, and as we take the time to go within and talk directly with our Soul, we begin to see our true beauty and light.

As you relax, and go into a space of love and intention from your heart you will begin to feel special warmth that comes from a deep place within your being. You may begin to see colors, and feel the electric energy of your Soul. From this special place you can re-connect in pure Synchronicity as you begin to ask and receive, and as you see and feel your Angels and Soul Guides gather around to listen, the answers begin to flow in pure unison.

They begin to take you into that place of perfection and opportunities begin to appear at every turn, for as you take the time each day to go into your heart and extend this warmth and love deep into your Soul you will be amazed at the outcome.

The power of Synchronicity surrounds the Earth

Surrounding our planet is a huge grid system, a conductor of sorts, etheric in nature, taking on all of the energies within and around the Earth. I liken these grids to special netting that holds the energy of thought, feeling and emotion within its perimeters. Since everything holds a vibration, either positive or negative, just imagine what these grids take on everyday. You get the picture. So now ask yourself this question; how can I contribute to the world? What can I do to make a true difference?

We often talk about having the desire to make a difference, thinking is has to be through a special job, or something we may do to help others. What if, instead, we could make a difference just by what we say and think? What if healing the planet is all about healing what flows into the Earth's grids?

Twelve Keys to Transformation

When I first created the Eight Week Soul Journey into Miracles and Joy and your Soul Mission, I was instructed by my Angels and Guides to create twelve special keys to help people shift and change their vibration. Each one has a special quality that helps to shift the vibration of ourselves, others and the planet.

Twelve is a very powerful number, and represents abundance and light. The digits added together become the universal number three and is filled with prosperity and good luck! Twelve is a multiple of three and so its vibration is extremely powerful. In Sacred geometry, it is a number that connects with the twelve layers of the human energy field and there were twelve at the Last Supper! So you can see that the number twelve has a great deal of power and energy surrounding it.

Each Key was created to promote a special energetic vibration around you, and as you use each key your vibration will begin to lift and change the world around you.

Each key helps you to attract like-minded people, and positive outcomes in your day. As your vibration begins to heighten the abundance begins to enter. All the amazing abundance of the universe is now on your door step. Be ready now to let it all in!

The twelve transforming Soul Keys

Pick one each day and repeat throughout your day. Know that your Soul is now contributing to the Earth grid, as you delight in being part of the healing of the planet.

1. *Today I will joyfully repeat: Love, peace and joy are who I am as I breathe in the pure lavender ray of grace.*

When you repeat this throughout the day, wonderful energies begin to follow. First and foremost you begin to see and feel that you are truly a being of light, and that you can turn on this light that shines from your Soul anytime day or night. Love opens the heart and Soul, peace brings forth glorious light from the divine and joy builds each chakra as they all begin to open and spin in perfect harmony. The lavender ray of grace is connected to the violet flame and pours through you and your entire etheric field, out into the world. Wow, what a great way to make a difference today.

2. *Today is a day of pure white light and miracles. I will send this miracle ray to everyone and to all situations as I feel my body, mind and Soul smile.*

Simple yet very powerful, the white light and the Holy Spirit come through loud and clear as you begin to see and feel the power and healing grace of the white light. As you send this white light into all situations you picture it bathing your loved ones, friends, family, work and all areas of your life, as it expands and begins to create a path of miracles. Imagine sending this light out into the world to strangers who now begin to heal, as miracles manifest and the planets smile. The grids of the Earth begin to shift and you become one with the divine. Smiling is a perfect addition to this key, for each time you smile you enhance your immune system and send love to each part of your being, and good energy to the planet. This is certainly a win-win situation for all.

> 3. *Today as I breathe into my heart I will tune into the channels of joy as soft amber rays of joy flow through me with ease. I will affirm; I am pure joy!*

The heart is the center of your being, a place where love begins to flow and nourish all that it touches. As you breathe into your heart your Soul expands and the two become one. Your Soul's mission and heart's desires begin to flow with ease, and you begin to set the stage for pure joy to come into your life. Your joy spreads out into the world touching everyone you come into contact with. Grand and glorious energies begin to flow to you and through you, as pure harmony flows through the grids of the Earth.

> 4. *My body is my Soul's vehicle today. I will check in with my body today and wherever it feels empty, painful or sluggish I will fill that area with the golden light of vitality and abundance.*

Your body is the vehicle for your Soul. As you check in with your body you are saying, I care about you, and want you to be healthy and whole. Remember that for your Soul to expand, and be able to enjoy all the many adventures that lay ahead, your body has to be in good condition. So remember to treat your body with tenderness, love, and respect each day and watch as your Soul flourishes, and the grids of the Earth vibrate to the beat of unconditional love.

> 5. *Today I will bathe myself and anyone who agitates me or seems to need extra help with the universal healing white light.*

Connected to the gifts of Jesus, this light is a profound healing energy that works in an instant. Each time we are stressed or feel that we want to lash out to those around us we become separated from Source. You know what I mean; the man who cuts us off in traffic, the boss that comes into the office with problems and seems to direct them at you, or the child or spouse that acts out in need of love. If we stop for that moment and begin to send this crystal white light into each situation, we become the vehicle for that light and great healing begins to take place for all concerned. Know that this special universal white light calms, soothes and heals and helps to dissipate all lower and negative energies.

6. *Today I will breathe pure mahatma rose/gold light into each Chakra as I say out loud I am willing to release the old to welcome the new. My Chakras are cleansed, cleared and free.*

The meridian systems of your body hold a special healing energy that when tapped into can heal all parts of our being and contribute to world healing. Each chakra relaxes and becomes receptive to receiving as each one becomes a magnet for all the abundance of the universe. Your energy soars, and you open the doors to grand and glorious abundance in your life, as the grids of the Earth shimmer and shine.

7. *Today I will sweep my entire aura with all the healing colors of the rainbow as I am one with the universal healing energies and all of the divine.*

Vibrant colors are one of the most powerful tools in the universe and your Soul resonates with each one. Branching out into your aura these colors begin to cleanse and clear anything that no longer serves you. The colors of the rainbow fill your heart and Soul, your vibration is lifted, love flows your way, and cords are cut, allowing your Soul and its mission to come forth into your life. You attract the highest and the best, bringing greater harmony and peace to the planet.

8. *Today I will fill my entire body top to bottom with the rich magenta ray of unconditional love. I will become one with the light of love and cherish myself.*

The Magenta ray is filled with the most divine Mother love. As the Angel Ray Magesta opens the channels and becomes a bridge for the energies of Mother Mary and Goddess Mother Quan Yin. Rich and profound Mother love flows through you with ease and grace. You feel nourished and cherished as you become one with all of life. The Earth grids began to vibrate with this love and all is well.

9. *Today I affirm that I am a radiant being of light that is filled with abundance and vitality as I breathe in and fill my entire body, mind and Soul with the golden light of Source.*

Intention is everything! Remember that what you say and think has energy and creates your reality. When you affirm that you are a radiant being of light, you are inviting all of the divine energies as a team to work with you in all areas of your life. The abundance and vitality flows as your body, mind and Soul become one with Source and the energies of the Earth grids are clear and cleansed.

10. *Today I will take my Soul's hand being fully present in each situation. I will listen and follow my Soul's advice as I call in my mighty "I AM" presence into action.*

When you call your mighty I AM presence into action, you are connecting with the God source within. A pure connection of rich golden light is made from the center of God's heart and Soul to yours. This is an energy that can move mountains, helping you to move forward with courage and ease in all situations. Rich light fills the Earth grids and empowers more positive energy onto the planet.

11. *Today my Soul is connected fully to my precious inner child. I choose to open my heart and Soul as together we play, dance and sing while the soft green rays of healing flow into my body, mind and spirit.*

Grand and glorious emotional healing takes place as the green healing ray flows through the emotions of your inner child. I feel that Archangel Raphael plays a huge role in this healing ray and as you access your creativity, your inner child is set free. Your creative power soars and you regain parts of yourself that have been missing through trauma or fear.

This is very powerful for the grids of the Earth and brings forth the energy of healing for all.

> 12. *Today I will stop and breathe in pure peace as a soft blue ray flows through me. I will breathe out all fear, as I repeat throughout my day, love and peace, and joy is who I am.*

Powerful and loving, this soft blue ray calms and soothes your very Soul. Your mind releases fear, your body becomes relaxed, as it fills with harmony and the energies begin to shift around you with ease. You feel light and free from worries, and the abundance of the universe is yours. Great clarity begins to flow and you clear the pathway for healing on all levels. The grids begin to vibrate to this peace, and harmony flows towards Earth and her people.

And so, as you pick a special key each day, you open your heart and Soul to receive all the blessings of this abundant Universe. Your vibration begins to shift and change and the many possibilities and gifts that have been waiting for a place in your life, begin to flow towards you. Your Spiritual Bank opens wide, and you have made a difference in the world. The grids of the Earth are cleansed and begin to fill with pure light, love, peace and grace.

Your Soul Yearns for Peace

Peace is an energy that flows softly with great light and grace. Think of a small child cuddled in their mother's arms, feeling warm, loved and safe. Peace is an energy that surrounds us each and every day if we are calm and allow it to flow. Worries and fears, doubts and sadness rob us of this wonderful feeling as it sits waiting for us to allow its soft and loving energy back into our lives. Peace waits patiently to bring us comfort, joy, and healing. Peace is the absence of fear, and we regain peace by slowing down and allowing our Soul time to sit and partner with God. Our Angels and Guides and all of the Ascended Masters are delighted to show us how we can bring more peace into our lives.

I believe that peace changes everything and that if we were to allow it to radiate from us out into the world, the wars would stop, the killing would end and even the world economy would turn around. Peace is something that cannot be bought or sold. Choosing this loving quality can be as easy as getting up into the morning and saying it is so.

Today I will walk in Peace. Today I will allow the things that normally would aggravate me to roll off my back. Today I will accept everything in my life exactly as it is, and know that with peace, trust and faith I can move mountains.

Remember that what we resist persists, so pour pure peace into each situation, claim peace, direct peace and attain peace. This is a choice, and as you choose to work with the energy of peace, miracles will flow easily into your life. Begin to think about where you would like to bring peace into your life. Tune into your Soul and write down all the areas in your life which you are ready to fill with peace. Remember that your Soul will thrive when it lives in the space of peace, so breathe in the soft blue rays of peace daily in all situations as it creates the foundation for glorious harmony and serenity within and around you.

Embracing my Soul Prayer

As my Soul expresses its many gifts out into the world today, I feel the love and acknowledgement from Divine Spirit that feeds its purpose. At the end of each day, I will notice all the wonderful things I have accomplished, letting my Soul know that we are on this Earth journey together, walking hand in hand on a pure path of synchronicity, peace and grace.
And so it is! Amen

My Soul's Embrace Review

How has synchronicity played a role in your life?
How does the power of synchronicity guide your Soul?
Where do you need the power of peace?
Which of the 12 Keys seem to resonate most with your Soul?

Chapter Eight

Your Divine Personality and Soul Types

"I embrace the perfection that I am"

Your Unique Soul

Did you ever wonder why you do what you do? Do you often question your personality or sometimes even dislike some of the things that you see about yourself? Like an actor in a play, our Soul has many roles. Each one is perfectly designed to act in different ways in different situations. For each action there is a reaction which is like a set of dominos affecting the universe as a whole. If we can remember that Earth is school, and that we're here to grow and learn, we see that there is a kaleidoscope of unique personalities that surround us.

Did you ever notice how your personality shifts and changes depending upon the people you're with or the situation you're in? You walk into a room of people, and you become the actor once again on the stage. You meet people daily, some you seem to jive with and others make you uncomfortable, even anxious. It's this unique part of self that knows exactly how to act as the lessons flow from person to person, situation to situation. Those we affect hopefully will grow and learn from our presence and our unique personality, as our Souls wisdom and knowledge

91

is activated. Acknowledging and embracing all of who we are, even the shadow side is all part of embracing the Soul and its uniqueness.

Soul Types

As far back as I can remember I was always on the go. I was told that I began to walk at nine months old and never stopped. As a baby, sleep was not on my agenda and over the years it was this profound energy that helped me to move forward over and over again in my life. Through the many challenges I overcame to the opening of the Angels of Light Center, the one thing I could count on was my desire to move, as the word transformation became my middle name.

Each one of us has a specific way of being on the planet. We all come in with specific planetary aspects that contribute to our personality and how we react to the people, places and situations in our lives. For me it was doing, and that was that. It has always been hard for me to just relax. I love being on the go! In the early eighties I became enthralled with astrology. I took classes at a local holistic center and began to learn more about my own personality which was linked to the stars. At one point, I sent away for a full print out of my chart, and when it arrived I was amazed at how accurate it was. It described me to a tee!

I began to do more research and had my daughter's chart done and some of my friends too, and lo and behold, each one's chart was right on. Today I have several wonderful astrologers as friends and I value their expertise in this proven field. The one thing that I know for sure is that the Soul has an agenda and picks our unique personality through our birth chart to expand, grow and heal during our time on the planet. Below you will find three specific Soul types. Have fun and see which one fits your unique Soul personality, remembering that this is only a small part of who you truly are.

The Being Soul:

You know who you are, you're that wonderful individual who can just relax and let go. You take life a little easier than the doing Soul which is always in the accomplish mode. As a being Soul you can observe and collect information and then make a conscious choice on how to proceed, directing your Soul's energy towards your goals and dreams. You have the gift of knowing when to pull back and when to move forward, and so the being Soul can embrace life as a perfectly balanced journey, filled with knowledge, deep wisdom and understanding. It is important that you acknowledge this part of your self, with acceptance and love as your Soul will flourish and open to the possibilities, attracting the right people, places and situations into your life to grow and prosper. Sometimes the being Soul procrastinates and can be accused of thinking too much, but in the long run if you just allow the process to unfold your Soul will guide you. Just be open and ready to move forward when you know in your heart the time is right, and above all, try not to beat yourself up for taking your time!

Soul Affirmation for the Being Soul

I bring balance into my life as I observe and then take action with ease and grace.

The Doing Soul:

Always on the move - You just can't seem to sit still and you have an agenda from the moment you open your eyes until the minute you lay your head on your pillow. Your energy is high and sometimes you are deemed a type A personality. You feel things very deeply and often have to keep moving to embrace the energies around you. You finish a task and move right on to the next, and you live life in the dash always ready for new challenges, as you delight in overcoming obstacles. You do plan, but for the most part you are spontaneous and filled with movement and magic. It is important that you make a conscious effort to relax and learn how to surrender. For you, this isn't always easy, partially because you truly love to take the bull by the horns. Stop for a moment and just be, as you make an effort to breathe deeply throughout the day and remember to ground yourself. Taking a deep breath into your body and allowing it to flow deep into the Earth is a perfect and quick way for you to ground. Visualize rich white roots flowing out from the soles of your feet, and with each step you take feel your feet connecting to the Earth.

Soul Affirmation for the Doing Soul

As I move throughout my day with ease, I breathe between each accomplishment, as smooth and vibrant energy flows to me and through me

The Having Soul:

You are filled with the knowledge and the desire to embrace the beauty and the gifts of the universe. You are ready and willing to receive at all times, and your desires seem to flow towards you with great ease and grace. Many say you came onto the Earth born under a lucky star, and maybe you did, but in any case you truly know how to create and embrace. Your Soul is receptive and ready to create and receive the gifts of this abundant universe. Others may pamper you, and give to you; even strangers seem to want to present you with something special. Your Soul's energy is a magnet for abundance and you often can cruise through life in an easy and carefree fashion. Remember not to become too attached to the material however, for the best gifts for your Soul come from connecting deeply with spirit. You can become an example for others, and although some may hold envy for what you have, you can let them know that they too can embrace the gifts that this abundant universe has for all of us. If you teach this to others it is truly a gift from your Soul, as you embrace the beautiful truth that God loves each of us equally and wants us all to have what is for our highest and best!

Soul Affirmation for the Having Soul

I balance the gifts of the universe with my connection to spirit, as I share my gifts with those who cross my path

No matter which category your Soul personality falls into remember you are unique and made from pure love. Once you begin to embrace all of who you are you can begin to see the kaleidoscope of possibilities that lay deep within the resources of your being.

Growing up I can remember my mother always saying to me, "You are just so different from the rest of us", as she added "in a good way". For some reason I always amazed her, and she would often tell me how proud she was of me. "I don't know where you came from", she would say. It was at those times that I felt very sad for my mother, for she couldn't see her own unique talents and gifts. Today I feel that many of my intuitive and healing gifts came from my mother, and yet she would never acknowledge that she had anything to do with this.

Now it is time for you to embrace your unique Soul and its many attributes. Without comparing yourself to others, begin to observe yourself and acknowledge yourself for your accomplishments. They don't have to be huge but authentic, and whether that's the special smile you give to others, or the kindness that comes from your heart, it all matters. This is all part of your beauty and the light of your Soul. So acknowledge yourself for your uniqueness, and then you can truly appreciate and value the uniqueness in those around you.

I am Worthy to Receive process:

Open your arms wide and let your Soul receive. Picture your Spiritual Bank filled with all of your good deeds from this life and all past lives opening fully, pouring down the gifts from all of your divine efforts. Now say out loud;

With open and loving arms I am now willing and worthy to receive, great prosperity, perfect health, divine love, peace, joy and abundance, great success and all the blessings that the universe has to give. I open my Spiritual Bank fully now as I embrace these gifts forever more. It is so and so it is!

Use daily and receive

Embracing my Soul Prayer

I thank Divine Spirit for showing me that I am a unique and light filled being ready to take all of my beauty and joy out into the world. As each day passes I am given the opportunity to spread my gifts throughout the universe, as I embrace all that I am with the purest form of love.
And so it is! Amen

My Soul's Embrace Review:

What did you learn about your Soul personality?
How did it change the way you view yourself?
In what ways do you want to expand your gifts?
What did you experience after doing the "I
am Worthy to Receive" process?

Chapter Nine

Embracing the Colors of your Soul

"The light of the Universe shines down upon me"

I absolutely love color. To me colors say it all, and when I ask my Soul which color it wants me to wear each morning, I seem to gravitate towards the perfect piece of clothing in my closet. So trust your Soul and give it permission to pick your colors today and everyday, as each color represents an energy that feeds your heart and Soul.

Color – the Vibration of the Soul

From rainbows in the sky after a warm summer rain, to the beauty of the leaves on the trees in fall, I have always felt the affect of color on my Soul. Perhaps this is part of the reason I live in New England. The colors of the season seem to move right along with the needs of my Soul. Think about it. Wherever you are, your Soul tunes into its environment and you are drawn to different colors at different times. Each situation in your life is supported by the colors you wear, and each mood and thought reflects the colors of this rich and abundant universe. Stop for a moment now and begin to think about your favorite colors. Write this down in your Journal and then next to each color write down a word or two about how these colors make your feel. How do they represent the inner stirrings of your Soul? This is but another way to tune in and connect with your Soul and its beauty and light. Begin to look in your closet each morning and ask your Soul; *what colors are best for us to wear today? Now listen and* see what happens. I like to have all my clothes color coordinated in my closet, which makes it easier to reach in and pick what's best for my Soul at any given time.

Colorful magic

The word Mandala is from the classical Indian language of Sanskrit. In translation it mean circle, but to me a Mandala is far more than a simple shape. It represents wholeness, and can be seen as a model for the organizational structure of life itself--a cosmic diagram that reminds us of our relation to the infinite, the world that extends both beyond and within our body, mind and Soul. I suggest that you buy a book on Mandala's and begin to color the ones that seem to feed your heart and Soul, as you awaken your inner Soul child's creative gifts.

A Soul Essence Reminder:

Remember that you are a beautiful child of the Universe and deserve to be happy – So spread your wings and fly and embrace more of life's gifts, remembering to open your heart and Soul and say "Yes" as you continue to expand your horizons fearlessly. Know that that age is just a number - have more - more fun, more love, more enjoyment - be willing to tell others about your dreams for the now and the future - expand each dream to include that which is for your highest and best - and hold on lightly, knowing that something even better could be coming your way - embrace and acknowledge yourself, and all of your beauty and light, as your Angels and all of the Divine Smile....remember that you are a blessing to the world, and that you are truly cherished and loved.

May you receive the blessings of this abundant universe!

The Gifts of color

Purifying White:

If the color white is chosen, your Soul knows how the healing grace of this color will vibrate perfectly for you. Your body, mind and Soul will connect in great harmony, reflecting purity and light out into the world. Pillars of divine light flow through you with ease as your 8th and 9th chakras expand allowing all of the divine to work with you and through you. Your Soul's affirmation connected to this color is as follows:

Divine white light flows through me today, as I walk with spirit, bringing in glorious cleansing energies that wash away the old to welcome the new.

Gracious Black:

Your Soul is preparing to hold onto its energy today and black is the color to do just that. The color black is made up of all of the colors of the rainbow, blended together in perfect harmony. Many light workers wear black from the waist down for protection on an energy level. Black will hold your energy in place and keep your foundation strong. If your Soul is calling for black, trust its insight. You are preserving your energy and your Soul knows exactly where it needs to be. So trust and wear the colors that speak to you today as you embrace the advice of your Soul. I love to wear black on the bottom and a pastel color on the top, bringing in a perfect connection with my emotional body.

As I cherish the energy that flows within, it expands and empowers me

Soothing Lavender:

Lavender is the color of the divine, along with the color white: it brings forth a ray of grace, protection and healing. It is soothing to the eye, and others will respond as they receive healing and grace from you today. Your Soul supports you as a healer and a source of light. Worn on the upper part of the body, this color radiates through you and out into the world, filling you with divine energies that vibrate harmoniously with those who cross your path. Your crown chakra and third eye expand with delight as lavender and purple of all shades vibrate with this energy. Allow your Soul to pick just the right shade as you walk out into the world filled with light and peace.

My body, mind and Soul vibrate to the healing energies that surround me as grace flows through me with every beat of my heart. I am connected, protected and cherished by all of the Divine.

Joyful Orange:

Playful and expansive the color orange brings great delight to the Soul. You are ready to celebrate, as this vibrant energy reaches out into all the cells of your body. By wearing orange, peach, salmon, rust, and amber, you are allowing your Soul to open into a joy filled opportunity. Each shade has its own special vibration which is connected to joy happiness and harmony. Your 2nd chakra smiles, as your goals, dreams and heart's desires begin to flow to the surface with ease. You step out into the world filled with glorious energy and light, as your inner child sings with delight.

My Soul is filled with great joy as I step out into the world, and those around me appreciate and honor who I am.

Beautiful Blue:

The soft and intuitive color blue and all shades of this divine color are especially helpful for communication. Whether it is soft sky blue or rich indigo this color is connected to intuition and great creative power. The 5th and 6th chakras will work perfectly with your Soul's creativity and will assist writing, channeling, or connecting with your deepest desires. Allow your Soul to pick the shade and trust that you will be guided throughout the day. I love dark blue on the bottom and light blue on the top, as it brings forth creative balance.

Harmony and peace flow through me today. My creative power is heightened and I follow my intuition with joy and ease.

Healing Green:

The color green brings forth great healing and love on many levels. The different shades all have their own special vibration, but will connect you to deep healing and heightened heart love. If your Soul reaches out for this wonderful color, the heart chakra will respond with gratitude. Your Soul will expand to embrace the healing that's taking place. You can direct this healing energy by going into deep heart and Soul, and sending this healing light to any area of your body. I always see Archangel Raphael standing by my side as the emerald green light is connected to his healing gifts. Your heart will beam with delight and your Soul will expand as this special color vibrates throughout your entire being.

Healing energies flow throughout my body, mind and Soul today, as I embrace all of my life with healing and rejuvenating emerald green light.

Spiritual Turquoise:

The vibration of this color is divinely connected to transformation and spirituality on all levels. When your Soul reaches out for the color turquoise, it is ready to usher you forward, bringing forth new beginnings. The turquoise ray will shine brightly through your body, mind and soul and great faith is encouraged and movement flows with ease. This vibrant and powerful color is filled with transformative potential, as it's known as one of the highest spiritual colors. Turquoise jewelry is one of my favorites, and I wear it daily to keep my vibration high and to encourage Soul growth.

I move forward today with great joy and ease as I listen to my heart and Soul. Faith guides me on my path of Soul fulfillment.

Expansive Yellow:

If your Soul chooses yellow, a strong vibration filled with vitality, abundance, confidence and positive energy will begin to flow through you. The colors yellow and gold connect you with the sun and all of its power and light. The 3rd chakra expands with delight when this color is present and you begin to radiate self-appreciation, luck and confidence. Your Soul is embraced and you will feel like you can move mountains. Vitality flows through you and you vibrate with sunny enthusiasm to all who cross your path. Like the sun, you are expansive and filled with warmth, divinely connected to Source.

Vitality and abundance surround me today, as I reach out into the world with great joy and enthusiasm, connecting deeply with the divine light within my Soul.

Energizing Red:

Vibrant and energized; today your Soul is ready for anything! Courage surrounds you and you feel good about yourself and your life. You are ready to move forward and this wonderful Soul enhancing color will empower you to be all that you were meant to be. Your heart chakra will expand as your root is secure and ready to move forward with great momentum and delight. Success surrounds you and you will be a magnet for your deepest heart's desires.

My body, mind and Soul expand today as I reach out with courage. Great prosperity flows to me with ease. I am grounded in the light of my Soul.

Shimmering Silver:

Choosing the color silver means your Soul is ready for miracles. Open your heart and Soul and ask for what you need. The divine spirit awaits and will fill you with the beauty and the light from the Holy Spirit. Celebrate your connection with all of the Divine. A perfect balance of male and female energies accompanies this color, and your Soul will shimmer with pure delight.

I feel the gift of miracles flow through me as I bathe in the beauty and the love of God. I am balanced in my beauty and my light.

Passionate Pink:

When your Soul reaches out for this gentle and loving color you are being told that it is time to love, pamper and honor yourself. Take your Soul's hand and connect with your beauty and light today. Pamper and adore yourself as you cherish the beautiful Soul who is ready to step into the world. Today it will be easy to share your love and understanding with all who cross your path.

I embrace and appreciate all of who I am today, with great love and appreciation. I cherish and love each part of that which I am. And so it is!

Prosperous Brown:

Secure and grounding, the color brown touches your Soul with abundance and prosperity. You are ready to be noticed as a person whose word can be trusted and relied upon. Your Soul is ready to expand and ready to be a true leader. It is anchored perfectly with the Earth's energies, ready to move forward into greater prosperity, abundance and achievement.

I am grounded and centered as my Soul leads the way to great prosperity and abundance in all areas of my life

This is a wonderful way to heighten and connect with your intuition, as you are guided by your Angels and Soul Guides. As I mentioned before I have all of my clothes in my closet, color coordinated. I find that when I do this it saves time, and my Soul can focus on just the right outfit for my day. So wear the colors of the rainbow and allow your Soul's vibration to shine bright!

The 8 Angel Rays of Light

For many years I have worked with the Angelic realms, cherishing their love and support. My Soul mission was clarified on the night of my dear father's passing, when I saw two angels carry him up to his divine home in heaven. From that moment on, I knew my heart and Soul were ready and open to receive, sharing the Angels' gifts with all who would cross my path.

As our lives and the energies continue to shift and change, it becomes more of a challenge for our dense bodies to receive the beams of light that is pouring down upon the Earth. Perhaps this explains why I was given the opportunity to become a channel for a group of Angelic beings who call themselves the 8 Angel Rays of Light.

It all began during one of my 8 Week Soul Journeys while teaching the students how to connect with their own Soul's name. Unexpectedly, the Angel Ray Majesta revealed herself to me, as we were all going through a process to connect with our Soul's essence, which had come through my Angels and Soul Guides. As I held my hand over the area beneath my left breast I began to feel a warm and loving sensation. I had experienced this many times before, but tonight was different. I became aware of a rich magenta light circulating throughout my body, and felt a presence that took my breath away. In my mind's eye I saw a beautiful Angelic being filled with unconditional love, and affection. She was adorned in a magenta colored robe, and she presented herself as Majesta.

At first I thought that this was part of my own Soul's essence, and of course in some ways it was. Over the days which followed, more and more information was to come through and on a snowy winters' morning in January of 2011, the next Angel Ray appeared. Rich and filled with vitality and abundance the Angel Ray Illumina presented herself to me. She told me that she had accompanied Majesta and was part of the 8 Angel Rays of Light.

One by one they made their presence known, as I began to listen and channel their divine guidance and love. At one point they began to come rapidly and as each new Angelic Ray appeared, I felt a pure bridge of light forming with the Archangels, the Seraphim and all of the Divine. Then on February 14th, 2011, as I stirred gently in my bed, they came one by one and I began to go through a Divine Journey with the 8 Angel Rays. They each brought their rich and life enhancing colors and attributes throughout my entire being.

Majesta was the first to join me with her rich Magenta Ray filled with the purest form of unconditional love, opening the pathways for Mother Mary, Quan Yin and all the divine universal Mother love energies.

Next the Angel Ray Illumina came forth as she began to pour her vitality and abundant ray throughout my body, mind and Soul, as the 12 crystals in the center of my being began to come alive and grand and glorious healing of past lives began to take place. Each crystal sparkled with her divine light, and I felt great confidence as my heart opened wide to receive her gifts.

Trinlar was next and brought the most amazing silver and white rays throughout, adorning me with miracles and light from the Holy Spirit. Every cell of my body radiated with the gifts from the Miracle Ray. I was instructed to take a deep breath as she anchored her many gifts deep within my heart and Soul.

A soft blue ray began to flow next, as the Angel Ray of Peace Stillaire bathed me from the top of my head out into my aura and down to the bottom of my feet with her pure blue ray of peace. I could feel myself relaxing like never before as the gateways to peace opened wide. All of the Angels of peace smiled as a portal for greater and grander peace began to open, spreading their gifts through me and throughout the world. At that moment my Soul was filled with anticipation of what was to come.

Rich and generous green rays of light began to flow with ease, bringing great healing and soothing energy, opening the pathways for the Archangel Raphael and all of the healing angels to enter. Linar the Angel Ray of Healing was flowing to me and through me, as I began to feel rejuvenated and renewed. It seemed as if I were one with the bed I was lying in, enjoying their light and love.

I began to feel a true sense of joy as the rich amber rays began to come through my crown chakra, and the Angel Ray Jazielle poured her light through me and around me. Huge Angelic wings filled with joy embraced me and I could feel my heart and Soul expand. It was one of the most amazing and delightful feelings I had ever felt; the purest form of joy flowing through me with ease. All of the joy filled energies of the universe seemed to follow and I felt adored and loved. I lay silent, in pure bliss, allowing my Soul to receive.

Generous beams of turquoise light began to flow as the Angel Ray Faeylore brought forth great faith, opening the pathways for trust and understanding on all levels. Rich turquoise rays flowed throughout my body, mind, Soul, cells, DNA and my aura. I felt a calm nurturing energy flow through me, embracing my heart and Soul. My Angels, and Soul Guides and all of the Divine seemed to follow, helping to instill the qualities of trust and faith deep within my being.

As I continue to breathe gently I felt a soft and generous lavender ray begin to flow down from above. The Angel Ray of Grace Shashielle was pouring her rich lavender light of grace throughout, filling me with light and clearing a pure path of grace for me to follow. Generous beams of light continued to flow, and when I finally brought my attention back to the room, I felt revitalized and renewed, with a sense of calm and a divine light shining all around me. My Soul had expanded and as the days followed the 8 Angel rays brought me more and more information. On one occasion they began to add to one of my channeling sessions, and on another occasion they brought me a guided journey for others. Most importantly they brought their 8 Angel Ray Attunement, a healing modality that enhanced all other healing offerings. This was another part of my Soul's mission and I was ready and willing to allow it all to unfold.

Gifts of the 8 Angel Rays of Light

Majesta offers a rich magenta ray of Love. These special Magenta rays fill the gap of separation between the self and the Divine. Majesta offers pure unconditional Mother Love, supporting and heightening our own capacity to love unconditionally, and enabling us to spread this love to ourselves and others. She works directly with the crystals caves and the Lords of the Akashic records as well as our DNA, clearing and cleansing, lengthening and fortifying each strand, as past lives are released and a return of clarity and unconditional love for our process is realized and embraced. Work with her divine gifts allowing her love to connect with yours, as together you expand your capacity for unconditional love for self and others.

Illumina offers a rich golden ray of Vitality and Abundance as waves of rich yellow light flow throughout, planting seeds for great vitality and abundance. Past Life trauma is lifted and the body expands with increased enlightenment. This is a wonderful ray to call upon if you need extra energy, strength or stamina.

Trinlar offers the purest of silver and white rays of Miracles aligning with our DNA as we grow and heal, connecting us with the Holy Trinity of the Father, Son and Holy Spirit. Creating the space for miracles to happen daily, bringing a sense of oneness with all of the divine.

Stillaire offers the soft blue ray of Peace, establishing peace within our hearts, filling our Souls with the intention of peace on Earth and throughout the universe. Breathe in her soft blue ray of Peace as it flows down to fill your physical, emotional and spiritual bodies.

Jazielle offers a generous amber ray of Joy filling our body, mind and Soul with joy and positive thought in all of our actions, creating great heart healing and a huge energetic shift for the planet. Take a gentle breath in and begin to see the rich amber rays of joy fill and expand into your chest. You will go about your day feeling and expanding joy out to everyone you meet.

Linar offers the soft green ray of Healing as she moves through all the layers of the physical body, strengthening and shifting past life trauma, illness, old karmic ailments on the physical, emotional and spiritual plane promoting rejuvenation and healing our DNA. This beautiful ray can be used for deep healing, to clear and cleanse your cells, organs and your aura, clearing the pathway for healing on every level. Coupled with Archangel Raphael and the healing Angels this special healing ray becomes a bridge for heightened healing on all levels.

Faeylore offers a brilliant turquoise ray of Faith, re-establishing faith in the heart of humanity allowing each person's journey to unfold with great clarity and perfect trust, as we move towards our true inner knowing. Breathe in the turquoise ray of faith daily as you expand your capacity to believe in all that is for your highest and best.

Shashielle offers a soft lavender ray of Grace, becoming a bridge for all of the Angel Rays of Light, bringing forth a smooth and flowing energy to replenish and renew body, mind and spirit. Shashielle ensures that all light rays are embraced, opening the pathways for the Archangels, the Seraphim and all of the Divine Universal energies. A wonderful time to work with Shashielle can be at the end of the day, as her lavender light is connected to Saint Germaine and the violet flame, clearing, cleansing and transmuting any stagnant energy that you may have picked up throughout the day.

Color Activation and the 8 Angel Rays

I offer this activation to my students and clients once they have been through the 8 Angel Ray Journey with me. You can also listen to my 8 Angel Ray Journey CD, and use the process below to activate the seeds and gifts daily.

Begin by taking a deep breath in and releasing your breath through your body deep into the heart of Mother Earth. Feel her embrace now as you feel light and free. Now you can begin to activate the gifts from each Angel Ray by saying the following: As you activate each one visualize yourself breathing in the color and expanding it from your crown through your physical body and out into your aura.

Activating the gifts of Divine and unconditional love – Magenta light
Activating the gifts of vitality and abundance – Golden Yellow
Activating the gifts of miracles – Silver/White
Activating the gifts of peace – Soft Blue
Activating the gifts of healing – Soft Green
Activating the gifts of joy – Joyful Amber
Activating the gifts of faith- Transformative Turquoise
Activating the gifts of grace – Soft Lavender

Now take a beautiful breath in, filled with all the colors of the rainbow, as it flows through your entire being, anchoring it deep into your heart and Soul.

The Eight Angel Rays will follow you throughout the day opening the pathway for purity and light, and expanding your capacity to work directly with all of the divine.

Look back at the list of the 8 Angel Rays. By following the process above you can bring just about any positive and loving attribute into your being. As the light ray branches out into your etheric field, your vibration shifts and you become a magnet for positive and uplifting energy. You have helped yourself and the grids of the Earth.

Embracing my Soul Prayer

I am grateful for the colorful Universe in which I live, and open my heart and Soul to choosing the perfect colors for me each day. With the help of my Angels and Soul guides I trust that each color will vibrate perfectly to the energies within me and around me, as each color brings my body, mind and spirit into perfect balance. And so it is!

My Soul's Embrace Review

What colors seem to truly resonate with your Soul?
How do colors in general make you feel?
How did you feel about the 8 Angel Rays and their many gifts?
Which of the Angels Rays did you seem to resonate with the most?

Chapter Ten

Numbers and your Soul vibration

"I embrace the gifts of the Universe"

Growing up I will always remember how math was a thorn in my academic side. Simple math was not the problem, but when I began to take algebra and higher forms of math, I was completely confused and more often than not, did not want to attend classes nor do my homework. As time went by however and I begin to work with energy and the power of numbers in numerology, and I developed a whole new appreciation for their power and wisdom. Today I love numbers because I understand them energetically. With this knowledge they excite me, and I can embrace them and the beautiful energy and wisdom they hold. If only they had taught us this in school. I love sharing numbers with others through my numerology readings, for I know that the vibration of each numbers holds a special gift, and can enhance ones understanding of energy.

What are some of your favorite numbers? What numbers seem to follow you throughout life?

Embracing your Soul Mission with Numerology

Numbers are a powerful and meaningful source of energy in the universe. Everything that surrounds us in some way is connected to a number. Think about this for a moment. You are born on a certain day. You have special

110

occasions such as anniversaries and holidays, all of which are connected to special dates. Your home office and even the license plate on your car all vibrate to certain numbers, each one holding a special energetic meaning that the Soul can easily connect to and utilize. A formula for the Soul, numbers play a huge role in our destiny. In the science of Numerology numbers are given a special meaning and thus can be used as a tool and a compass for the energies at hand. Below you will find each number and their meaning. Be aware of the numbers that you see each day and begin to see if certain numbers keep presenting themselves to you. They are connected to special messages for the Soul. The formula for calculating your Soul number at birth is as follows: You will end up with a singular number for the most part.

For example: 12/27/1953 add 1+2+2+7+1+9+5+3=30+the number 3

This is my Soul number at birth, and represents idealism, and positive energy. The number three is also the divine universal number.

Embracing your Soul numbers at Birth

The Soul Vibration One brings forth Leadership and Originality

If you brought the essence of the number one in at birth you have grand ideas and come up with new and exciting formulas for living life to the fullest. You can be stubborn and a bit arrogant and your Soul is always ready to be honest. Your Soul is filled with leadership skills and qualities, and you yearn to be the boss. Having your own business can be one of your deepest Soul's desires, and your greatest challenge is to stay open minded and see the other person's point of view. This will help your Soul to live a well rounded life.

The Soul Vibration Two - You are the Peacemaker

You have a beautiful and diplomatic nature. You use your intuition to connect with other people's moods and needs and often think of others before yourself. Being surrounded by those who love you is important and can lead to success in your life. Sometimes shy, the two vibration often times needs a boost to their self-esteem and tends to put things off. Always ready to create peace and harmony, your Soul's lesson is to learn to speak your truth and create boundaries. This will help you to expand your gifts and gain the respect of others.

The Soul Vibration Eleven is filled with Intuitive Insight

Since the number eleven is a very powerful number for the Soul, you have the ability to tune into everything in your environment. You are deeply spiritual and idealistic by nature. Often labeled the dreamer you have a natural understanding of the Earth and the Heavens. People are drawn to you, for you open your heart and Soul and listen to their needs. Eleven is the light worker's number and you are a humanitarian through and through. The lesson for those who embrace this Soul number is balance. It is important that you take time for yourself and bring a balance into your life.

The Soul Vibration Three ushers in Idealism and Positive Energy

You are very creative, positive, social, charming, and romantic and can often times be called easy going. You love to make other people happy and will go to great lengths to give and give until you achieve this. You hold a wonderful reputation and others seem to really like your wonderful and positive energy. You look at the bright side in most situations and believe in the gifts of the universe. Popular and idealistic, your Soul's lesson is to learn to see the point of view of others, appreciating and learning from each lesson and each person who crosses your path.

The Soul Vibration Four - The Conservative

You are filled with good sense and traditional in your thinking. You love order and routine and love hard work. Your Soul thrives in the great outdoors, and you have an affinity with nature. Stubborn and persistent you get the job done. You vibrate nicely with the four directions, and could have a pull towards Shamanism or Earth Science for your work. Your Souls lesson is to allow your self to more flexible and less ridged. This will make your Soul grow and flourish all the way to the top.

The Soul Vibration 22 - The Master Builder

Just like the other double digit numbers the twenty two master number draws its strength from the spiritual realms. Always connected, no matter what they are doing, the physical world is very important to them. You can become a great leader and hold a solid foundation for those you support. You have great ideas and your idealism helps you to create your goals and dreams. The Soul twenty two vibrations lesson is to be more connected to your own personal energy and take time for meditation and your inner self.

The Soul Vibration Five – The Non-conformist

You need your Freedom. You love to explore and you are naturally curious. You love taking risks and you can be over enthusiastic which sometimes lands you in hot water. You need to have changes flowing in your life at all times and it is important that you stay moving and not get stuck in a rut. The Soul five vibration's lesson is to look before you leap and get all of your questions answered.

The Soul Vibration Six – The Romantic

You love to feel useful. You have a strong family connection and love to help your family and community in any way that feels helpful. Your emotions can rule you and you often use your feelings to make your decisions. You have a strong urge to take care of other's and are very loyal with those you love. You are a wonderful teacher and healer and love music and the arts. Your Soul lesson is to learn to differentiate between what you can change and what you cannot. Balance and spending time to replenish and rejuvenate is also an important lesson.

Soul Vibration 33 - Filled with Compassion

Love, Grace and Beauty are the word you are connected to. You feel deep compassion for the world and those in need. You can often become the victim and take on a martyr role if not careful. Self-sacrifice is also a trait of the heightened six vibration. Your Souls lesson is to become the observer and teach rather than take on other people's problems. Make sure you are clearing your energies and keeping your chakra's balanced and in tip top shape. In this way you will avoid getting burnt out.

Soul Vibration Seven – The Intellectual

You search and search. Questions must be answered. Your Soul is constantly looking for information, you are the detective. You question everything in life and hold a deep need to know why. Slow and steady is your motto and you will make it to the finish line. Your Soul loves to spend time alone, and you love secrets. Sometimes living in your own world you are a seeker of the truth. Your Souls lesson is to step out of your comfort zone and participate more with others. This will open many doors for your Soul to expand and grow.

The Soul Vibration Eight- The Problem Solver

You are the problem-solvers of the universe. Professional and very blunt you get to the point. You do have good judgment and stand out in the crowd. You are the boss and feel that you are capable of teaching many. Your Soul lesson is to make sure you have a balance and not allow your ego to rule you. Underneath it all you are kind and loving. The Soul eight vibration often has to learn how to balance their desire to let money rule them. It is best if you look at money as icing on the cake and not the whole pie!

Soul Vibration Nine – The Actor

You are a natural born entertainer. You are caring and generous and would give people the shirt of your back. Your Soul is filled with charm and you have no problem making friends. You embrace strangers and they become part of your family and you are ever changing and blending in with your environment. You have wonderful luck, but sometimes are moody and changeable. Your Soul's lesson is to find and build a strong and loving foundation for yourself and those important to you.

Life cycle numbers and your Soul

I feel that it's very important that my clients understand the life cycle they are in at any given time. Each year we all go into a special cycle, beginning on our birthday that runs for twelve months and sets the tone for the energies that surround us in that particular year. I believe that by knowing this, we can make healthy and Soul filled decisions. In my Angel and Soul guidance readings I always share the current life cycle with my clients. I also find that our Soul and our intuition are so aligned, that these numbers follow suit with the readings.

Formula: Your Birth cycle number in the current year

Once you know the meaning of the numbers you can use them daily to see exactly what kind of energy is available. This is a perfect way to connect with your Soul and its mission in that day, month or year.

For your Birth cycle: Take your birth month, day and the current year and spread it out as seen below:
12/27/2017 - The formula- 1+2+2+7+2+0+1+7=2+0 =4

On my birthday, December 27th 2017 I will be entering into a four cycle. Your life cycle is always calculated by adding the month/day and the current year we are in. This will give you the energetic vibration of your Soul at this time, and the very best avenue to take for the year. On the next page you will find the meaning of each cycle. Enjoy!

The One Cycle - This is a wonderful cycle because you are working with the purest of energies and can begin to take on a new path and direction. The old is a thing of the past and opportunities are just waiting for a place in your life. Begin to think fresh and let the past go. Your Soul guidance is to take the lessons and the gifts from each person, place or situation and leave the rest behind. Whatever you begin to build at this time will grow over the next eight years until the tree bares fruit!

Soul mantra for the One Cycle:

I open myself to the new and fresh and vital energies at hand. My Soul is ready to release the old to welcome the new.

The Two Cycle - Is connected to the creative part of your heart and Soul. As it builds off the one cycle you begin to open more and more to your creative talents and unique self expression. This cycle encourages you to journal and really tune into what it is that you want to create. Writing and all creative talents are heightened at this time. Music is a powerful tool to use creatively, so listen to it often. Your Soul is helping you to create the life you truly want, and your intention will go a long way.

Soul mantra for this cycle is:

I am a creative being filled with new ideas and inspiration" "I allow my creative power to flow and grow.

The Three Cycle - This is a grand prosperity cycle is filled with luck and enthusiasm. It's time to take all that you began to create in the one and two cycles and expand into action. Luck is on your side and as you ask you will receive. One of the best ways to use this cycle is to think positive as you move forward into pure joy. Asking = Receiving, so remember that your intentions are magical at this time leading to abundance and prosperity on all levels.

Soul mantra for this cycle is:

I open my heart and Soul to all the prosperity and abundance in my life and so it is. I am filled with light, luck and enthusiasm.

The Four Cycle - A special cycle filled with divine help as all of your hard work and effort will be rewarded. I like to call this the 401K cycle of the universe. Your team of heavenly helpers will match your efforts so that what you put in will return to you doubled. This is a great time to really put extra effort into all areas of your life. Great rewards are on the horizon.

Soul mantra for this cycle is:

All of my efforts are rewarded and I am supported at all times. Divine Spirit works with me to create the foundation for my dreams.

The Five Cycle - This is a time of great freedom and expansion. This is a time to spread your wings and fly. Adventure is around every corner now, and attaining knowledge is important for the rest of your journey on Earth. Make sure to go where you feel pulled without judgment, and take in and assimilate all the knowledge around you. This special knowledge will help your Soul to expand its gifts even further.

Soul mantra for this cycle is:

I trust the freedom that is given to me as I expand and move into my joy. I am filled with knowledge and personal power, as my Soul expands with delight.

The Six Cycle - This is a time of commitment and balance in all areas of your life, a time to look over each area and see where your heart truly wants to place a greater focus and commitment. Work, family and life purpose is all highlighted at this time, and it is important to stay true to you. Ask yourself the question "Where do I want to put my time and effort"? This is also a time when your heart is open to helping others in need. You may take in a stray animal or begin volunteer work. Whatever choices you make, be sure to check in with your Soul stirrings.

Soul mantra for this cycle is:

My heart and Soul are open to improving all areas of my life as I am committed to bringing in greater balance and joy.

The Seven Cycle - This is a time of great reflection as you begin to plant the foundation of what is to come. Quality time spent alone is very helpful as you begin to see who you are and where you want to go. Positive affirming goals and visualization are recommended, as each one is a seed that is planted and begins to grow. You are releasing the old and letting go of what is no longer needed. Meditation is a must, as it deepens the connection with your Soul, Angels, Guides and all of the Divine on a deep and profound level.

Soul mantra for this cycle is:

I go within and listen for answers, connecting deeply with my heart, Soul and all of the divine.

The Eight Cycle - You made it! The tree is ready to bare the fruit of your efforts. This is a time of focus and being willing to receive the gifts from your Spiritual Bank. Doors will open for grand manifestation and prosperity on all levels. This is a great movement cycle and many of your goals and dreams begin to unfold. The most important suggestion I can make is to stay positive and focused and as each gift is manifested stop and show gratitude for as you do, more will come!

Soul mantra for this cycle is:

I open my heart and Soul to the many gifts that I am about to receive. My spiritual bank is open, pouring down all the blessings of this abundant universe.

The Nine Cycle - This is a time to deeply cleanse the old to welcome the new! It's time to re-evaluate once again. People, places and situations are being looked at from a new perspective and as you let go of the things that no longer work in your life you open and create the space for your Soul to move into the new. If you are true to yourself and listen, release and let go, this can be a rejuvenating and healing time on all levels. Your Soul is in preparation for new beginnings. Look over your life, and see what needs to be released; this could be old beliefs, old matters, or anything or anyone that is holding you back.

Soul Mantra for this cycle is:

Letting go is easy, as I release the old to welcome the New. I am cleansed, I am clear and I am free.

Heart and Soul Release for Abundance process

Place your hands over your heart and take a deep breath in and release. In your mind be willing to release anything that has held you back. Your Soul knows exactly what it needs to do, so give it full permission to start the release process. Say aloud; "I am ready to release all that no longer serves me."

Take another gentle breath in and allow your heart to expand as all remaining stagnant energy begins to transmute and fade away. Feel the freedom as your heart and Soul merge together and become partners on your journey from this day forward. Feel your heart begin to fill with loving pink light, as the energies around you shift from the past into the present. Creativity, freedom, and new beginnings are entering your energy field, so take a deep breath in and allow these energies to embrace every cell of your body. See your cells expand as they are bathed in the richest form of abundance. Take another deep breath in, expanding your breath through each chakra deep into the heart and Soul of Mother Earth. Now one more deep breath in to seal the pact with your heart and Soul, bringing forth all the many blessings that have been waiting for a place in your life. End by pouring the richest golden light of abundance over your crown and allow it to expand through each chakra and out into your aura, as it bathes all twelve layers of your energy field. Now bring this amazing light filled energy back into your heart, taking one more nice gentle breath in, as it is anchored within you from this day forward.

Embracing my Soul Prayer

*I am grateful for the power of numbers, and how they work with my
Angels and Soul Guides to bring me their messages of hope, and faith
each day. My Soul loves to show me which numbers are vibrationally
perfect for me, and as I ask for signs my Soul sings. I am one with
the Universe and know I am truly worthy of all good things.
And so it is! Amen*

My Soul's Embrace Review:

Did you discover your birth cycle number from this chapter?
How do numbers play a role in your everyday life?
Which numbers do you feel your Soul truly resonates with?
How did you feel after going through the heart
centered Soul Abundance Process?

Chapter Eleven

Soul Chakras

"My personal healing creates wholeness in the world"

I will never forget the first time I heard the word chakra. I was studying Applied Kinesiology (Muscle Testing) at Massasoit Community College, as part of their Holistic Studies program. Being a massage therapist at the time, it seemed like the perfect healing tool to add to my work. I was enthralled with the concept of meridians and chakras which ran throughout the body, enhancing our energy system and wellbeing. I was thrilled to be given the opportunity to experiment and share this wonderful and exciting modality with family and friends. As I began to appreciate and understand the fascinating energy system that ran throughout our bodies, I began to work with pure energy like never before. I continued to learn and practice energy medicine, channeling many techniques to enhance the wellbeing and balance of each chakra. In this section of the book, you will learn about these circles of light that move energy and channel emotion throughout our being.

A clear & powerful energy flow

Our body systems are amazing. When you think about all the many things that your body does everyday, you have to smile, for the energies that circulate through and around the body are truly divine. The chakras are a powerful set of energy vortexes that pulsate continuously both day and night, working with the entire endocrine system as they try to stay in balance. Each chakra has a corresponding organ and contributes to our breathing, circulation, digestion, reproduction and secretion. From the top of our head to the bottom of our tailbone these special chakras respond to our Soul and our life situations.

The chakras change energy from one level to another by distributing life force energy, also known as chi, qi or prana along the meridians inside the physical body. Each gland and organ responds as hormones are formed and distributed throughout. Physical problems are often the result of a blockage in the energy flow of this system, causing the organs or glands to not function properly.

How does this apply to the Soul?

Soul energy in encased within the energy field, and is a constant moving energy which can truly never be destroyed only transformed. Would you believe the body actually houses over 2000 chakras? In Sanskrit, these energy vortexes are called Nadis, and are affected by our everyday life. Foods, emotions, stress, and our environment have an affect on each one. The seven chakras are the main energy systems that keep it all moving smoothly; each energy pathway crisscrosses another, expanding energy out in the form of a vortex.

Before writing this part of My Soul's Embrace, I began by clearing each chakra with a special process I will share with you at the end of this chapter. Once cleared and balanced I tune into each chakra and ask for information in the form of a channeling. The chakras are a great support system for the Soul, and below you will find the perfect energies to expand and nourish each one. I have included a channeled affirmation that will energetically inspire each chakra to spin in perfect balance.

The Root/1ˢᵗ Chakra – Ruby Red

Great security and safety, protection, trust and power, lay within the resources of the Root Chakra, and are just a small part of its many gifts.

I am your root chakra and here to strengthen and secure your Soul to the supportive energies of Mother Earth. I am here to expand and secure safety, protection, and instill trust, as I help your Soul to achieve a stance of connection, and power. I am ruby red in color, and as my center spins, I encourage you to ground yourself daily to the gifts of the Earth, as she will hold you in a space of power and conviction. Worries and fears keep your Soul in limbo, as they only cause you to disconnect from your strength. Losing this connection keeps you ungrounded, and blocks the grounding forces of Mother Earth and her many gifts. Breathe and feel my energies expand, as rich white roots flow deeply from the soles of your feet into the Earth Star chakra remembering that you are safe, nurtured, supported and loved.

Soul chakra affirmation: I am grounded and secure in Mother Earth's support and love.

The Sacral/2ⁿᵈ Chakra – Brilliant Orange

Your creative power center, the inner child, embracing and loving oneself, pleasure, and balance are all part of the 2ⁿᵈ chakras gifts.

As my rich orange energies spin in perfect balance, your Soul can expand, for the essence of self-awareness, self-love, and creativity is endless. I spread my gifts and ask that you honor your feelings, as I enhance your connection with your beautiful inner child. I am your pleasure center, and help you to bring in a perfect balance of give and take. Low self esteem and feeling restricted create an imbalance, so please remember that you are a divine spirit having a human experience, and deserve all the blessings of this abundant universe. Give me permission to expand and create as together we can communicate from a place of magic and child-like wonder.

Soul chakra affirmation: I receive pleasure in perfect balance, as I create my universe

The Solar Plexus/3rd Chakra – Golden Yellow

Your Soul's personality, self-confidence, worthiness, wisdom and emotional balance are the gifts of the 3rd Chakra.

As my brilliant yellow energies spin in perfect harmony, your Soul fills with the wisdom of the ages. Within the resources of my center lay twelve sparkling crystals which vibrate to the heart and Soul of the Creator. I delight in connecting you with your unique gifts. My only request is that you fill me each day with the light of God, as together we can re-unite the beauty and the power of Source within your being. Please remember to believe in yourself, knowing that the only opinion that truly counts is yours.

Soul chakra affirmation: I am a powerful and light filled Soul, brimming with great wisdom and self-respect as I expand my gifts to all who cross my path, with joy and ease.

The Heart /4th Chakra – Emerald Green

The capacity to expand love and forgiveness are a major part of the Heart Chakra. Unconditional love for self and others expands and keeps this divine chakra whole and filled with peace.

As my loving emerald green energies flow out into your body, mind and Soul, great healing begins to take place, for it all begins from a place deep within my core. Be compassionate and forgiving with yourself and others, as your love becomes a healing force for the universe, remembering that you are part of the Divine Heart; loved and cherished by God and all of the divine. Release all feeling of bitterness, and extend pure rose colored light from your heart and Soul, for as you do, you heal yourself and the world.

Soul chakra affirmation: The love of the universe flows to me and through me, as I compassionately share my love with the world.

The Throat/5ᵗʰ Chakra – Sky Blue

Creative self-expression and communication flow through the Throat Chakra, as great inspiration works hand and hand with your Soul.

Soft blue light expands the gifts of my center, as the butterfly spreads her wings to fly. Creative inspiration flows throughout your Soul, helping you create your world. I speak the truth, and expand my gifts out into the world as communication is my greatest gift, and I bring truth out into the world with ease and grace. Being open and honest and telling the truth will enhance my gifts, as you let go of all fear of who you truly are, and express your beauty and light out into the world. Believe in your creative self and allow your dreams to come to fruition.

Soul chakra affirmation: I create magic and beauty in my world, as I teach others to express their own beauty and light. I believe!

Third Eye/6ᵗʰ Chakra – Indigo

Great vision, intuition, and understanding are the gifts that the 3ʳᵈ eye brings to the Soul; great clarity is the outcome.

As my indigo light expands, a portal of pure intuition and insight begins to open. I am connected deeply to your heart and Soul, and as I spin in perfect balance, you will begin to have answers to your questions. Your path begins to open to your purpose and your mission, as I connect you deeply with your Soul and its many gifts. Be sure to stay focused on your hunches, and allow your intuition to guide you in all situations. Meditation is my greatest friend, and as you visualize what is truly in your heart and Soul, it will be so! Relax, breathe and receive as together we walk hand in hand on your path of grace.

Soul chakra affirmation: I see with pure clarity and light, as my Soul expands on its path of grace

The Crown/7ᵗʰ Chakra – Lavender

Pure enlightenment is the gift of the Crown Chakra. Great unity and oneness with all of the divine expands this chakra, opening a pathway for communication with the Divine Umbrella of Spirit.

We are one, as you are bathed in unconditional love and acceptance, from the Father/Mother God and all of the divine. Your angels delight, for as you open the twelve petal lotus, your crown is complete. Great love and insight flows down from above, as you allow the Divine Heart to become one with yours. I am here to bring forth enlightenment as you connect with the beauty and light of your true essence. Please remember that you are not alone, and that separation only causes loneliness and confusion. See me, and allow me to touch your Soul with my light, as Source smiles down upon you and your heart is filled with the purest form of divine love.

Soul chakra affirmation: I am one with all of the Divine, as their love flows deep into the resources of my heart and Soul. I am one with God.

The 8ᵗʰ Chakra –Shimmering White

Filled with transforming energies, the 8ᵗʰ Chakra is a perfect companion for your Soul, as it helps to process our life lessons and karma.

I am a blueprint for your physical body, which is the vehicle that houses your Soul. I am all about transformation, as my crystal clear energies spin above your head. I am never affected by death, because I am all about transformation and new life, and I carry to you the wisdom of the ages. Your Soul believes I am its perfect companion, as I dwell in the higher realms and truly know who you are. Together we are one with God and all of the Divine.

Soul chakra affirmation: My connection with God, the angels and all of the Divine is enhanced, and my Soul smiles.

Higher Chakras as above, so below

In my experience and study of chakras, I have worked with the 9th 10th 11th and 12th chakras all of which are important for the Soul. These higher chakras are to be used when we are ready to expand beyond our earthly beliefs, knowing that once again we are spirit having a human experience respecting our limitations, as we reach up for higher knowledge and wisdom. As you venture out into the heavenly realms, you will be supported in opening these chakras and receiving their many gifts.

Balancing the chakras is important for your health and wellbeing, physically, mentally and emotionally, and I believe spiritually. They affect how we function in our everyday lives whether it is traits such as psychic ability, psychic shielding, mental stability, mental clarity, emotional stability or just the ability to feel safe, confident and whole within ourselves.

Chakra energy centers power the body, bringing life and keeping it healthy. Each chakra is associated with different parts of our being and need to spin in total balance in order for us to also feel healthy and energized.

Chakras absorb energy that comes from thoughts, feelings and outside environment, clothing, television, books and so on and feed the accumulated energy to our body. The body is affected by the quality of the energy that passes through these centers. For example, if we have negative feelings, we will be feeding negative energy through our chakras and into our body. Over time this can make our body ill. These centers also absorb energy from the environment. Other people's negative emotions or a room full of clutter, negative television and media, books with negative focus will all produce an unhealthy energy that we absorb.

We can't always avoid negative energy in our current contextual experience on our planet, nor can we avoid feeling down at times, but there is much that we can do to change our feelings from negative to positive and to protect ourselves from harmful energy in the environment. Keeping the chakras in good condition is the key, in other words keeping them spinning in balance. Chakra balancing can be akin to giving your car a tune up.

Seven Chakra Balancing process:

Stand up with feet hips width apart, and take in a gentle breath directing it through the soles of your feet into Mother Earth. Repeat two more times, as you become grounded in your space. Now bring your attention to the upper part of your body, as you raise your palms up above your head to the Divine Umbrella of Spirit. Say out loud,

I invite all the highest universal healing energies to pour through my hands as I open my palms to receive

Now begin to experience this rich life enhancing energy as it flows into the palms of your hands. You may feel tingling as they fill up to the brim. Once you feel each palm is filled (you will feel a fullness in the center of your hands) direct your hands below your feet at your Earth Star chakra and visualize the light pouring in from your hand – allow it to circulate throughout this chakra for a moment or two and take a gentle breath in anchoring the light below your feet.

Now, repeat this same process all the way up, as you direct your hand between your knees, allowing the healing light to circulate through your knee chakra, often called the 10th chakra. Make sure you breathe gently to anchor the light, and move up to your root chakra, sacral chakra, solar plexus, heart chakra, throat, third eye, and crown, allowing each one to fill with healing universal light. Once you have moved all the way, place your hands over your crown, and breathe in the remaining healing light as it makes one more sweep through all of your chakras deep Into the heart of Mother Earth, as you go about your day feeling revitalized and renewed.

Star Chakra color activation – This is a powerful and quick way to enhance each chakra

Close your eyes, and in your minds eye begin to see a beautiful shimmering star. Now visualize this golden star moving down to your Earth Star chakra. Begin to see and feel it expanding out to fill this area beneath your feet. Now bring this same Star energy up between your knees to your 10th chakra and see it expanding – now work all the way up from your root to the crown chakra expanding this pure star quality. Now visualize a group of stars circulating around your aura, and go about your day feeling your own Star quality and light. This special energy will expand out to everyone you meet, bringing in a greater sense of beauty and abundance that will follow you throughout your day.

Foods that nourish your Chakras, body, mind and Soul

Organic is always best – fresh better than cooked if possible

Root Chakra delights:

Root vegetables: carrots, potatoes, parsnips, radishes, beets, onions, and garlic
Protein-rich foods: eggs, meats, beans, tofu, soy products, peanut butter

Herbs and Spices - horseradish, hot paprika, chives, cayenne, pepper

Second Chakra delights:

Sweet fruits: melons, mangos, strawberries, passion fruit, oranges, coconut, cherries, papaya, banana's and all melons
Honey & nuts: almonds, walnuts, pine nuts, and all tree nuts/Omega's 3's.

Herbs and Spices: cinnamon, vanilla, carob, sweet paprika, sesame seeds, caraway seeds

Third Chakra delights:

Granola and grains: whole grain pastas, breads, cereal, rice, flax seed, sunflower seeds, sesame seeds, pumpkin seeds- Dairy: milk, cheeses, yogurt, kefir, buttermilk, and all cultured milk
Herbs and Spices: ginger, mints (peppermint, spearmint, etc.), Melissa, chamomile, turmeric, cumin, fennel, star anise

Heart Chakra delights:

Leafy vegetables: spinach, kale, dandelion greens, romaine lettuce, and all green vegetables, beets, broccoli, cauliflower, cabbage both green and red, celery, squashes – Green Tea

Herbs and Spices: basil, sage, thyme, cilantro, parsley

Throat Chakra delights:

Liquids in general: Spring water, natural fruit juices, herbal teas
Tart or tangy fruits: lemons, limes, grapefruit, kiwi, orange, tangerine
Other tree growing fruits: apples, pears, plums, peaches, and apricots

Herbs and Spices - salt, lemon grass, seaweed and almonds

Third Eye Chakra delights:

Dark bluish colored fruits: blueberries, red grapes, black berries, raspberries, and all fruits and veggies with a deep blue tone

Liquids: red wines and grape juice

Herbs and spices: lavender, poppy seed, mugwort

Crown/Eight and higher Chakra delights:

Air: fasting / detoxifying – cleansing with fresh fruits, veggies and herbs
Incense and Smudging Herbs: sage, copal, myrrh, frankincense, and juniper

Special sounds to enhance and activate your Chakras:

I like to repeat each one 3-9 times
Soul Chakra sounds:

Earth Star and Root Chakra – LAM

Sacral Chakra – VAM
Solar Plexus – RAM
Heart – YAM
Throat – HUM (pronounced HOOM)
Third Eye – and Crown – OM
Crown & 8th Chakra – AH

May your Chakras be filled with the abundance of the universe!

Embracing My Soul Prayer

*As my chakras expand and contract with my thoughts and actions,
I am grateful for the Divine Guidance that each one receives. My
Soul gets involved when my chakras close down and seem out of
balance. Right away my Soul signals my body and symptoms appear.
I listen and act as I embrace each sign, refilling each chakra with
divine light, bringing me into a state of balance and good health.
And so it is! Amen*

My Soul's Embrace Review:

What did you learn about your Chakra's from this chapter?
How will you apply it daily to your life?
Is there one Chakra that seems to need more attention than the others?
After using the processes in this chapter what did you discover?

Chapter Twelve

Soul Crystals the gifts of Mother Earth

"I celebrate nature and her many gifts"

Growing up in a suburban neighborhood had its advantages. We had the convenience of stores being close by and the woods which bordered our back yard. I remember how much I loved the woods, and how mystical and magical it seemed to be. Often times my little sister, Suzy and I would sneak off and go into the woods and sit under a group of trees, listening to the birds and taking in the delicious smell of pine. I always felt supported and safe and nature was something we both loved. Near the house where we lived was a beautiful meadow that ran though the woods all the way up to the Pond Meadow Reservation. A small babbling brook and expansive tall trees lined the pathway to the pond. In the spring when the waters were flowing high from the winter snow, we would go down to the brook and collect rocks. There the crystal cool waters would run over our hands, accompanied by the shimmering gems below.

My sister Suzy loved to collect rocks and had them all over her bedroom. I loved to see her giggle and laugh as she found each stone, unique in color and size. I think I loved watching her joy more than I did finding my own stones, and as we got older we ventured out to the beach and places were Mother Earth's treasures were plentiful. I noticed over the years that I seemed to have an affinity for finding heart shaped stones, and always felt that they were messages of love from the universe. Yes, Suzy and I were mesmerized by the feeling, shape, size and colors of the stones we found, and we could feel their energies and their gifts.

When my daughter Cristina was little, she too would collect colorful rocks and would delight in picking up stones and bright colored shells. It seemed so natural and right, as she tucked them under her pillow before bedtime. Just like my little sister and I had done, I believe our Souls have an intuitive love for these gifts from the Earth, available and free of charge. I have always been drawn to crystals, their properties, shape, size and color. Later in life I became friends with a Shaman, who told me that stones held special and unique energies that were used in healing ceremonies and were tools of guidance for the Shamans, and the Native American Medicine men and woman. Today, at the Angels of Light Center, we have an abundance of crystals and information regarding their energetic meanings for our clients. Cristina has developed a whole array of Crystal Grids and Crystal Classes that her Soul shares with others.

Crystals are the Gems of the Earth and gifts from God. They hold unique energies that can bring forth greater healing, enhance our energies, support our chakra system and enhance our Soul journey. Modern research is discovering more and more about the healing and energetic properties of these special gems. I feel that crystals were given to us by the divine as tools for the body, mind and Soul and to support our evolution on the planet. Crystals have been used over the years by Talisman in the earliest recordings of Shamanic work as tools for healing, meditation, initiation and magic. The people of Atlantis used crystals for healing, communication, weather control, and as record keepers.

Crystals can be used to enhance and perpetuate deeper healing in your body, and can be a very valuable tool for your consciousness and your Soul development and growth. Crystals come in all shapes and sizes, and are often carried to protect and bring forth greater clarity, understanding, and draw love closer. Crystal Skulls are ancient in origin and are said to carry great powers and wisdom. The Mayans used crystals in their temples of healing, and for inspiring their people into greater vision and insight. The Incan Temples of the Gods were lined with mirror-like stone crystals which were said to illuminate the Soul.

Crystals hold a high vibration, and are used in everyday technology such as computers and machinery. Crystal bowls have been used and played for centuries and are said to enhance and clear the aura. Crystals at their simplest functional level will store light and discharge light, or convert sunlight directly into electricity, and since our bodies are in a pure electrical field, you can see how the power of crystals can blend and balance our entire energy system.

Below you will find an array of amazing crystals, their uses and their Soul message. With the help of my angels and Soul guides I was able to connect with each crystal personally for the purpose of sharing their many gifts with all of you! There are many more crystals for your Soul to discover, these are just some of my favorites

The Spiritual Awakener

One of favorite healing crystals is Amethyst

This crystal has amazing healing powers and helps to strengthen the entire endocrine and immune systems, as it cleanses the blood and energizes the Soul, bringing great inspiration and intuition, spiritual/psychic awakening, creativity, and courage.

It automatically transmutes one's lower nature replacing it with greater understanding and heightened potential. Purification and regeneration on all levels of consciousness are one of the many gifts that the Amethyst crystal as it brings forth and enhances right brain activity and pineal and pituitary glands and enriches the heart and Soul. The third eye is very fond of this gem and will respond by opening to greater intuition and light. As I tuned into this rich purple gem it gave birth to this channeling;

Your Soul has the wisdom to bring your body into a state of wholeness. You have divine gifts that are waiting to come forward, and your light is beginning to

shine brighter and brighter each day. Allow the energies from my rich purple essence to flow deep into your third eye, as I open the pathways for even greater knowledge, wisdom, healing and soul transformation.

This made total sense to me, since I have been going through many shifts and changes since the beginning of this book. I suggest that you carry this powerful and light filled stone with you, keep it by your bedside and use it in your meditations. It will connect you deeply with the Angelic realms and help you to open to your true Soul mission.

Spirit of the Ocean Selenite

Selenite and I have a deep appreciation for one another, as its oceanic vibration is formed from rich gypsum beds at the bottom of the Ocean. Rich in salt and cleansing properties, Selenite to me is one of the highest vibrational crystal formations on the planet. Often referred to as liquid light, gypsum occurs on every continent in the world, and is the most common of all the sulfate minerals. White in color Selenite crystals have many healing and mystical properties.

Named after the Greek Goddess of the Moon, Selene, this soft, yet powerful mineral is filled with metaphysical benefits, as it clears, cleanses, stabilizes and balances the emotional body.

Each season as I create a special Crystal Grid for my Meditations and Sound Healing at the Center, I incorporate 8 pieces of Selenite in a circle projecting out at the group. Along with the other Crystals it is a pure revitalizing and cleansing energy that moves through each person's energy field to create greater healing and movement on all levels.

There are many ways to use Selenite in your daily life, and one that I truly love is to sleep with a Selenite rod placed at the center along the torso chakras. This powerful crystal will begin to absorb all lower negative energies that may have been picked up during the day, and will bring you into a state of harmony and balance. Feel free to program your Selenite, telling it what you would like cleared and healed, and allow it to work it magic.

As I hold my Selenite wand I begin to feel a sense of calm, and peace. Here is the message I received

As I blend my energy with yours, I am honored to clear and balance your physical, emotional and spiritual bodies. We were together in Atlantis, where you first learned to work with my energies, and our connection is strong and meaningful. Your Soul understands and truly appreciates the energies in which I emit, and together we can teach others how to expand their awareness and their gifts.

All I can say as I hold the Selenite is that I feel the ocean waters moving softly over the land, on a warm sunny day, and my Soul feels rejuvenated and renewed.

Stilbite the radiator of love:

Stillbite stimulates the heart chakra and radiates from energy of love, compassion and openness. Great for meditation it brings in a sense of peace, and helps the mind to relax and receive. A perfect stone for astral travel when you meditate it will guide you on to other worlds, and helps you to feel safe and protected.

Holding Stilbite when you sleep will bring about profound dreams as it helps you to spread your wings and fly. Great clarity, wisdom and enlightenment follow the energies of this crystal and as your heart and Soul fill with the energy of happiness and joy, Stillbite has accomplished its purpose.

One of its many purposes is to help unlock the messages from dream, so before going off to bed place this crystal under your pillow. Remember to keep some paper or a journal next to your bed, and hold the Stilbite as you channel the message

As I work directly with the Stilbite today I feel a sense of kinship and purpose. I feel my heart opening with greater compassion as the messages flow through with ease.

There is no need to be afraid; your heart is ready to embrace love once again. You have learned so much about yourself and whets important to you at this time in your life. Trust that the love that is about to unfold is nurturing, and that you deserve to receive. Feel your heart heal as each tiny crack is mended. You will begin to feel my energy sealing off and clearing the pain of the past as you embrace the vital love of your future.

All I can say is thank you, my appreciation runs deep, as I feel confident that a richer love that truly nourishes all concerned is on the horizon.

Apophyllite the supreme intuitive healing crystal

Apophyllite is used in Reiki, meditation, and crystal healing. With its pyramid shaped peaks it in a conductor of energy, and magnifies any healing. I love how it connects to the higher realms and links the material and spiritual world in balance. Working with heightened psychic energies is one of its many gifts, and can help you to open your third eye, bringing in a deepened state of wisdom and enlightenment.

Using Apophyllite brings forth a greater sense of introspection, and I love using these properties to enhance the healing and light of my crystal grids at the center. As I hold this shimmering pale green stone, I begin to feel its message coming through loud and clear:

Allow yourself to blend your energy with mine, as I clear and expand your third eye, bringing greater clarity and wisdom to your Soul's purpose. You are truly ready to move forward, as new and exciting information from the higher realms is about to present itself to you. I invite you to work with me daily to enhance these expansive gifts.

The Soul Revitalized

Joyful Amber

Rich in color and joyful energy, amber is a stone that will bring forth great healing with its calming, purifying and revitalizing energies. It will help your Soul with its spiritual development and aid in the transformation of negative energies that get stuck in the body and the aura. Your Soul will thrive with this powerful stone, as it promotes a sense of well being, luck and success. As I was working with the Amber stone, my Soul opened up completely to receive its messages of light. A wonderful stone for the third chakra, it is said to empower all those who hold its beauty and light in the palms of their hands. The messages flowed with ease and grace.

Success is here and in the now, be receptive to the energy that surrounds you at this time, as my rich amber color and prosperities of success and good luck flow deep into your Soul enhancing your many gifts, and leading you in the perfect direction for abundance, expansion and joy.

I could feel the energies flowing deep within my heart and Soul, and suggest that you use this powerful and light filled stone with your goals and affirmations, as it will help to open the pathways to your Soul mission and success, connecting you with your mighty "I am presence."

The Angels embrace my Soul

Rockport is one of my favorite places, and I often go there in the summer. I love to go into the Metaphysical shops and look for unique stones and crystals. On one occasion, I came across a display of Angel Stone. Right away I got very excited, for anything to do with angels always makes me smile. It was a beautiful stone filled with energy and light and as I picked it up I could feel my angels joining me, as they admired its beautiful color and energy. Angel Stone is an uplifting spiritual energy that invites angel guidance, deep peace during meditation and purification. It promotes joy, light, and optimism, activating the throat chakra, and can help you to find your Soul purpose, as it channels higher knowledge, and helps you to reach deeper meditative states. It is said that the highest order of the Seraphim and the Archangels delight in working with those who hold this stone close to their heart. As I hold the Angel Stone in the palms of my hand I begin to receive this message from my angels and Soul guides;

We love and respect all that you do and all that you are, as we surround you each moment of everyday. Gratitude flows from our heart to yours, as you spread good cheer and enhance the light of those who cross your path.

You have such a beautiful and light filled Soul, and our vibration can blend easily with yours. Please use this stone to enhance our communications with you, as we help you to further your personal growth and connection with all of the Divine.

I suggest that anyone who is truly ready to connect deeper with their angels carry this stone, and use it in their intuitive and healing work, for your Soul will expand to embrace the energies of your Angels and their many gifts.

Smooth Soul sailing

Rich in color the Aquamarine will embrace and enhance your spiritual clarity and understanding. It will bring healing energies to your body, mind and Soul as it enhances your immune system and brings calming and soothing energies into your meditation. A stone of release, Aqua Marine will help you to let go of that which no longer serves you, as it is known as the "water of the sea stone" and filled with cleansing and clearing properties, helping you to let go of old issues and fluid retention. Folklore says the Aquamarine will protect against gossip. It is also said the Aquamarine will lift your spirits. The Romans used the Aquamarine for diseases of the stomach and believed it could cure liver and throat troubles; it has an affinity for the throat and third eye chakra.

As I hold the Aquamarine in the palms of my hand, I automatically felt soothing and calming energies begin to pour through my hand chakras. This is what began to come through

Delight in the opportunities to play and have fun. Relax, let go and allow the joy of life to flow through you. Sail with ease on the waters as you clear and cleanse the old to welcome the new. Great adventure is on the horizon, but there is no need to worry, for it is time for you to embrace all of life as your Soul expands with pure pleasure and joy.

Wow, I was really happy to hear this, since I just went into a three cycle as I write this book, and feel that many changes are on the horizon. I suggest that if you are experiencing any kind of change that you work directly with the energies of the Aquamarine. A wonderful stone to use in all meditations and to help clear out all that is no longer needed by the Soul, as it will help you to express your feelings in a safe and productive way.

The Soul aligned

Green Aventurine is a powerful and precious stone for the Soul, it helps the fear based ego to become silent and brings forth great courage and stamina, as it ushers in a positive mental attitude, emotional clarity and pure joy. A stone that will help you to align with your true Soul purpose and mission, bringing forth good luck, heart healing and greater creative insight to all relationships. The heart chakra is enhanced and balanced with the energy of this stone.

Green Aventurine will help to bring you all the energy you need to accomplish your deepest Soul's desires as it balances your energies in perfect harmony with your Soul intentions. I suggest that you carry this stone daily using it to clear away cobwebs and bring in greater clarity and wisdom.

As I held the stone in my hands this came through loud and clear;

Purify, purify, purify, cleansing your physical body is of the outmost importance at this time. New and light filled energies are waiting to flow through, heightening your gifts of intuition and healing. Eat the highest vibrational foods and drink the purest of waters for it is the pathway to greater movement and harmony as you continue to progress on your spiritual path.

I suggest you use this stone as a cleansing and clearing tool to help the body to purge old stagnant energies that are ready to be released. Along with a good cleansing program, this stone can help to bring about greater purification, clarity and much needed movement.

Energizer for the Soul

Carnelian is a pure energizer and helps us to reproduce our deepest Soul yearnings. Filled with the properties of creativity, balance and curiosity, this stone will help you to understand and see what is most important in your life at this time. It is a stone that opens the portals of empowerment and works hand in hand with the solar plexus chakra and the heart chakra, bringing in greater wisdom, empowerment and activating self love and prosperity on all levels.

Holding the Carnelian in the palm of my left hand felt very empowering and began to bring a sense of clarity to my thoughts. I loved the way the energies flowed up and down my arm, filled with adventure and movement. I could see and feel the energies of the Carnelian as a rich wave of golden/orange light begin to flow through the upper part of my body. I could feel its light and joy filled energies flowing in many directions and moving into what seemed to be denser areas of my body, mind and Soul. For several minutes I just sat and allowed this beautiful stone to vibrate throughout my being, as I became the observer. It was amazing, and as I tuned into the energies of the crystal a bit more, I began to hear it speak to me

Release the old patterns that have only held you back. You are a divine and creative being filled with ideas and teachings from your many lifetimes on the Earth. Believe in yourself and your capabilities for they are many. The energies of your mind, body, and Soul have been intertwined, reminding your Soul of its many gifts and the many gifts to come. Be open and ready to receive, for you are loved by your Angels and Guides, and as you open your heart your Soul will expand with greater understanding and wisdom.

Intuitive enhancement for the Soul

Celestite brings a calming and creative energy to the Soul, as great intuitive gifts flow from its center. Clarity and a sense of wellbeing accompany the gifts of the Celestite and your Angels and Soul guides will celebrate as you work with the precious energies of this crystal. Detoxification and empowerment of psychic gifts, this powerful crystal also reduces stress, brings in greater relaxation and creative expression, along with higher consciousness. A wonderful stone to use in meditation, it works strongly with the throat and third eye chakras. This special gem had the following to say:

It is important to take the time to pay attention to your dreams. Messages from your Angels and Soul Guides are flowing down at a fast pace at this time, and being quiet and taking the time to receive is of the utmost importance. Greater wisdom and clarity are on the horizon, and movement is in the now, so be willing to just be, as you slow down and listen as we express our deepest insight and knowledge.

I felt so many Angels around me as the Celestite shared its wisdom with me that day. I feel so honored to work with the energies of this precious stone and for me this stone is perfect for quiet time and meditation. Its messages come through with ease. All you need do is take the time to listen.

Soul empowerment with Citrine –

This amazing stone releases into the owner a sense of self worth and empowerment as it aids the 3rd chakra and the body to improve digestion, as well as to balance creativity, self-esteem, clarity of thought, mental processes, self-confidence, helps in letting go of addictions, psychic connection to higher self and can open the Soul to its many gifts, as success begins to flow in waves of energy towards the one who works with this stone.

As I held the Citrine in the palms of my hand I began to feel courage, and the qualities of strength and stamina. These energies began to flow from my hand up through my arm, traveling down into my stomach area. I could feel the power of this special stone, and it was as if my Soul literally began to draw energy from its rich golden color and light. I could feel my Soul expand, and I had the thought at that very moment "I can do it, I believe in me" this thought went through my head several times, as I felt the positive energy flowing throughout my entire body. I then stopped and listened as the Citrine stone began to speak to me:

Feel your personal power now flowing throughout your body, mind and Soul, as my energies bring to you a pure path of abundance and light. Allow my rich golden light to flow into the past, clearing away all doubts and fears that have been lurking deep within. Allow your cells to expand as you see that you are so much more than you ever imagined, and allow your 3rd chakra to expand *with courage and movement, as you have now been attuned to the truth, and of course the truth will set you in motion and set your free.*

It felt so good to experience the energies of the Citrine, and the beautiful messages that it brought to me. Truly a wake-up call, as I began to feel tremendous possibilities. I began to feel as if I could move mountains, as I felt perfectly in sync with my Soul.

Rose Quartz perpetuates Love

As you hold the Rose Quartz over your heart you begin to feel a deep connection, for this semi precious stone emits the qualities of divine love. Rose Quartz can help us to connect with those around us and even to those in spirit as its essence is one of pure love.

For me, Rose Quartz connects us not only with our heart and Soul, but with the heart and Souls of our loved ones in spirit. As I began to share more and more of my mediumship gifts with others, I was guided by the Angel Mihr to gift a Rose Quartz to each person who was ready to connect their heart to the heart of a loved one who had made the journey home. A wonderful process began to unfold, as I took each one through a guided journey, asking that they hold their Rose Quartz close to their heart and think of their loved one in Mihr's garden. They were asked to extend a rose beam of light through the quartz to the loved ones heart and allow it to return back to them. This process began a whole new way of connecting them easily with the love that is always available, from the Heavenly Realms. Try this and you will begin to make the connection with joy and ease.

Messages of love flowed from the Rose Quartz:

Divine love surrounds you now and always as your loved ones in spirit send you their most complete and lasting love. Your heart is ready to heal, allow me to fill it with my love and healing as it becomes whole and ready to receive the most perfect and divine love from those around you.

I could feel the love pouring down deep into my chest, and I am filled with gratitude.

Turquoise- Soul transformation

A total support for the Soul, Turquoise tones and strengthens the body, and nervous system, promotes nutrient absorption, tissue regeneration, circulation, respiratory system, aligns subtle bodies, protects against harm, environmental pollutants, psychic abilities, calms the mind, creativity, communication, friendship, takes on the characteristics of the owner. Turquoise is one of the oldest stones known. This is a stone that a person must learn to attune to instead of the stone attuning to the person. It is important that the owner of a Turquoise give it the proper attention. It is connected to the throat chakra, and brings about great movement and transformation for the Soul.

For several years now I have been wearing an array of Turquoise rings, and feel that it has brought great movement into my life. I am very attracted to Turquoise, and have many pieces that I wear daily. As I tune into the energies of my ring I am given this special message:

I am here to support your Soul's movement, for your Soul is one that is committed to transformation. I am helping you to let go of the old, easily, as your Soul is ready to experience the next chapter of your life. Listen to your inner guidance, and believe in what you hear. Your goals and dreams are attainable, if you believe. Know that whatever you choose, that you will be supported by all of your Angels and Guides. Allow my rich energies to open the portals of greater spiritual wisdom and knowledge. Feel your spirit soar into heightened dimensions as you spread your wings and fly.

Chakra balancing Blue Kyanite

Today as I write this chapter I am wearing a Blue Kyanite pendant. I can feel its calming nature, as it is a stone that will balance all of the chakras. I love to meditate with this stone as well, and feel it centers and clears the pathways for me to go into a deeper meditative state. Kyanite will help you to make a deeper and lasting contact with the spirit realms as it soothes and relaxes the body, mind and Soul. As a very powerful healing stone, it is great to place it on any part of the body, and especially good after surgery of any kind. This wonderful stone is truly an energizer and will bring back a sense of wellbeing and heightened energy throughout. It is also a wonderful stone to clear the meridians and pathways of the chakras, bringing a smooth steady flow of energy throughout.

The Kyanite speaks

You are about to graduate from a very long process of transformation. I am pleased that you have chosen to wear me today, as together we are bringing in a better sense of purpose and balance. The transformation that is taking place has been deep, as many layers of old stagnant energies have been lifted off of your physical, emotional and spiritual bodies. Today is a day of celebration, and as my energies flow perfectly with yours, I can feel your strength return. Your meridians are vibrating much quicker now, and great movement is at hand. Continue to wear me over the next several weeks, as together we create an environment of great transformation and joy.

These are just a few of the many semi-precious stones and crystals that can help to support your Soul and its Earth journey. I suggest that you see which ones call out to you and whether you choose to carry them in your pockets or wear them as jewelry their energies will continue to bring you the gifts from Mother Earth.

Bountiful Milky Quartz

While I was almost at the end of writing this book, I had a magical crystal experience and would love to share it with all of you. This also shows us the power of asking, and being patient as your Angels and Soul Guides go to work on your behalf.

For sometime I had been searching for a large milky quartz crystal. I had found one several years back on the edge of the woods near by. I saw its tip peaking out at me and I began to dig until I pulled it out of the ground. It was covered with dirt, but I could feel its high vibrational energy flowing through. I couldn't wait to get it home, and when Cristina saw it she asked if she could put it in the healing room at the center. I agreed, and life went on.

It was the beginning of summer and once again I began to get the urge to find large milky quartz. I was making plans to build another crystal grid in the center of the meditation circle, and felt called to use a large milky quartz crystal in the center. I decided once again to ask my Angels and Soul Guides and once I did I surrendered my request to a higher power, knowing that in the right time I would find the perfect one.

It was a beautiful warm sunny day, and a perfect time for a walk in nature. I began to walk through my neighborhood and felt called to walk up to the High School which boarded the woods. It had been some time since I thought about the milky quartz, and felt guided to look down as I walked along the wooded path. I no sooner looked down when low and behold I saw a white shinny tip poking out from the dirt. I looked around me for a sharp stick, and found one nearby, and I began to dig. The dirt was rather loose and as I continued to dig deeper and deeper more of the crystal revealed itself. It was huge, and took sometime to get out, but when I did I had to smile, for I know that my Angels and Guides had brought me here at this time to find the perfect crystal for the center of my grid. I lifted it from the dirt and placed it on the ground, as I began to take some of the dirt off of it. I knew I would have to wash it in the tub with special cleansing solution, but was thrilled that I had found it. I decided to continue my walk and pick it up on the way back, when suddenly I looked down again and another tip was protruding from the ground. I began to dig once more, and by the end of my walk, I had harvested twelve large milky quartz crystals in different shapes and sizes. I was totally amazed at how they were all together in a row, just waiting for me.

Before taking them from their home in the woods, I stopped and asked each one if they wanted to go with me. They seemed to answer yes, and seemed happy that they would be part of my grid. I felt great gratitude and shared that with Spirit, as I took them back to the car and drove home.

I was very excited, and began the cleansing process. It took quite sometime, but when all was said and done, I had mined twelve beautiful milky quartz crystals, and planned to use them in the crystal grid at the center. My clients were amazed and asked me where I got them, and I said I mined them, telling them the story of my request.

Since then I have gifted several of them to clients and friends, and kept several for myself. I find that crystals pick their owners, and then their owners pick others who they feel would benefit.

The moral of this story is that when you ask, be patient, and know in the right time and for your highest good you will receive –probably a lot more than you expected.

Embracing my Soul Prayer

My Soul knows exactly what energies and gems will do to support and enhance my purpose and mission. I hold the perfect stone close to my heart feeling Divine Spirit connecting us, and as I listen I begin to connect with my inner child bringing in its healing qualities and light. My inner Soul child smiles and comes alive and I hold this precious gift close to my heart with love and appreciation. And so it is! Amen

My Soul's Embrace chapter Review:

Which crystals seem to connect deeply to your Soul?
How do you feel you can use crystals in your daily life?
Which crystals do you feel would be most beneficial to you at this time?
Do you feel you could use crystals in your work?

Chapter Thirteen

Sacred Shapes & Sounds enhance Soul energy

"I step back as Divine Spirit leads the way"

For many years I have been interested in energy and how everything works. I truly believe that God has given us many esoteric gifts to experience, and as I continued to ask, I continued to receive. I was drawn to books about energy and how the universe works, knowing that God had placed each one on my path. I would no sooner go into a book store or metaphysical shop, and lo and behold, a book would be noticed on the shelf, or fall in front of me at my feet. It was times like this that I paid attention.

I happened to be in a metaphysical book store in Salem, when I was introduced to Sacred Geometry. The cover on the book looked like a nautilus shell and it really caught my attention, so I picked it up and started to go through the pages. It was fascinating, and as I looked over the contents, I just knew I had to buy the book. As I began to read the book it brought me back to the time I had taken classes in Alchemy. The instructor had used many sacred geometry shapes in the processes that we used. I had been using the Octahedron for some time in my morning meditations and felt it was a wonderful tool for protection and energy work. As the Angels of Light Center began to grow I began to connect more and more with Sacred Geometry and began teaching it in many of my Energy Workshops.

On the Metaphysical Journey Certification that I offered at the center many of these tools came to me just in time to use and teach. What always amazed me is how they were easily accessed and available to use anytime day or night. I consider them to be one of my Soul's best friends, as each shape brings about a special energy, and each shape is within our very being. Our DNA, our cells and the skin that covers our body, are all connected to the shapes in Sacred Geometry.

This morning after going through my morning spiritual practice, a special Soul clearing and enhancement process was given to me by my angels and guides. I would love to share it with you, as it is another energy tool, to enhance and embrace the beauty of your Soul, and the amazing energies of the universe. |I suggest you go on line and look up each sacred shape as each one will energize you in its own special way.

The Octahedron

Known as the diamond sphere – This wonderful sacred shape will help to protect and build boundaries around you, so that your Soul can move throughout the day with ease.

The Octahedron creates harmonious frequencies, purifying and balancing the body, mind and Soul. It can be hung in large spaces for purification creating a harmonious atmosphere. It is considered a true shape connected to alchemy/energy because it represents many molecular structures which means it transforms itself into different materials.

Sacred Soul enhancement process with the Octahedron- Creates purifying and balancing harmonious frequencies

Begin by calling in your angels and Soul guides. They will immediately be by your side. I will take you through this special process that will ground you and create a wonderful force field for your body, mind and Soul. (I suggest you have a friend or family member take you through this process, until you become familiar with it).

Take a gentle breath in and hold it for a moment. Now begin to direct the breath through your body, into the heart and Soul of Mother Earth. Take another gentle breath in, and bring your attention the top of our head. In your mind's eye begin to see a large white pillar of light above you. Now begin to visualize yourself pulling this white pillar of light from the heavens into your crown chakra, allowing it to flow down through your body gently landing on your tailbone/root chakra. Visualize a pure clear channel extending from your root chakra as it all flows deep into Mother Earth. Let's do this again; Begin with the white pillars of light coming down from the Heavens through the crown, touching upon each chakra, and landing on your root, forming a channel of clear light that goes from the root into the Mother Earth.

Bring your attention down to Mother Earth where you begin to see this light coming up through the channel from the Earth, and then flowing from the root chakra and going up to the navel filling your whole lower half of your body with pure white light. Continue to allow it to rise slowly from your navel up to your breast, front and back filling this whole area with white light, now visualize it coming up to your neck front and back and slowly pull this light through your crown so that it over flows around each side of your body.

Now begin to visualize this light creating the Diamond Sphere. It flows from the top of your head encompassing your whole body. Allow this to flow from your head around you back into the ground 3 times. Now gently begin to pull the light back into your crown allow it to slowly go down to your neck filling each area along the way with white light, now down to your waist, your root chakra and back into the ground. The outline of your Diamond Sphere is surrounding you and you are filled with white protective light. You can use the color silver to boost immunity and pink for self-love and green for body and mind healing, gold for self-worth, gentle blue for peace and violet for protection. It's up to you. Build your Diamond Sphere each day when you rise from sleep and feel the energizing affect that it has on your body, mind and spirit. You are supporting your Soul when you build this sacred shape as it helps to keep out any negative energy or static. This way you can truly follow the guidance from your Soul.

Taking it one step further:
The Highest Vibration in the Flower Kingdom is the White Rose

Use the White Rose to place below you, above you and to each side of you to absorb all tension, stress, and negativity that crosses your path. In the morning you can put a set of new white roses around your diamond sphere. The roses will continue to absorb anything that tries to remain in your aura. This will keep you more energized and balanced throughout you day, supporting your Soul on its journey.

One step further – let's close our eyes and put a closed up white rose in the center of each chakra – we will begin by placing the white rose on the root, sacral, solar-plexus, heart, throat, 3rd eye, crown and move up to the 8th chakra 2 feet above the head. Now when all roses are in place they will begin to absorb anything from your chakras that may be blocked or any lower energies that your chakras may have picked up.

Give your chakras a few moments to absorb – o.k. now bring your attention back to your root chakra and visualize that the rose is open, having cleared your root completely – see yourself removing the rose with your hand and placing it in the violet flame of St. Germaine – the intention is all you need to do this – and you can picture the violet flame right by your side ready to transmute the energies of the rose – now you will work your way up, 2nd chakra, 3rd chakra and so on until you reach the 8th chakra two feet above your head – now take a gentle breath in and place a set of new white roses on each chakra.

This process is best done in the morning – placing the white rose on each chakra in a closed form. At night when they have taken on the energies of the day and are in full blossom you can remove and place into the violet flame – at night when you sleep, you can ask your chakras to spin freely moving in perfect harmony with your Soul.

Embracing your Soul Mission and your Soul Gifts through

The Flower of Life

The Flower or Fruit of Life consists of thirteen spheres holding the laws of geometrics. The Sacred Shape represents the whole universe, bringing forth the gifts of longevity, good health and universal life. It is found in all major religions in the world. As I was working with this beautiful sacred shape, my soul guides gave me the following process. This special tool will help to open all the channels to your true Soul mission and gifts on Earth.

Take a gentle breath in and choose a flower that you really love. Visualize the flower in your minds eye, and ask your Soul to give it a special color. My Soul gave me the color magenta to use with this process. Now imagine that you smell the flower and take in and allow it to flow first into your heart and then your soul. Your flower of life begins to build now automatically. Now expand the light from the flower out into your body, then your aura and then out into the world. See yourself in a pure bubble of light. Take a gentle breath in and allow the flower of life to settle in the center of your third chakra where it will enhance your Soul's essence.

The Christ Grid – Healing light for body, mind and Soul

The Christ Consciousness Grid holds a subtle yet powerful energy for healing, body, mind and soul. It is made up of a combination of two sacred geometry shapes, the dodecahedron and the icosahedrons. This sacred shape can bring about great healing when placed within the body. Remember the body is the vehicle for the soul. This is a simple yet powerful healing process that my Soul guides and the angels brought to me.

Begin by taking a gentle breath in and allowing it to flow through each chakra and then see it flowing deep into Mother Earth. Feel your feet connected to the ground as strong white roots begin to flow from the soles of your feet into the core of the earth. Feel Mother Earth embrace you now, grounding your energy to hers. Now with your eyes closed open your hands and place them in front of you as if you are ready to receive a gift. Feel the energies of the Christ Grid as it is placed in the palms of your hand. Begin to feel its warmth and healing light. Now bring your attention to an area of your body that needs healing. This could also be an emotion. Feel where it is in your body and see yourself placing the Christ Consciousness Grid in the center of the issue. Feel and see its rich golden light moving throughout the issue, until it feels warm and tingly. Now ask the Christ Grid to remain in the area or emotion until it is healed. Go about your day, feeling rejuvenated and renewed, knowing that your body, mind and Soul are in perfect balance.

Soul Peace and Light – The Nautilus Shell

The Nautilus Shell has been on the earth since the beginning of time, and unchanged for 450 million years. It is called the Living Fossil and I believe it can expand the essence of the energy field, and the Soul. Nocturnal in nature the Nautilus spends most of its time in the depths of the ocean. It is lined with mother of pearl, and is a Soul symbol for expansion and renewal.

Energy/Alchemy process using the Nautilus Shell

Begin by sitting in a comfortable position and take a deep breath in visualizing your breath moving into your Earth Star chakra below the soles of your feet. The Stellar Gateway chakra begins to open automatically as pure blue light begins to move through creating the energy of peace. Feel this peace flowing through your body now and relax. Visualize yourself placing the Nautilus Shell in the center of your third chakra as it begins to swirl through all twelve layers of your third chakra. See the Nautilus Shell spiraling deep into the twelve crystals at the center of your body. These special crystals are attached to the Akashic Records, your past lives and your Soul. Take a gentle breath in and begin to see the shell pouring soft blue light into each crystal, bringing peace and renewal into all areas of your life. Remain in this place for as long as you feel you need to. This is a wonderful sacred tool to use at bedtime, as you will fall asleep peacefully. As an added bonus the energy of the mother of pearl will spread light throughout your body, mind and Soul.

Activating you deepest hearts desires- Metatrons' Cube

This is a special channeled process that came to me as I wrote my Soul's Embrace. The Angel Metatron advised me to use this process whenever I wanted to give extra power and energy to a special goal or heart's desire.

Take a gentle breath in and connect with your earth star chakra beneath the soles of your feet. Once again this will automatically open your stellar gateway chakra. Begin to visualize Metatrons' cube sitting above your twelfth chakra at the top of your head as it prepares to connect with your energies. See this golden cube of brilliant light flowing down through the higher chakras until it moves through your crown and into your third eye. Here it sits gently in the center of your third eye as you begin to visualize exactly what your Soul wants to create. Once your heart's desire is fully visualized, place it within Metatrons' cube as you visualize the cube traveling down into your heart and Soul. Great movement begins to take place as your heart and soul prepare to manifest your goal in the right time and for your highest good.

Angel Metatrons' Soul clearing

Begin by standing with your legs hip width apart. Get comfortable and begin to lift your palms up towards the heavens as you call in your angels, guides and all the divine universal energies. Feel the palms of your hands filling with their love and support. Now bring your attention to the top of your head and raise your arms up as far as they will reach. Now you will begin to move your hands back and forth, in and out, clearing a pure pathway for their guidance and light. Move your hands back and forth four times and then bring your hands down about seven inches above your head repeating the process.

Now right above your crown four times back and forth and then place your hands on your head as you allow the energies to flow through you. Now begin to sweep your hand in a downward motion moving over the front of your body. When you get to the bottom of your feet sweep out into your aura and then sweep down the sides of your body. Sweep your aura again to the top of your head and then direct your hands down to the back of your head and picture the energies flowing down your back until it reaches your heels. Now scoop up the energy in front of you bringing into your heart and Soul.

The Cube (Hexahedron) – Activating Soul peace and joy

The cube is a perfect sacred shape to enhance your connection with your Soul. Connected to the grounding forces of the earth, the cube is a perfect home for your Soul, and will enhance its energy and light.

Begin by bringing your attention below your breast on the left side, and begin to rub your hands gently until they become warm. Now place your hands beneath your breast into deep heart and Soul, and begin to let the warmth radiate into that area. Take a gentle breath in and feel your Soul come alive.

I always see my Soul as a wonderful white electrical light that begins to shimmer and dance. Before continuing you may want to check in and see what your Soul feels like. Once connected begin to visualize the cube around your Soul, as it begins to cocoon your Soul in pure Earth energy and light. Your Soul will feel cherished, nurtured and loved, and will thank you. Go about your day connected to your heart and Soul in pure peace and joy.

The Dodecahedron -Soul Clarity and Light

The Dodecahedron has given me great clarity and expanded my awareness. This is a process that my angels and Soul guides gave me one afternoon in meditation.

I was feeling rather stuck, and as I began to travel with this special sacred tool I found that my Soul came forth quickly with the answers I truly needed to hear. I began by taking a deep breath in and visualizing this soccer shaped ball of light. I asked that my higher self be present, and right away I felt a stirring within my Soul.

I could feel my Soul connecting with my heart in a figure eight which is also the infinity sign, as the energies appeared to be golden in nature. I began to fill the dodecahedron with the violet flame, sending thousands of them up through the figure eight from my heart to my soul. Tiny little Dodecahedrons filled with transmuting light flowed in a pure path of grace, from my heart to my Soul, and back again. I began to see that once I brought the energies down to my heart, they automatically connected with my Soul, activating great wisdom and clarity.

My third eye began to open fully at that point, and I could feel a gentle pressure in the center of my head, as if a spotlight was turned on and the answer became crystal clear. My soul was fully engaged as my ego stepped out of the way. I suggest you try this anytime you feel stuck, for the answers will flow from the truest part of your being, and you will have embraced the beauty and wisdom of your Soul.

Cleansing the Vehicle for the Soul Process

I love to use the Dodecahedron to clear my energy field, my blood stream and all the fluids of my body. Begin by picturing a pure white light flowing down into the soccer shaped Dodecahedron, fill each one half way and fill the remaining half with violet flame. Once filled begin to see each one flowing throughout the fluids of your body, and then expand them out into your aura five feet, as they sweep all twelve layers of your energy field. Go about your day, knowing they are in place, clearing away anything that doesn't enhance your wellbeing. Remember the body is the vehicle for your soul, treat it with kindness and care, and above all keep it energetically clean!

Divine Sound and the Soul

For many years I've been interested in energy enhancement of all kinds. Whether it was through the teachings of Chinese medicine, my transcendental meditation practice and forms of energy movement such as Tai Chi and Chi Gong, to tracing my meridians daily, to how thoughts and communication affect everything in our world.

The desire to work with and shift the energies within me and around me has truly been a desire that has unfolded over the years in many ways. Eventually I began to work with the energies of sound. After I opened the Angels of Light Center, my good friend and gifted Astrologer, Mantra specialist and Healer, Rev. Jill Jardine began to lead an evening of Sanskrit Chant once a month. I had always been drawn to Buddhist teachings and their culture so the Mantras fascinated me. As I began to practice the obstacle -removing energies of the deity Ganesh, the rich abundant sounds of Lakshmi, and the powerful planetary mantras, I begin to experience a sense of greater balance, clarity and Soul enlightenment.

I am a big believer in the sounds that flow from the Mantras and can feel how they lift my heart and Soul to a higher sense of self. For the past seven years I have been chanting and have found the power of Mantra to be truly amazing. Jill is an amazing Mantra teacher, and has taught me so much about the power of the Chant, another one of my many teachers Jill brings her expertise to the Center monthly, and shares many of her expansive Astrological workshops with us.

The Sacred sounds of the Mantras go deep into the heart and Soul. They expand out to all of the many systems of the physical, emotional and spiritual bodies, as their soothing sounds clear, cleanse, heal and enhance our wellbeing. Each divine deity that is associated with the Mantra practice brings their commitment to the chant. It can help us to remove obstacles, bring greater health and well being, clear lower and negative energies, and bring greater abundance and prosperity to our daily lives.

Free from Ego, each mantra vibrates throughout our energy field, and is said to have great karma releasing properties reaching into the deepest resources of our Soul. I have experienced these sacred times when I chant as a way to empower my being, enliven my spirit, and clear and heal my body on all levels. Truly a gateway to higher consciousness and enlightenment, chanting has become a part of my daily life, in a way that I can say has truly moved me closer to the divine part of myself.

I would like to share several Mantras with you that I've learned over the years and suggest that you try them and see how your feel. Mantra's can be done in denominations of nine up to 108 – I love using my citrine chant beads to keep count, remembering to place my middle finger and thumb on each bead, leaving the index (Ego) finger out. Below you will find a special group of Deities, and their Mantra gifts:

OM GUM GANAPATAYEI NAMAHA - Ganesh remover of obstacles through the power of unification – Depicted as an elephant, Ganesh truly clears pathways for the Soul to expand and move forward: I love working with Ganesh and have used this special Mantra almost daily for many years with intention behind it, the pathways to our true Soul desires become crystal clear and open with ease.

OM SHRIM KLIM MAHA LAKSHMIYEA NAMAHA - The Goddess Lakshmi, enhances the energies and gifts of prosperity and abundance: One of the ways I love to use this special manifesting mantra is to direct it towards my Vision Board. Each time I chant I visualize waves of energy from Lakshmi filled with prosperity and light moving through my deepest hearts desires.

OM EIM RHEEM KLIM CHAMUDAYIE VICCHE NAMAHA - CLEARING AND PROTECTION: I love this Mantra and have used it to clear lower energies that I feel around me. I have used it at the Angels of Light Fairs to clear a high vibrational pathway for people to join us – it seems I no sooner finish this chant and people are walking through the doors with ease.

OM HUM HANUMATE VIJAYAM – A wonderful Mantra that brings healing, strength and enhances life prana. I have used this Mantra whenever I feel tired or like I am coming down with a cold, or feel rundown. It truly enhances the immune system, and lifts my spirit.

OM VIGHNA NASHANAYA NAMAHA – Remover of obstacles – Whenever I feel as if things are not blocked and negative energies from this life or any past life is in my way, I begin to chant this wonderful Mantra. Right away I feel a lifting and things begin to move again.

AHAM PREMA -The Divine Love Mantra – This special Mantra brings pure peace and love out into the world. As it is chanted it vibrates through all layers of the heart and Soul, and re-connects us with our true divinity. Its meaning of "I am divine love" reminds us that that is truly what we are, love, pure and simple.

OM SHANTI OM/OM SHANTI OM – Inner peace and peace for the Planet.

Here is a list of the short Planetary Mantra's that bring body, mind and Soul into balance:

The Sun: OM SURYAYA NAMAHA – Supports the energies of the heart and circulatory system, thymus gland, and upper back.

The Moon: OM CHANDRAYA NAMAHA – Supports the digestive system, female reproductive system, breasts and nervous system.

Mars: OM ANGARAKAYA NAMAHA – Supports the muscles, urogenital system, gonads, adrenals, red blood cells, kidneys, and sympathetic nervous system

Mercury: OM BUDHAYA NAMAHA – Supports the respiratory system, nervous system, thyroid gland, arms, gall bladder, sight tongue and vocal cords

Jupiter: OM GURUVE NAHMA – Supports the liver, gall bladder, posterior lobe of the pituitary gland.

Venus: OM SHUKRAYA NAMAHA - Supports the veins, parathyroid glands, kidneys, throat, chin, lips, navel, neck and olfactory nerve.

Saturn: OM SHANAISH WARAYA SWAHA – Supports the skeletal and sympathetic systems, ears, calves, cartilage, ligaments, spleen, knees, joins, teeth, and tendons.

Rahu – North Node of the Moon: OM RHAVE NAMAHA

Ketu – South Node of the Moon: OM KETUVE NAMAHA

These are just a few of many wonderful Mantras that I have learned to incorporate into my daily life. Each one addresses a special situation and activates the gifts of abundance, healing, protection, love, and joy into my heart and Soul.

Embracing my Soul Prayer

The sacred shapes and sounds of the Universe make my heart and Soul sing, as a pure channel of light comes through from Divine Spirit. I become one with all of the Divine, as each sound represents a special gift that is being bestowed upon me today, and my vibration is lifted to a place or pure divinity and love.
And so it is! Amen

My Soul's Embrace review:

What did you learn about the sacred shapes in this chapter?
Did you use any of the processes? And if so what did you experience?
Where can you apply these processes in your daily life?
How did the Mantras make you feel?

Chapter Fourteen

Temple of the Spirit Butterfly

"I open my heart and Soul to the power of Grace"

From the time of our birth we are vulnerable to what I call a "Soul Storm". This dark night of the Soul is all part of our growth, for each challenge brings about great opportunity and Soul transformation.

In the summer of 2005, on the fourth of July to be exact, my body began to show me that there was another great transformation on the horizon. I was fifty two years old and had been experiencing some hormonal changes. My menstrual cycle began to come and go, and was erratic, accompanied by hot flashes and night sweats. I had begun peri-menapause and all of its many gifts!

I was visiting friends and celebrating the fourth of July at a cookout, when nature called, so I went into the bathroom to take care of business! As I stood up I could feel a stream of liquid coming from my body, and as I looked down I saw a perfect stream of red blood in the toilet. I was very surprised, and thought oh well, this is just all part of the process, and so I went back outside to celebrate the fourth!

As the days passed I began to experience pain and my angels and Soul guides told me it was time to see the doctor. As I sat in the office, a sense of peace came over me, letting me know that everything would be o.k.

I always trusted this special voice and knew that whatever was about to unfold would be part of a bigger picture and lessons and gifts would be the outcome. I was called into the office and told my doctor what was happening. She examined me and took some samples and said she would call when the test results came back, and so I waited with a sense of peace. The following Tuesday the phone rang and I answered only to hear that my doctor was concerned and that she had scheduled an ultra sound for me. She told me that my uterus was very thick and she didn't like the numbers that came back on the blood test. I agreed to go and have the test, and once again waited for results.

I received a call a few days later and was told I should see a specialist in Boston. Now I was beginning to feel a bit concerned, but something deep inside of me said, it will all be o.k. As I met with the doctor in late August, my friend accompanied me. I sat waiting, nerves on edge, and then was called into his office. He was very blunt and told me he thought I had uterine cancer. His words cut through me like a knife. I remember sitting straight up in the chair and asked "Why do you think its cancer?" He said that the blood test and ultra sound produced some evidence, and that he wanted to do an MRI. He told me I would most likely need a full hysterectomy, and that it would be the best avenue to take no matter what the results of the MRI were.

I was in shock, and told him that I had been treating my body with natural methods of healing for over thirty years, and I would find a way to deal with my issues naturally. He smugly smiled and said, well it's your life, but if it were me I would have the surgery. It's funny because at that very moment I could feel my Soul answering him back with great determination and intention. It brought me right back to the time when doctors told me I couldn't have children. My Soul stepped up to the plate and together with my angels and guides and the grace of God, I overcame the odds. I knew that this was very similar and that I had a choice.

I knew that somehow with the help of my divine team of angels, and the healing energies within and around me I would be o.k.! I agreed to have the MRI, and made the appointment feeling confident that everything would turn out o.k. By now it was mid December and I remember leaving my friends' Christmas gathering a bit scared, but very determined to heal. My friend drove me into Boston, where I waited patiently to have the test. It didn't take very long, and all the way home I remembered thinking that they would find nothing at all, but my next visit with the doctor told a whole other story.

He had the MRI results and pictures to show me. He told me I had a large growth inside of my uterus and that it must be removed. He told me that they would do a complete hysterectomy and take everything. He also said that my bladder would be involved and that he wasn't quite sure how to get around it. How could this be happening, I thought? I don't smoke, drink, and take any kinds of drugs or medication. I eat healthy food, exercise, meditate and live a pretty clean life? But the evidence was there, and so I turned to my angels and Soul guides for help.

I knew in my heart that this doctor might have been the messenger, but he wasn't the right surgeon, and that I would have to be open and honest with him about that. I can remember one time going back into Boston for more tests and as I walked through the streets to the hospital I saw a truck parked in front of the entrance that said, "Angels on Call" yes that's right! It was crystal clear that I was being supported all the way. I had to laugh when I saw the telephone number 1-800-444-…. Right away I knew that I was being guided and that I certainly was not alone. I smiled and my vibration lifted as I went through the hospital doors, knowing that the power of grace was by my side.

Each night I would pray and say "Thank you God for the healing that is happening to me and through me" as I invited Archangel Michael in to protect me, cut cords and guide me, followed by asking Archangel Raphael who would wrap his emerald green wings around me and heal me as I slept. And so my healing journey had begun. Over the next several months, many who knew about my condition offered me Reiki and healing Sessions, and I found an amazing Holistic cancer specialist who gave me guidance and supplements to enhance my immune system. I had begun to practice Tai Chi each morning and ate a pure diet, taking supplements and herbs to enhance my immune system. I turned to God and prayed, affirming my healing. I worked diligently with my angels and guides who brought through many healing sessions.

I am reminded of one night in particular when the healing angels showed up to work on me as a very powerful wind and rain storm was going on outside. I had just gotten into bed and it was then I felt them ready and willing to bring in their healing gifts. The rain poured down in buckets on the roof, and with each drop I could feel a grand and glorious cleansing going on deep with my body, mind and Soul. Archangel Michael was cutting cords all around me and I could feel him pulling in the area of where the tumor was. With each pull and tug I felt lighter and lighter. With each raindrop that pounded on the roof, I felt cleaner and cleaner, and the grand finale came when Archangel Raphael poured his rich emerald green light through me over and over again. I was all but frozen in my bed as it went on for over an hour. The rain would stop and start again, and each time another layer was lifted off of me.

I was pretty positive that I would not be having surgery with this doctor, and then the rains began to subside and I drifted off to sleep. I began to go into a dream state, and saw myself in a hospital setting with a female doctor by my side. She was telling me that I was going to be fine. I felt her love and kindness, and at that very moment I knew my angels and guides were at work helping me find this woman doctor. Several days had passed and the doctor called me one more time. I told him that I was getting a second opinion and to please stop calling me. I thanked him for his advice and told him I didn't feel comfortable with the way he wanted to treat me. He didn't speak for a moment, and than said, "I'm sorry you feel that way" and with that, I never heard from him again.

I do believe in some way he was a catalyst for my healing journey, and when I look back I have to thank him for being who he was, as he pushed me towards a whole new realm of possibilities, but now I would have to wait, and have faith that all was unfolding perfectly. Several days had passed and a good friend who was aware of my situation called me to say that her daughter who was a nurse had a recommendation for me. She told me about a female doctor at Mass General hospital who was ahead of her time, and holistically minded. She was an Oncology Surgeon and also an Acupuncturist, and had an amazing reputation. I remember taking the information, feeling something deep within my Soul confirming that the path I was about to take was perfect. I called the next morning, and much to my dismay, she was booked up for a full year.

I couldn't believe what I was hearing, and thanked the receptionist for letting me know. I left my name just in case anything changed and went back to talk to my angels and guides. Deep down inside of me, I knew somehow that it was all going to turn out fine, and that the right doctor would show up. Two days had gone by, and the phone rang, it was the doctor from Mass General, she had called personally to talk to me. I was absolutely amazed, especially when she told me that she had a cancellation and could see me the next day. I knew deep in my heart and Soul, that a pure path of synchronicity and grace had opened wide and that all of the divine had orchestrated our connection. The next day couldn't come fast enough.

My friend, who had told me about the doctor, drove me to Mass General Hospital in Boston. I remember thinking that this was a miracle and that many more miracles were on the horizon. We entered the hospital going directly up to the 6th floor and waited patiently, and when she entered the room I smiled.

I could feel her warmth and her love, and she made me feel at home and safe. My dream had come true. We spoke as if we knew each other forever, and she listened to my story. I told her about the other doctor and how I just didn't feel comfortable with what he had to offer. I also shared with her that I worked with angels and was a spiritual teacher. She smiled and said she believed in angels whole heartedly and that she also had a great respect for holistic healing. She was very familiar with Reiki and the herbs I had been taking to build my immune system and she knew the holistic Oncologist I had been seeing. She asked me if I would be willing to have a DNC, to confirm the diagnosis, and I agreed. I left the hospital, feeling optimistic and uplifted.

The day of the surgery my friend drove me into the hospital in the early hours of the morning. As I was taken into the operating room, I remember falling off to sleep quickly, having a dream that I was sitting with God. In my dream I appeared as a small child dressed in white. I was looking up at this all loving figure also dressed in white who told me that I was needed on the Earth, and that all would be well. I was told that whatever was about to happen would turn out fine, and that many great avenues were about to open for me. I was told to follow the path that would be unfolding, and that I would heal. "Be ready to follow your Soul's Mission" were the words that flowed from God's lips and I remember feeling great love and understanding, experiencing myself as this young child sitting on the lap of God. I could feel God's compassion and love for me, and I remember feeling so safe and at home.

When I awoke I remembered it all and began to share it with the nurses. They kind of looked at me like I had three heads, but I didn't care, for I knew I had been with God. So I got dressed and was then told that the doctor would call me as soon as the test results were back. I took a big sigh, and reminded myself that everything that was happening was for my highest and best and that God was with me and wouldn't let me down. The morning that doctor called me, she gently and with great compassion told me that I had stage one uterine cancer. In a way this was good news, because it was very treatable. She told me not to worry, and had me come back to sit with her and go over everything. She was such a wonderful, loving woman, and made me feel as if I was really being supported and taken care of. I shared my concerns with her, and she told me exactly what she would be doing. I had been listening to a specific healing CD every night since I was told about my illness, and asked if she would allow me to listen to it with head phones during the surgery. I also asked if all those who were participating in the surgery would be willing to say positive affirmations for healing during the procedure. They all agreed, and the day that they wheeled me into the operating room, I had a set of positive affirmations and the CD to listen to as they removed my uterus, my ovaries, and my cervix.

I remember thinking "What if I lose my intuitive gifts? What if by working on the second chakra and removing what was right in the middle of it, there was no longer a creative pathway for me to channel?" I know it all sounds silly, but when you do the kind of work I do, you know that this whole area is an intuitive portal for the 3rd eye and other intuitive and creative centers in the body. I remember sharing this with doctor, the morning of the surgery and she told me that there was nothing to fear. "You will be better than ever," she said, and with that I was wheeled into the operating suite and fell into a deep sleep. I remembered thinking about what God had told me and a deep sense of comfort filled my heart and Soul. I was wheeled back to my room after the surgery and my friend Preston and my daughter Cristina came into the room, smiling and told me that the cancer had been contained to a tiny polyp, and that it hadn't spread.

I was still half asleep, but I could feel my Angels right by my side, telling me that I was again going to be fine. When the doctor came into the room she was very pleased, she told me that the large tumor on the MRI had somehow shrunk to a pea size polyp and that without any complications my uterus had been removed. I had to smile, and thank my healing angels and all those in the community that helped me treat my condition naturally. It was evident that it had paid off, and that I was on the road to recovery. She told me that everything I had been doing had truly made a difference and she told me that I was the first patient at the hospital to ask to listen to a healing CD and have the operating team recite affirmations while doing the surgery. She said the whole hospital was buzzing about it, and that everyone who had been in the operating room with me experienced the power of positive energy. She told me to rest and that she would check in with me the next day.

During the night a wonderful nurse came into my room and offered me Reiki. To me she was an angel sent from heaven, as she spent over an hour with me and as I feel off to sleep I smiled, feeling supported, nurtured and loved. As the days passed and I came home from the hospital I healed in record time. All the tests came back clear and I was given a clean bill of health. God, the angels and my Soul guides had been with me every step of the way, and the lessons I had learned were many. From the very beginning of my healing journey to the very end, there was a path of pure synchronicity and grace that had unfolded. It had taken nine months before the surgery to discover this path, and nine months to give birth to better health. Looking back it was a true gift and I felt blessed to have gone through it. It was a time in my life for pure Soul growth and transformation, and as I lay in my bed at home, the morning after coming out of the hospital, another amazing journey began to unfold.

I remember feeling so happy to be home in my own bed, and when I awoke, I decided to listen to one of my healing instrumental CD's. I had no sooner begun to listen to the music when in my mind's eye a beautiful monarch butterfly appeared. I began to feel my second chakra pulsating and a surge of energy began to flow deep below my naval. A beautiful orange monarch butterfly was anchored in the center of my 2nd chakra. She told me that I had been reborn, and that my gifts would be heightened from this moment forward. She told me that the area where my uterus lay, had become a pure temple of intuition and insight, and that by agreeing to have my uterus removed I had released an immense amount of stagnant energy that was interfering with my gifts.

At that point I was in total amazement. My second charka began to pulsate and radiate a pure warm glowing light that began to flow through my body, filling my heart and Soul. I almost felt high, as it continued its journey throughout every inch of my body. I had been taken on a personal life enhancing journey with the butterfly, and from that moment on we were connected in spirit. I'll never forget that summer because it seemed wherever I turned I was greeted by butterflies. When I was out in the yard the monarch butterflies would appear out of no where, swooping down and often landing on my shoulder for a brief moment, only to remind me of my transformation. They were a true reminder that I had survived only to be better than ever, and that a whole new realm of experiences was about to come my way. The following November my first book 'Americo Michael' surrounded by Angels' was born, and in the spring the Butterfly Awakened CD came to fruition. Amazing and life changing gifts had come my way, and I am reminded of the butterfly each and every day as she continued to share her wisdom and transforming gifts. My heart and Soul was inspired to write this poem.

I dedicate it to all who are ready to enter the
Temple of the Spirit Butterfly,
You are truly ready to spread your wings and fly!

The Temple of the Spirit Butterfly

As I reach up to touch her wings
She flutters by my side
She soars above the sky so blue
Touching heaven with her glide
The gifts she brings are many
Her temple filled with light
Her heart and Soul are part of mine
Transforming me each day
My Soul is light and filled with peace
She shares her gifts this way
I thank her spirit fully now
As she embraces mine
She soars into eternity
Our hearts and Souls entwine
My temple houses all her gifts
Expanding with her light
I thank you Spirit Butterfly
My heart is filled with love
Your wisdom fills my very Soul
With grace from God above
I feel your Soul reach out to me
As you adorn the sky
You are a gift forevermore
On wings of grace you fly

The energy of the Butterfly is filled with transformation and grace, as we are reminded of our own Soul's essence, learning to spread our wings and fly!

My Soul Journey Experience by Cristina Burke

Whether you realize it or not from the moment we are born we begin our Soul Journey here on earth. The journey we experience during our short time here can be absolutely amazing while at the same time presenting us with heartache, loss, fear, and hardship.

Through my personal Soul Journey and spiritual growth I have come to realize that the good, bad, and ugly life experiences are all equally amazing because they all offer extremely valuable gifts. To have never known true sorrow how are you able to fully appreciate true happiness?

Through my own personal Soul Journey with the guidance of my beautiful mother I was able to connect with my true-life purpose and to heal on a very deep level. I discovered that there is so much more to life then meets the eye and I live my life by following the guidance of my Soul and higher self rather than relying solely on my ego. I have learned that life can be so very beautiful and aw-inspiring in the most simple every day experiences. I have also learned that living in the moment and having faith is truly the key to happiness.

Everyday is a chance to start fresh and to see where your Soul wants to take you. It is important to trust and surrender so that new positive opportunities can flow freely into your life. Set your intentions daily for a positive, prosperous, and uplifting day and be open to receive. I have learned so many wonderful techniques on my Soul Journey and thanks to my mother's guidance I'm mentally, emotionally, and spiritually balanced in a way I never knew could be possible.

Your Souls transforming gifts:

It's your turn now so take out your Soul Journal and begin to think of a Soul Storm that brought you gifts, transforming your life and moving you forward on your path. Below you will find a process given to me by my angels and Soul guides. This is a wonderful tool, that will help you connect with your Soul, and the next step of your journey, enjoy!

Feeding your Souls power center process

You will be working on your Soul's power center, a center which feeds our ability to expand and move forward fearlessly. Sit quietly now in a space that is peaceful and energetically light. Take a gentle breath in and allow it to flow deep into the heart and Soul of Mother Earth. Begin to feel Mother Earth holding you in safety and grace. Remember that your angels and guides are right by your side as you repeat this process two more times, feeling grounded and ready to proceed.

Bring your attention now to the center of your stomach area where your third chakra resides. In your mind's eye see your body miniaturize and step into a bubble of pure golden light. Once you feel secure begin to travel in the bubble of light deep into the center of your third chakra and begin to explore. Begin by looking all around the area and see if there are any dark patches or blockages.

Begin to see your third chakra as a pure circular ball of energy and tune into its color. Is it bright yellow and brilliant filled with golden light and circulating in perfect harmony? Or is it dull and weak, moving slowly? Take a deep breath in and continue to observe. Be the observer now without judgment. You are only here at this time to access the situation. Once you have a perfect picture on the condition of your third chakra bring your attention two feet above your head. You will be opening and connecting with the higher chakras and a greater volume of light will be able to flow through you.

Above your higher chakras is the Divine Umbrella of Spirit. Here resides the Father/Mother God, Jesus, the Holy Spirit the angels and all of the divine ready and truly willing to connect with your center, bringing you into a state of clarity and light. Rich beams of golden light begin to come through the higher chakras now moving through all upper body chakras and landing gently in the center of your third chakra. Deeper and deeper their energies flow circulating into the 12 crystals in the center of your core. Feel and see each crystals expand as you take in the golden clarity light, cleansing and clearing the pathway to greater and greater clarity.

As each crystal vibrates to the divine energies you are balanced and purified, pure golden light begins to expand into the circular energies of your third chakra. You are standing in the middle of this energy now and you can feel and see your third chakra begin to fill with this pure golden vitality light. With each rotation your chakra is fed, as this rich golden light begins to empower and remove all doubt and fear. Time after time the crystallized energies are mixed with the golden flame and a deeper sense of self appears. You embrace all that you are and your Soul smiles. You begin to feel strong, vibrant and renewed. All dark areas are now filled with light. Richer and richer the golden light builds into the very heart and Soul of your third chakra, each layer of your chakras energy field is enhanced and greater and greater understanding, courage and clarity becomes the outcome.

When you feel you are filled to the brim begin to see the little you in the bubble coming back into your full body. Take a gentle breath in and bathe in the clarity and the light. Now go about your day knowing that the energies you have created support your Soul journey, bringing greater movement, wisdom and enlightenment. Remember to do this daily for one month as you begin to see that you are in a state of perfection, connected to Source, and worthy of all good things.

What did you experience on your inner journey?

Embracing my Soul Prayer

As I take the hand of Divine Spirit I know that my Soul is ready to help me move forward into a state of action today. In a positive and uplifting way my intention goes directly into my deep heart and Soul space as it begins to draw towards me the abundance of this amazing universe. And so it is! Amen

My Soul's Embrace Review:

How do you connect with the stories in this chapter?
What are some of the obstacles you have overcome?
What lessons did you learn from each one?
How do you feel your Soul is stronger for experiencing these challenges?

Chapter Fifteen

Reuniting the Soul

"I embrace my brilliance in this new day"

From your small Soul child to your grown up adult, you have grown in stages, throughout your life. As we embrace each part of our Soul, a wonderful energetic and divine team begins to form. Once we reunite all parts of our Soul, self sabotage becomes a thing of the past and we can move forward into our bright and brilliant life. God is here to guide us, as we trust in the hands of the Father/Mother God and their pure and unconditional love.

Your Inner Soul Mate

From the day the Soul is ready to come into your physical body, it is filled with pure and unconditional love. This love is stored deep within the etheric field of the Soul and can be called upon anytime one is ready to open up to pure and joyful love. This very special love is the foundation for healing and one of the most powerful energies in the universe. You can set yourself radically free with this kind of love, and by giving yourself these self love offerings each and every day you can strengthen this gift, being able to share love with others with ease and grace.

Creating a relationship with your self is the key. Respecting the beautiful you! When you offer yourself compassion, freedom, and forgiveness, amazing things begin to happen. Your Soul surfaces in all of its glory and its etheric field hums with the vibration of love. In turn this powerful energy flows out into your auric field and begins to attract just that, love! You become a love magnet, and the people, places and situations around you respond accordingly. You know what I mean! Now think of a day when your hair comes out perfect, you love the outfit you are wearing and how it looks, and you woke up on the right side of the bed. You feel good about yourself and life. The energies around you vibrate to the beat of harmony and acceptance, and you feel on top of the world. The day unfolds and you notice that everyone is being rather nice to you, as they open doors, smile and let you out in traffic. You begin to think, "Wow this day is my kind of day". It's all cause and affect, and you have released what I like to call good Soul hormones out into the Universe. This is just a taste of what is available to you. Imagine if you did this daily no matter what you looked like or what you were wearing. Imagine if you just loved you, no matter what! Each day would be a parade of good Soul hormones and you would be receiving the benefits from everything and everyone that crossed your path.

Remember that when you create a loving relationship with self, and top it off with a bit of compassion you discover something amazing, a direct connection with the God source and the light of your Soul. You have a pure connection with your inner Soul mate, and begin to appreciate all of who you are.

As we venture out each and every day we have the opportunity to spread this loving energy from our Soul into the world. This of course becomes a win-win situation for all and can create healing within our bodies, as well as those around us. Your Soul smiles as you embrace the rich and unconditional love that is radiating from your intentions.

Everything in this world needs love and attention. It has been proven that the structure of water molecules change in our bodies and are affected directly by the words, sounds and thoughts that we allow to flow through us. Self- love is contagious and the key to having the kind of loving experience that you have always desired. As you love yourself, you are loved.

When you are filled with this kind of Soul mate love, your relationships become rich and full of life. You become the mirror of your Soul and attract those who are a perfect image to that mirror.

Kind and loving words fill your thoughts and your lips speak the language of love as you embrace the part of your Soul that knows how to truly love. Based on the laws of attraction, the only way to manifest a deeply loving and beautiful relationship to another is to have an equally loving and profound relationship with you. The inner self is where all love stems from. Love increases your ability to relax deeply inside, eliminating those stagnant and energetic blocks in your body that stop you from manifesting. To be able to accept yourself exactly as you are is one of the greatest experiences there is. You can make this something that you strive for daily as you learn to embrace yourself and your Soul. Laughter is a great tool for this, for it will help you to relax and let go of your own inner judge.

Embrace your Soul right now process:

Deep Inner Soul Mate Connections:

Begin by rubbing your hands briskly together and place them over your heart allowing the warmth of your hands to go deep within your Soul once more. Take a deep breath in now and gently allow this warmth to go even deeper into deep heart and Soul. Rich pink and emerald green light begin to flow together now in a vortex of light with ease. Now connect your heart and soul in a perfect Divine Love link. Begin to feel your heart reaching out to your Soul and your Soul reaching out to your heart as they meet in perfect love and harmony. See and feel the rich pink and emerald green light moving back and forth with ease and grace. Be with this powerful energy for a few moments and breathe. You are now connected with your inner Soul Mate; this is truly a place of perfection and unconditional love. Note: (If you feel disconnected at any time repeat this process of visualizing your heart connecting to your Soul in a beautiful heart link dance of love and light.)

The Soul yearns for love

Love is a powerful energy that feeds the universe. Without love, there would no longer be an existence, for it is the solid foundation of everyone and everything. Your Soul yearns for love and will reach out to others through the personality to make that special connection and begin to build a loving relationship. Some loves seem carefree, easy and filled with joy, while other loves seem to challenge our souls to the very core. Each love however is a stepping stone to the evolution of our heart and the transformation of our Soul. Contracts made in heaven, long before we stepped onto the earth plane, persuade two Souls to come together to fulfill karma and embrace heart healing

We spend much of our life looking outside of ourselves for safety, love and trust. Yet, the richest experience of that state rests in our own heart and Soul. The following questions will connect you deeply with your inner child and its many loves. Remember your Soul yearns to be happy, and alive.

Now it's your turn, now take out your Soul Journal and begin to write. Ask yourself what did I love to do as a child? Eight is the number for transformation so feel free to write eight special delights that filled your heart and soul with joy.

Begin with: When I was a Kid, I loved to:

Example: When I was a Kid, I loved to spend time with my Grandmother in Quincy

A kaleidoscope of rainbow energies-

It's time to allow your Soul's imagination and your inner child to come out and play, as once again we will do this 8 times. Now close your eyes and begin to see and feel rich and colorful rainbow energies starting at your feet. Now see this same rainbow energy moving up throughout your body as you feel a huge surge of color flowing from the top of your head all the way around your aura. Feel and see the rainbow rays clearing a pure pathway of energy into your deepest Soul's desires. Now come back and open your eyes and answer the following questions:

When I grow up, I want to:

Now let's take it all one step further and create some positive and uplifting Soul memories;

What's your favorite memory of your Mother, Father, Siblings, and Grand parents?

The house you grew up in, your school years, your first kiss, your first job, you're your greatest triumph at work.

Let's take it one step further;

What kind of work do you love to do? How did you learn this?

Going a bit further now;

What did you love about your teenage years?

Your twenties?

Thirties?

Forties?

Fifties and up?

What do you love about your life now?

What forgotten piece or pieces of yourself did you discover from this exercise?

Embracing the desires of your Soul with enthusiasm

What really makes your heart and Soul sing? An example of this might be: "I am enthusiastic about my new commitment to my health and wellbeing" For now list eight scenarios in your life that you are willing to be excited about – keep the possibilities open without restriction – this gives your angels and Soul guides full permission to help you to manifest. Remember the number eight is the number of discovery and transformation so see if you can list eight things that expand your enthusiasm. Please use your Soul Journal for this process.

Embracing the Gifts of your Soul process:

For the most part, many of us move from accomplishment to accomplishment without ever truly acknowledging what we accomplished. We move forward quickly and forget to acknowledge our gifts. You know what I mean! Most forget how to just relish their success and allow the joy to become their power and their strength. So here is a wonderful process that my angels and Soul guides gave to me in one of the Soul Journey Classes. Please practice often. For when you do you will begin to see that you are so much more than you ever realized and your will feed your Soul as you embrace its beauty and light.

Begin by bringing your hands over your heart center and imagine a rich golden light building in the center of your heart. See it glowing and growing, and then begin to send it out into your body as it flows through every bit of your being. See it expand out into your aura, bathing all 12 layers and then gently bring it back to your heart space. You have just opened your heart and Soul to receive! With paper and pen ready to write, take a wonderful life affirming breath in and allow it to flow through your body deep into Mother Earth. Repeat this several times until you feel your energies flowing through you with ease.

Now begin to think back as far as you can remember and start to write out each accomplishment. I believe just making it down the birth canal is quite an amazing accomplishment, so you might start with that. Now expand your thinking as you begin your journey of Soul accomplishments. Remember that many times what you accomplished took courage, so acknowledge yourself for that, as well as all of your wonderful attributes, such as kindness, generosity and so on. Keep writing until you feel you have created a wonderful list filled with the energies of acknowledgment and joy.

Now look over your list. Read it slowly several times and then place your left hand over the list. Close your eyes and begin to feel the energy of all these wonderful accomplishments and attributes flowing up into the palms of your hands and up into your arms, eventually moving into your heart and Soul. Soon the energies will be flowing deep into the cells of your body, bathing your mind and bringing greater and greater awareness to your personal gifts and strengths. Sit for five or six minutes and just allow the wonderful energy to flow. Remember at the end to anchor these beautiful gifts deep into your heart and Soul, where they will reside forever. This process will enhance your wellbeing, your confidence and empower you to move forward on your Soul Journey with ease.

Process to open your heart and Soul to great healing and Soul love

Begin by rubbing your hands together very briskly until they feel warm. Now with palms up next to your ears repeat after me: "I now invite all of my Guardians and Angels and all of the divine universal energies in at this time, as they connect their heart and Soul to mine. I give them full permission to bring forth extra support and healing today, as fragments of my Soul return, and my Soul begins to heal and move forward with ease and grace".

Now as the energies have filled your hands (they will begin to feel tingly) please place them over your heart and allow the energies from your guardians, angels and all of the divine to flow easily into the chambers of your deep heart and Soul. Feel and see your Soul stirring as it comes alive, ready to receive the gifts from the universe.

Embracing my Soul Prayer

My Angels and Soul guides remind me daily that deep within my heart lay my inner Soul Mate. I call forth this special love daily as it radiates out into my physical, emotional and spiritual bodies. I am empowered by this special love, and will embrace its many gifts, as I open the doors to pure and unconditional love from all who cross my path. And so it is! Amen

My Soul's Embrace Review:

What did you learn about your Soul from this chapter?
How can you apply it to your life now?
At what age or ages did you feel the greatest Soul growth?
What did you experience after doing the processes in this chapter?

Chapter Sixteen

Soul Mission a Path of Grace

"I see all through the eyes of the Divine"

As each year passes and I look back over my life, I begin to see that life offers each of us the opportunity to step onto the path of grace. Since the beginning when Cristina and I opened the Angels of Light Healing and Intuitive Center, I began to see this path perfectly and began to feel the energies within my heart and Soul expand. I could feel these special energies connected to my angels and Soul guides moving me in the perfect direction. I could feel my angels and Soul guides saying to one another "She's getting it" "She is really listening." I began to think about the hundreds of books I had read and how the Soul knows it all. I knew from my years of meditation study that when you take the time to go within and follow the stirring of your Soul, you automatically connect with your angels and guides.

What a wonderful path this can be, for it's a path without struggle, where faith is never ending, and where adventure and awe reside. Grand and glorious synchronicities begin to take place and the energies of the divine celebrate each waking moment, as your heart and Soul begin to listen and respond with ease. The stories I am about to share will illustrate this path of grace, enhanced by my heart's desire and my Soul's purpose and life mission. I trust you will begin to recognize your own Path of Grace like never before.

The Divine Plan

As I recall it was a cold but sunny day in January with a brilliant winter's blue sky. I remember waking to the feeling that my angels were up to something. They had come to me often over the years to let me know that it was time for this or time for that! Everything from the creation of my 12 month Angelic Soul Forecast to my custom Guardian Angels, to the 8 Angel Rays of light, they would encourage me to open my heart and Soul to receive.

I could feel another level of my Soul's growth ready to expand and welcomed it with open arms. The feelings I began to receive were very similar to when I was working on a temp job in one of the office buildings close by. Gentle and loving voices began to speak within my mind and I heard, "We are going to write a book." I responded," We are?" And they said," Yes, its time." I could feel my father Americo Michael as well, and together with the angels he had agreed that the time was right. But where would I start? And what would I write about?

And as I asked these questions, the path of grace began to open wide. Great ideas and inspiration began to flow, leading to the many experiences that I would write about in my book, 'Americo Michael Surrounded by Angels'. Day after day they brought me channeled messages, energy tools for transformation and poetry as the book took on a life of its own. Three years to the day I began writing it was sitting on my shelf, complete and ready to share. To this day it still amazes me, and I often wonder how I created that. Well, my Soul knew the answer and as I write this book, I can feel it stirring deep within me, compelling me to write and share my deepest thoughts and wisdom. So again, I saw my path of grace open once more with new beginnings and another chapter in my Soul's mission and evolution.

I remember feeling excited, not even knowing what was to come, but something in me knew it was monumental and so very important for my Soul's growth and mission. Shortly after I received a call from a friend who told me that Reverend Kimberly Marooney had created an Angel Ministry. She told me a bit about it and my heart started to race. My Soul came alive, and I knew at that very moment that this was meant for me. I had been channeling information and guidance from the angelic realms since 1995 and using Kimberly's Angel Blessings deck in my work. I had always loved her work, and although I had never met her I felt very connected to her teachings.

Without hesitation I picked up the phone and made the call. I wasn't surprised that she answered, for I knew the time was right for this to unfold. As she answered the phone I could feel her gentle and loving energy. I felt so comfortable with her and I knew the minute she spoke that I was going to become one of the first Ordained Interfaith Angel Ministers. We talked and she told me a bit about the Ministry. It had taken her seven years to bring it to fruition. She shared that it was a nine month program and that at the end there would be a special Angel Ministry Ordination retreat in California. As she told me more, I could feel my Soul stirring with excitement. I was so sure, and knew that nothing would stand in my way. I asked her how much it would cost, and when she told me I knew that I would find a way to pay for it. Everything had been set in motion ahead of time for me to succeed. A path of pure grace was open and ready for my arrival, a path that began that winter morning as I listened to my heart and Soul.

Soul expansion and light

I was one of the first to sign up for the Angel Ministry, and worked hard for nine months, studying, doing homework until all hours of the night, working, taking care of my home, my own work, my mom and more. It didn't matter because somehow I was given the strength and stamina to accomplish what my Soul had set out to do. It was a calling deep within me, and I wanted to succeed. I was one of twenty two Ministers from all over the world that had joined the group, and I felt blessed and honored to be part of this amazing and new direction. As the retreat grew closer, Kimberly was looking for a photographer to take all the pictures. Of course, I could see my daughter, Cristina, flying to California with me, and sure enough the path of grace opened once more. She was invited to be there and take all the pictures, and in December of 2009 we arrived at the Mount Madonna Retreat Center in San Jose, for four amazing days of bliss. What a gift, to have Cristina experience the retreat, and for her to see me being ordained. For those of you who have never been to Mount Madonna, California all I can say is it is a piece of Heaven.

I remember that the rooms were high up in the mountains above the clouds and when you looked down from the mountain top the clouds appeared to be below you. I truly felt like I was up in the heavens, looking down upon the Earth. It was an amazing place to be, filled with magic and light. I will never forget the morning of the ordination, as I went out onto the balcony of my suite and looked up into the sky. I couldn't believe my eyes, for there against the bluest sky I had ever seen was a pure set of large angel wings. They seemed to be etched from the clouds over the retreat center, large and proud letting us all know that they were celebrating with us. I ran and got Cristina and she took pictures which I now display on our website. I had allowed my Soul to expand its mission and purpose, and felt nothing but joy from the moment I arrived until weeks after I returned home. It's funny but when we are on the right path, our Soul automatically expands with delight, and we feel refreshed and renewed.

My Soul had forged forward and in December of 2009 I became an Ordained Interfaith Angel Minister. My daughter who had grown up in the holistic world since birth, transformed over those four days as well, and a whole new path opened up for her. She had received a special sacrament and blessing from Kimberly at the retreat, and when she returned home her own Soul's mission began to unfold. She was compelled to take her healing gifts out into the world and began to pursue Reiki and a host of divine healing modalities. Together we became a Mother/Daughter team of Intuitive Healers.

When I returned from the retreat, I was excited that I could actually marry couples. I had never thought about doing that in the past, but now it became crystal clear that it was one of my Soul desires. I also saw myself creating the Angels of Light Sunday Service, which would be a non-denominational, uplifting, affirming and light filled Interfaith Service that everyone could join, feeling nourished and supported by spirit. The path of grace went on and on, and in May of 2010 the path took Cristina and my self to 320 Washington Street in Norwell, Massachusetts. We walked onto the 2nd floor of the building into the most perfect space for the Angels of Light Healing an Intuitive Center.

Cristina and I, with very little money opened the center literally on a wing and a prayer, yet the path of grace continued to bring me the right people, the right situations, and the most divine support from the entire angelic and universal realms. To me, it was Divine Intervention, for everything fell into place with ease. Over the years the Angels of Light Center has grown and flourished and continues to surprise us year after year. The path of grace is never ending, and it is our blessing to be supported by the divine universal forces that love us unconditionally and are here to guide and support us. The gratitude that fills my heart and Soul grows stronger each and everyday, as I thank myself for listening to my Soul, and following my heart.

Divine Intervention:

As time goes by, I begin to see more and more of my Soul gifts emerging. Sometimes I remember in awe at how far my journey has brought me. I often ask "How did I get here?" and then I feel a little stirring in the center of my heart and Soul. A quiet and loving voice assures me that I am never alone and that as I continue to listen, so I will I continue to grow and expand my life Mission and Purpose. I have begun to view life as a great never-ending adventure, an adventure that, if allowed, can become a pure and joyful expansion of the Soul. Timing is everything, and trust and faith play a huge role in the process, but I have to say I truly believe that with patience and love, everything unfolds for us at the right time and for our highest and best.

Discovering my Soul's Mission:

Shortly after graduating and being ordained, I was given the opportunity to meet another Minister who lived in North Carolina. She was an Interfaith Minister like myself and had been taking a long distance class with me. We began to talk one night after class and she asked me if I had created a Soul Mission Statement. Much to my surprise I had to answer, "No". She took me aside and told me to call her later at home, and so that evening I did just that. Before calling her I checked my e-mail and noticed that she had sent me a copy of her Soul Mission Statement. I began to read it and something began to stir deep within my heart and Soul. I felt compelled to open a word document and begin to channel. I had been channeling messages from my angels and spirit for many years, but this was different, because I could feel it coming from a deep place within me. I continued to channel until at last I seemed to be finished. I stopped for a moment and took a deep breath and began to read what I had written. I would like to share it now with you:

My Soul's Mission Statement: By Rev. Cathi Burke

I am a beautiful being of light that is here to share and heal myself, and in turn I have chosen to bring this healing out into the world so others may experience their own unique self and healing. I am here on the planet at this time to bring forth a greater understanding and to become enlightened in a way that helps the masses. I am here to share my heart and Soul with those who cross my path, and to open my heart to many different avenues of self-expression, wisdom and divine knowledge. I see my path as a never-ending journey of learning and healing, as I embrace my Soul each day.

I am a clear and conscious channel for the Divine Masters, Angels and Planetary energies as I open my heart and Soul to embrace enlightenment, continuing to ask the questions that are necessary to stay on the path of grace and light. My satisfactions come when I see others blossom into their full potential and I feel blessed to be part of their unique journey and transformation.

Transformation is what I have come here to accomplish, as I continue to incarnate over and over again as each transformation brings me closer to the perfection that I truly am and enhances my connection with God.

> I am here to embrace spirit and to share the divine energies
> of the universe with all of those who are ready, open and
> willing to grow and expand their Souls mission and light.
> My spirit yearns to teach and expand great wisdom onto the
> planet, helping Mother Earth and her people to heal.

I am delighted to offer this gift to others and cherish each waking moment that I have here on earth. My energies are shifting each day towards the beautiful expression of spirit having a human experience on the earth, and I feel blessed to have a strong angelic Soul guide team of divine helpers that have partnered with me on my Journey.

I honor my Spirit and my Souls Mission. And so it is!

As I read each word I began to feel a great amount of energy building in my throat chakra. I felt as if I were about to cry, and so I let the tears flow. This statement had brought me to the realization of who I truly am, and what I was here to do on the Earth plane. It gave me chills, and at the same time it brought me a sense of peace and joy. It was then that I decided not to wait and called my friend, Carolyn to share what had come through. She answered the phone and was very happy to hear from me. I told her what had happened and for a moment she was silent on the other end. Then she spoke. "Somehow I knew once I mentioned the MIssion statement that you would have no trouble writing it," she said, and then asked if I would read it to her. When I was finished, she was silent for another moment and then said in her southern accent, "Well my dear, I believe your Soul has spoken," and with that we both laughed and promised to keep in touch. I have to say that I am very grateful for Carolyn as she had compelled me to expand my horizons and write from a space deep within my heart and Soul. To this day I have my Mission Statement close by, reading it often, as each time it connects me with my true Mission on Earth. For this I am truly grateful.

Stepping onto the path of grace process:

Begin by tuning into deep heart and Soul, as you begin to create your path of grace each day. The path is there for you to call upon anytime day or night. I have found that morning is best for me, so follow my lead and step onto the path of grace. Take a gentle breath in before getting out of bed in the morning and clear your mind. Let all the thoughts that may be filling your head just drift away. Now begin to see a pure lavender path in your mind's eye. See it as rich and expansive and never ending, as you sit up and swing our legs over the side of your bed. Your path is right over the edge, so place your feet directly on the ground with the intention that you have stepped on the path of grace for the day. Now go about your day, knowing you are fully supported and guided towards the right people, places and situations as your Soul expands with pure joy.

Planet Earth and your Soul

For many of you reading this book, you may already have an understanding of what I am about to say. As we continue to shift and change along with Mother Earth through the twenty first century and beyond, we are becoming more aware of the power of our own special energy, and how it affects everything and everyone around us, including the Planet.

Many are starting to realize that the Grids of the Earth are so much more than we ever imagined, and that energy accumulates each and everyday and feeds the Grids in a positive or negative way. These powerful Grids cover the Earth, collecting information and energy, which in turn affects the whole. As we continue to expand this awareness our Soul comes alive, and the possibilities to be part of a new way of thinking and being are activated. We begin to see that who we are truly does affect more than just our selves, that it is a driving force on the Planet, and can be a supportive source for all that is occurring at this auspicious time. It is said, that just one or two enlightened workers giving energy towards a positive outcome can change reality. The things that you do daily feed the Grids of the Earth for better or worse, and so your Soul has the opportunity like never before, to make a difference.

We all remember the doom and gloom forecasts for December 21st 2012. This was a time when the Mayan calendar ended, and predictions of the world ending were in the news. I can recall tuning into my Angels and Soul Guides, as they assured me it was a shift in consciousness that needed to take place, and so the ceremonies, prayers, and a more spiritual way of being began to unfold for many. Could this have changed the outcome? I say it did, and so do many of the Metaphysical teachers in the world. This is proof that what we do, say, and act out truly does make a difference.

So now it's your turn. I invite you to look over your own life and begin to see your own path of grace before you. Tune into it and feel your Soul sing, for it will be the path of least resistance and filled with light and abundance on all levels. Take your journal and begin to write from that space deep within your heart and Soul and see what appears. Ask yourself the question "How can I respect and support our Planet each and everyday?" and see what your Soul tells you. Whether it's a whole page or one sentence you will be on your way to reuniting with your true Soul purpose.

A special offering to Mother Earth process

Begin by bringing your attention to your breath and allow it to flow through you moving deep into the heart and Soul of Mother Earth. Repeat this several times until you feel relaxed and centered. Now begin to see the Planet before you as you bring your attention to the top of the North Pole. At this point you can call in St. Germaine and the violet flame, and begin to see a rich lavender light building at the top of the Earth. Visualize this transformative light expanding out and slowly see it moving from the top of the North Pole to the South Pole below. Repeat this several times, knowing that the Planet is being bathed from pole to pole in this clearing and cleansing light. Once again bring your attention to the top of the North Pole. Visualize the Master/Healer Jesus at the top holding his palms over the Earth as the richest and most unconditional loving light flows from his hand over the Earth – through the Grids, and every person, place and situation. See it flowing through the mountains, valleys, and streams, and know that you are being bathed in the deepest and most profound love. Repeat this three times and allow it to land softly on the South Pole where it is anchored and great healing and transformation continues to take place. How do you feel? What is your Soul telling you? Know that your intention holds the key for healing of the Planet, and be proud of the energies that you have just created and gifted to the Earth. Go about your day feeling light and free!

Embracing my Soul Prayer

I feel the divine guidance from my Angels and Soul Guides as my Soul's mission begins to unfold. I am fully aware of all that I am and all that I am becoming, as I give myself full permission to expand my Soul's mission out into the world. I embrace my Soul's mission as together I am empowered in bringing my beauty and light out into the world. And so it is! Amen

My Soul's Embrace Review:

What did you learn about your Soul from this chapter?
Did it awaken you to new possibilities?
How did it feel to begin your Soul Mission Statement?

Chapter Seventeen

A New Soul Journey Begins

"I deepen my connection with Divine Source"

Each time I share a Soul Journey Certification I feel exhilarated and alive. My Soul is filled with purpose and light as I anticipate the positive transformation the eight week journey will bring to my students' lives. The Soul Journey is much like taking all natural homeopathic medicine. For those of you who are not familiar with homeopathic tinctures, they are small but powerful doses of natural ingredients that when mixed at the perfect speed and taken at the right dose, begin to subtly change the vibration of the person for the better. With this being said, I feel that the Soul Journey is filled with similar healing potential, helping each person to move forward, bringing forth healing and light. Step by step they begin to shift and change their vibration, so that their Soul can expand and their true desires and Soul Mission can surface. It is my honor to share this wonderful journey with all who are open and ready to expand their horizons, agreeing to be all that they were meant to be. The journey is never ending, but the doors that begin to open just amaze me.

I always love to start the Journey on the New Moon or within a day or two after. The New Moon is known for being a catalyst for our goals and dreams. Seeds that are planted begin to grow and blossom, as our Soul intentions work perfectly with the energies available at that time. Each Journey has its own unique flavor and gifts. Below you will meet a special group of men and women who opened their heart and Soul to the light that shines within us all.

These wonderful and courageous men and women have given me their input on the transformation they felt and continue to feel while opening to the gifts of their Soul. The Journey of the Soul is unique to each individual and this group was truly open to expanding their Soul's Mission and purpose. I want to thank each and every one of them for sharing their new found connection and joy. May your lives be filled with great Soul expansion and love.

Students of the Soul Journey and their wonderful transformations

As I connected deeper with my Soul and its many gifts, I began to feel a sense of peace, calmer and more connected to my true essence. I could see that I truly was a spirit having a human experience and could value this in everyone. I feel more connected to the divine energies and my Soul, and have a greater understanding of my purpose here on Earth.

-Joanne Castricone

I had always been an over-achiever, and my accomplishments had been many. Since a small child, I had been encouraged by my parents and peers to succeed. I began to believe that this is who I was, my accomplishments, but as my Soul expanded I began to feel much more intuitive, and feelings and emotions began to flow from me that I had never experienced. I know now that I am so much more than my accomplishments, and that I don't have to fix anyone anymore. With this one belief change, I feel freedom to express who I am in a diverse way. My Soul is Free.

-Heidi Roy

My Soul and I are re-connected in a way that is very nurturing. By connecting with my Soul and all its many facets, I feel empowered and full of courage and strength. I have more clarity and understanding. I feel lighter, with a better awareness of who I truly am. I also see that I have a choice, not to allow others to bring me down. I can be the observer and feel the light within my Soul.

-Rachael McDermott

I am aware of my deepest heart and Soul desires and can now feel my Soul drawing me closer and closer to a profession in the Healing Arts. I had a belief that I had to fill other people's expectations, and now I see that I no longer have to extend my energy in this way. My voice has come alive and I know that by connecting my heart and Soul with all parts of who I am, I can take care of myself and let go of all that no longer serves me.

-Patty Whitcher, Doves Flight Healing

I can actually feel my Soul and its guidance, each and everyday. A whole series of events began to occur and miracles have flowed into my life like never before. I have found my true purpose and essence as a Healer and Spiritual Teacher and have been able to express this now as my profession. I am so grateful for the gifts of my Soul, and opened my heart to true love.

-Cristina Burke, Divine Healing Light

The 8 Week Soul Journey course was liberating and challenging at the same time. During the course I was gently pushed, in the best way possible, to confront the depths of my being. I discovered new passions and parts of myself I never new existed. I came to terms and healed old thoughts, habits and feelings that were holding me back. As a result of the Soul Journey course, today I can confidently say I feel a much greater sense of wholeness in myself."

-George Ghantous

After taking the 8 week Soul Journey I was able to expand my healing and energy work and take it to a whole new level. I felt that working directly with my Soul helped to feel more empowered and focused for my journey ahead. It was a wonderful experience, and I would recommend it to those who are ready to move forward towards their Soul Mission in life.

-Jodi Griffin St. Onge, Blue Angel Healing

This is but a few of the many who have opened their heart and Soul through the Soul Journey. My own Soul feels honored and filled with joy, knowing that my own Soul Mission continues to bring light into the world.

As the teacher for the Soul Journey all of my wonderful students also helped me to expand my Soul and my healing and intuitive work and teachings to a whole new level. I feel that the Soul Journey has helped me to have a deeper and more profound connection with my mission and my life purpose, and for this I am grateful.

-Rev. Cathi Burke, Angels of Light

Your Soul Mission

Many ask me, "How can I discover my true Soul Mission?" This question always makes me smile, for I know the answer and love to share it. I begin by telling them that it is their own unique authentic self together with their many gifts and talents that bring forth their true Soul Mission. I go on to say, that it isn't important if you are a Doctor, Lawyer or Shaman. What's truly important is their unique essence and beauty that they bring to whatever profession they choose. There is no need to identify yourself with a particular profession, remembering that whatever you do, you bring your own unique Soul and its many gifts to the table. Your Soul Mission is also connected to the contracts you agreed to in this life as well, and how you choose to fulfill each one, bringing forth healing and enlightenment. For years my angels and Soul guides remind me to "Just be who you are" and I have to smile for it takes a great burden off my shoulders and reminds me that there is no-one quite like me. So cherish all parts of your being. Share with others, and know that your unique essence is making a difference in the world. Smile and feel your own beauty and light and remember that your Soul is all knowing and when asked, will lead you onto a path of pure grace and light. Remember that you are part of the Earth at this auspicious time, and that this time in history is like no other. As you share your light and your Soul's calling each day, you are helping the planet to balance and heal. You are truly so much more than you think. So step up to the plate, share your love and make sure you give that love back to yourself as well.

Staying connected to your Soul's Purpose and Mission with the help of the Archangel Gabriel

A special Channeled Journey and a gift from the Archangel Gabriel

Take a gentle breath in and begin to feel your crown chakra opening as you begin to see a pillar of pure white light flowing down from the heavens through your crown. Allow the light to flow softly as it bathes your entire body, mind, Soul and energy field. Like soft and gentle snowflakes allow them to gather one by one into the center of your 3rd eye. Begin to see this rich ball of pure white light as it begins to gently turn to pale lavender light. Continue to see this light flowing through your 3rd eye, each time it circles through preparing your third eye to open and expand to receive. Take a gentle breath in and begin to see the pale lavender light begin to grow deeper and deeper in color, until it turns to a rich purple light. Allow this light to flow through all 12 layers of your 3rd eye now, as it expands and begins to turn once more into a pure indigo light.

Take a gentle breath in as the Archangel Gabriel is now present. See and feel Archangel Gabriel taking your hand, as together you walk on the path of pure joy. See yourself walking along the path, feeling the energies of joy flowing from Archangel Gabriel's hand into yours, as it travels softly up to your shoulders and begins to expand into your heart and Soul. Feel and see this rich light of joy being anchored deep within your higher and lower heart preparing you for Gabriel's heart and Soul link. Breathe and receive as you begin to see yourself back at the beginning of the path now as the Archangel Gabriel gently releases your hand and smiles, telling you that you are on the most perfect path at this time. Thank Archangel Gabriel and begin to bring your attention back into the room, knowing that the power of joy has begun to flow deep within your heart and Soul. Take a gentle breath in and allow it to flow through your body deep into Mother Earth's heart Begin to stretch, bringing your attention back into your body and into the room. When you are ready you can open your eyes.

Seasons of the Soul

The energies of the four seasons are a perfect example of the path of the Soul. For everything there is a season, and for the Soul this is especially true. We can see that during our lives on Earth, there is a certain ebb and flow of energy that accompanies us. This is a pure divine path that when followed can lead us to a new connection with who we truly are. As I write this chapter of the book it is autumn, and what a beautiful autumn it has been. The trees are an amazing kaleidoscope of shapes and colors that symbolize not only the changing and shifting of the seasons but also of the Soul. Walking through my neighborhood, I am truly impressed at the beauty that surrounds me. The past year has been both challenging and life affirming and I feel at this time in my life my Soul is once again at a crossroads and I am ready to move forward.

I have just returned from a wonderful vacation in North Conway, New Hampshire, accompanied by my daughter Cristina, my friend Diane and my cousin Suzy from California. It was a light and fun-filled vacation, and looking back I smile, feeling a bit sad that it is over. My Soul needed the rest and rejuvenation and the mountains of New Hampshire are my sanctuary in the fall. I feel connected, protected and grounded there. We were very lucky for the trees were filled with majestic colors, the streams flowed with ease, the waterfalls full and overflowing and our days were filled with the balmy temps of a late Indian summer. My Soul was inspired by the beauty, the friendship, the love and the laughter all around me. It was a time of rich enjoyment and light. Each day upon waking I felt deeper and deeper peace and gratitude for where I was in my life. My angels and Soul guides and I worked hand in hand to orchestrate this most perfect get-away as for several months as I had hired the heavens and asked for a specific tone for the vacation. They came through for me better then I expected with a few added surprises to boot.

From the country Inns, to the Bed and Breakfasts, to the home cooking and the beauty that surrounded us, my Soul began to feel the nourishment it had yearned for. I returned home with gratitude in my heart and the desire to do it all over again. That was the hard part. I would have dropped everything in a heart beat to go back and stay another week, or month or perhaps even longer. The joy that I felt had been long overdue and although the vacation was a pure delight, it allowed me time to reflect upon my everyday life. I had been running the Holistic Center now for quite sometime and although my Soul's work had been truly at the helm of the ship, I could see that I had given out a great deal of energy to my work and had forgotten the joy of just being. I had allowed myself to get caught up in the doing and the have-to-get-it-all-done mode. I had somehow left out the joy and the fun from my daily existence.

This doesn't mean that I hadn't accomplished a great deal or that I hadn't felt great purpose and satisfaction in helping those who came my way, but it did mean that I had forgotten about the simple pleasures in life and just being with my Soul one-on-one. So my autumn vacation had been an eye opener for me; a crossroads of sorts and a time when I knew that, above all else, I needed to learn how to bring balance back into my life. I thank the mountains and the streams, the fall leaves gently falling to the ground around me in their most magnificent array of colors and my wonderful friends and family who traveled with me that most memorable week in October, for after all is said and done, it was not only a rejuvenating time for my Soul but also an awakening. Now it's your turn as you take out your Soul Journey and begin to answer the question below:

What's holding you back from experiencing balance and joy in your life?

Divine Timing and the Soul

In 2010 I was giving the opportunity to open the Angels of Light Healing and Intuitive Center in Norwell, MA. It was an amazing opportunity for me to expand my gifts, contribute to the community and make a difference through the desires of my Soul. I love to help people and teach them that they are so much more than they believe. I receive great satisfaction from seeing them transform into the beauty and light that they have always been. The doors to the center opened on May 4th and from that day forward, it has been a steady commitment to healing, coaching, and bringing forth just the right energies to help those who come through our doors.

My daughter, Cristina, had been told at a very young age that she was a healer too, and I could see that she was truly blossoming. At the age of 30, she began to share her wisdom and healing gifts at the center. You could see that it was exactly what her Soul was meant to do, for the energy that flowed from her hands was healing, nurturing and light filled, and her teachings were rich and filled with higher knowledge and divine energy. Yes, the two of us were now a Mother/Daughter team of Healers and Spiritual Teachers that were ready to do what it takes to make a big difference on the planet. It felt so right and filled us up to the very core. I loved my work and I could see that Cristina was very committed to sharing her gifts with all who came to see her. We worked day and night to create a Sacred Space that others could come to, to heal, grow and transform.

For quite sometime we were giving most of our time to the Center, and then it began to feel as if something was missing. In my dreams and my meditations I could see that I was truly living my Soul mission and purpose, but forgetting about the rest of my life. I was no longer able to go out on weekends, and took very little time off. It was as if I was addicted to my work! So little by little I began to see that I was out of balance. Being a Creative Life Coach for many years and helping others to see that they need to bring energy into all areas of their life; I began to feel that it was time for me to take a long hard look at my deepest desires and needs. I could see that my work and what we had created was a beautiful and sacred piece of my Soul, and that it was the work that I was meant to do, but now it was time to connect with the other parts of myself that weren't being nourished. I knew if I asked my angels and Soul guides for assistance they would show me the way.

So for several months I began to tune in daily and ask them to show me what was missing. As soon as I did that an array of ideas and yearnings began to flow into my consciousness. My Soul had yearned to be out in nature, to play, to dance and to sing. My body which housed my Soul was feeling under exercised and undernourished, even though I was a big believer in natural foods and eating healthy. The homemaker in me began to yearn to make a delicious dinner, paint a room and go shopping for new curtains, and the explorer in me wanted to venture out and discover new places to walk, and enjoy nature. At first it was all a bit overwhelming. How was I supposed to fulfill all of the above, run a home, and a full time Holistic practice? Where would the monies come from to support me if I slowed down? How could I just take a week off and not feel guilty? These and many more questions began to flood my conscious mind and I began to feel as if I just wanted to pull the covers over my head and tune it all out.

Time out

Again, I asked my angels and Soul Guides for help. I told them I just had too much on my plate and that I needed some down time. I told them that I needed help to make money to finance all of my needs. I asked that they help me to delegate more of my work and trust those who were capable of helping me out. Once I asked and continued to speak with them daily, a plan of action began to take place. I began to encourage other healers and spiritual teachers to work at the center which helped me financially while affording me time for myself. I gave myself permission to have two days off every week in order to have more balance in my life. I started to go for polarity treatments and other healing modalities with people I trusted and then with more faith and trust I saw that my Soul's work would be supported by the Divine. I began to see that I didn't have to do it all by myself and that all I had to do is ask.

Little by little my work began to grow, classes filled up and the times I spent away, whether it was to cook a good meal, take a walk in nature or go out with family and friends, began to flow with ease. As I changed my belief system to "I am supported by life" and "I can joyously ask others for help" my life became more balanced and joy filled. Over the years I have seen many Light Workers crash and burn because they gave and gave and gave some more. Their Souls, like mine, had a deep yearning to make a difference for others, and yet they were forgetting that the most important person to take care of is themselves. I started to realize that I had to be fulfilled before I could fulfill the needs of others, and that I had to be physically and emotionally sound to be able to do my work.

Now it's time for you to begin to look at your own life and see where you feel out of balance. Perhaps it is the opposite of me and you yearn to be out of the house sharing your creative gifts or that you travel too much for work or not enough. Whatever it is that is out of balance, be open and honest with yourself. Give yourself permission to accept balance into your life and commit yourself to being more concerned with your needs at this time. Ask your angels and Soul guides for help. Then listen and watch as doors begin to open with ease and grace.

Embracing my Soul Prayer

With joy in my heart, I invite all of my Angels, and Soul guides to walk with me each and everyday. The Ascended Masters and all of the divine are by my side, and together as a team, they help me to expand my Soul and its unique gifts out into the world. I am filled with gratitude and I send them my love and appreciation now. And so it is! Amen

My Soul's Embrace Review:

Do you feel you are truly living your Soul Purpose and Mission? If not, where do you feel called to begin? Are you willing to allow your Angels and Soul Guides to help you?

Chapter Eighteen

Soul Growth and Rebirth

"I now release the old to welcome the new"

After December 2012, a whole new energy was ushered onto the planet. A rich cleansing of sorts, that everyone and everything would experience. There was no time left to dwell on the past, as a whole new way of being was on the horizon. Each of us had been preparing for this grand transformation since birth, and some still going through their day-to-day routines, were not even aware of what was happening around them. All they knew was that something was up. Our Souls began to bring about situations that perhaps we hadn't dealt with before, and it was time to truly grow into our fullness. For me it was a challenging yet amazing time; a bit of sweet and sour all wrapped up together. This was a time of great potential, movement and Soul growth, which would take me to the next chapter of my life. I would like to share this story with all of you.

My daughter Cristina had met and fallen in love with a wonderful young man who seemed to fulfill her in all the ways she yearned for. He was bright and loving and they were like two peas in a pod. They enjoyed many of the same things and finished one another's sentences. I was thrilled, since she had been asking for this kind of true love to show up in her life, and then the challenges began. In November of 2013, Shamus began to feel great pain in his right foot. His doctors decided that it was a growth and the treatment began with doctors appointments, tests, samples and then came a date for surgery. The tumor turned out to be quite unusual and cancerous. It was a form of melanoma that had grown in the sweat gland of his foot. It was very painful and would require several surgeries to remove since it was so deep. In January of 2014, the surgeries began. First they went in to remove the tumor and left a gaping whole between his big and middle toe. This would require a skin graft and would be done weeks after the original surgery. It was amazing to see how my daughter stepped up to the plate.

She was an angel, taking care of him both day and night, encouraging him, taking him to the hospital, doctors appointments, cooking, cleaning, and filling prescriptions and more. She was calm, deliberate, and all she knew was that she wanted to see Shamus heal. I saw a part of my daughter's soul come forth and her strength and stamina amazed me. Then my own transformation began.

Cristina moved in with Shamus and stayed with him day and night. For the first time, I was alone. Living in my house with three cats I felt a bit abandoned. From birth to age 60, I had never truly lived alone. From my childhood, to marriage, to having a daughter, to having my mom live with me, to sharing my home with a friend, I had never had the chance to live on my own. Although very independent by nature, it was a change for me, and rather uncomfortable. I just never had the opportunity to live day to day by myself. So my life was about to change. My Soul was ready. It was a time of letting go completely of old fears and patterns that for years had dictated parts of my life. You know those parts, you have them too. So now it was my turn to move forward and transform the past into the bright and brilliant life I had always dreamed of.

The first night I slept with the light on and then woke up and thought, "This is nuts! I have my angels surrounding me and have no need to be afraid", so the light went out and instead I put my little night light on. I fell asleep and was so proud of myself the next morning when I awoke to the sun shining brightly outside my window and the birds singing. "I did it!" And it felt good. Night after night went by and even though I spoke daily to Cristina, I began to feel that it was ok to be alone. I started to think of the single women who came to the center, and of my single friends who had been living alone for years. I began to feel like a young girl who had left her parents' house for the first time to live on her own. It was refreshing in many ways. Night after night flew by and it was two months before I realized that here I was, a single woman living on her own.

I was still teaching classes and saw Cristina here and there at the Center but I was truly independent and feeling good about it. It dawned on me that I had been running everything on my own since my husband died at age 28. I had been an independent woman ever since and although I did have my daughter living at home, she was still a young child and I was the one making decisions and holding it all together. So this was another step up in my Soul's evolution, and it was time for me to just be with me!

I have to admit that there were times that I did feel lonely and yearned for Cristina to be next door on her side of the house but for some reason it was different than before. I could see what was happening and just felt the feelings in order to be able to cope and grow. My Soul was being given time to expand and learn more about being on my own, teaching me that I was even more capable then I had ever thought. It was a great awakening for me, and a kind of freedom I had never experienced. I could eat what I wanted, when I wanted, go shopping when I was ready, go to bed and get up whenever it felt right. I could be in a silent house with me! And be ok. I also had the opportunity to connect deeper now, because of the silence that I found at home. The cats did keep me company at night as they hovered around me while I watched television. I really did appreciate their love and support.

Yes, this was a very special learning time as both Cristina and I began to see more of what we were truly made of, as the gifts from each situation continued to unfold. Shamus would recover nicely and learn many of his own lessons. It was amazing to watch the whole process unfold. As Souls we all interact with one another and for each action there is a <u>reaction</u> – contracts are made in heaven to be played out on the Earth plane, at the right time and for each person's highest good.

I invite you now to take a look at your own life. Take out your Soul Journey notebook and write down your challenges. What are they? And what are you learning from each one? Pure clarity and understanding will follow your questions, and your Soul will show you your truth as you allow it to expand and grow. It's time to embrace all that your Soul was meant to teach you.

My Soul challenges at this very moment are:

How is my Soul nudging me to change and to grow?

What Lessons am I learning?

What gifts are beginning to unfold?

Age is just a number: A story of Soul growth and expansion

It has always amazed me how everything just seems to fall into place and how universal divine timing surrounds us at all times. I believe that the plan for our Souls' transformation is never ending and that age is just a complication we buy into. I would like to share a story with you that I hope will get you thinking about your hearts' desires and connect you with the next level of your Soul creative journey.

For many years I had thought about playing an instrument. When I was a kid I thought about playing the guitar or maybe the drums or the flute and as I got older it was the piano. I never ended up playing any of them, even though I bought a piano that sat in my house and collected dust. I encouraged my daughter Cristina to take lessons but I could see that her heart wasn't really in it, so eventually she stopped. I finally sold the piano, and that was that. I just continued to think I wasn't very musical and that I would probably never play an instrument. I was given a small Tibetan singing bowl as a gift at one point and just couldn't seem to get the hang of it, so it sat in a pretty spot at the center for others to play.

So I put the thought of playing an instrument to rest and continued to expand my intuitive gifts and channeling. For several years I had been holding a Monday evening Journey Meditation at the center and I truly loved the special channeled energies that came through each week, helping those who participated to heal. On one occasion I was told by my Soul guides and angels to take everyone on the 8 Angel Ray Journey of Light. I had been offering their special Journey off and on at the center and at local centers in the area. The Angel Ray Majesta was very present that particular evening and as I began to work with the energies of the 8 Angel Rays, I began to have a vision of a beautiful set of colorful crystal chakra bowls. I laughed inwardly, and asked, "Who is going to pay for this wonderful set of bowls?" And then the answers began to flow.

I was told that there was a set of Rainbow Crystal Chakra Bowls just waiting for me to purchase on online and that the 8 Angel Rays would like me to begin to use them in all of my Journey work and so my musical desires would be fulfilled. I went home that evening and went onto a site on the internet that has everything. I had ordered crystals from them before for the center and now I was searching for the Chakra Crystal Bowls. As I clicked on the tab, lo and behold one beautiful set appeared. I remember thinking how beautiful they were and then as I looked closer, the description read," Last set." O.K. now I had to make up my mind fast. The next thing I thought about was how would I pay for them? I had a credit card that I could use but was trying at the time to pay it off. I looked at the price, which was very affordable, and then I saw it. The seller was offering a monthly payment plan! I could feel the excitement building as my Soul seemed to come alive and began to say, "Just do it!" Then, as I looked back at the screen I could feel the bowls calling me and my Soul seemed to open up fully, filled with excitement and anticipation. There wasn't one thing about this transaction that couldn't work. I even received an extra twenty dollars off as a first time buyer.

So I took a big breath in and with a huge leap of faith, I bought the bowls. Now remember I had never played the crystal bowls before, so I thought. The transaction was complete and the bowls would be sent to me over the next couple of weeks. I remember thinking that night as I went to bed, "What if I get them and can't play them?" My Soul guides gently reassured me that it would all work out perfectly. So I fell asleep knowing that a whole new Soul journey was unfolding. When the bowls arrived several weeks later, I couldn't wait to open them. Seven boxes were on my porch, each one holding a different colored chakra bowl. The color was the indicator of each chakra to which the bowl was attuned and when I finally unpackaged them, they sat on the floor in unison.

They were beautiful twelve inch bowls, frosted with all the colors of the rainbow. Each one came with a padded striker to use and right away I picked it up and gently thumped the side of each bowl. The sound was amazing: it vibrated throughout my entire body. I felt light and carefree. Next I took one of the bowls and gently began to run circles around the edge. It felt as if I had been playing the bowls forever, as each circle began to create a beautiful tone. I remember each one brought a different sensation to parts of my body. I began to play all of them, over and over again. At one point I saw a temple in Atlantis and knew I had played the bowls there in a past life. It happened so naturally. I just knew what to do, as my hands were being guided by my angels and Soul guides. This was a dream come true.

The first night I brought them to the Center I was so excited. I set them up in order of color and when the group arrived they were delighted. That evening I took them through the 8 Angel Ray journey with the seven bowls and the addition of the 8th chakra bowl that I had previously ordered for myself and never played. It amazed me how my hands went back and forth to different bowls with ease. I was very excited for the group, many of whom had been joining me each Monday night for almost five years. I knew that the bowls were a tool for clearing and enhancing the body's abilities to heal and my intention with all of my meditation and offerings were for movement, manifestation and healing. The group shared their experiences and each one said they felt deep relaxation and release that they had not experienced before. Many said they didn't want the bowls to stop, and felt the vibration flowing through every cell of their body. It was amazing, and I felt so honored to be able to bring this new and heightened healing to the group.

Since I began playing the bowls have taught me many new things. I have since been given several other high vibration instruments to go along with the bowls. At this point I have a wonderful gong and several different kinds of musical chimes that I use along with the crystal bowls, and I have also been working with the Crystal Pyramids, all of which have been included in the weekly journey. I have been using the Native American Rattle and Drum as well, and seem to have activated a whole new musical part of me. I also believe that many years ago when I studied Transcendental Meditation, that my Soul guides were preparing me to offer my special form of Journey Work that seems to flow each week with ease and grace.

My connection to my Atlantian lifetime has grown and each time I play the bowls I feel myself back in a time of pure peace, joy and light. Over the holidays I was gifted a beautiful heart healing Crystal Pyramid, which I also use to clear and enhance the group's energy, bringing great heart healing and clearing. As I embrace these new tools and gifts, I have given my Soul the opportunity to grow and expand. My Soul smiles and it all feels so right. Recently I have been directed to offer the bowls as a charity night, giving back to those in need. I feel so good about my new or should I say, rediscovered musical talents, and see now that at any age we can enhance our Souls' gifts. We are truly timeless beings of light on a pure adventure of self discovery.

Adventures of the Soul

Over the years, I have asked for certain things to manifest and I have always tried to stay open to the outcome. If we surrender control of the outcome, magical happenings begin to take place. When we let go of the result and trust our angels and Soul guides to bring us our highest and best, we will be pleasantly surprised. The magical formula is in the power of intention, holding a supreme vision, and then allowing spirit to connect us with the right people, places and situations for it to unfold. Mix this with a few drops of faith and trust and a whole lot of gratitude and like magic our adventures unfold in a state of grace and joy! Remember to hold on lightly for something even bigger and better may be on the horizon.

Now it's your turn – take sometime and begin to write in your Soul Journey a Soul Bucket List of sorts – see where your Soul wants to take you and allow your creativity to explode with possibilities.

Embracing my Soul Prayer

I give my Soul full permission to experience life and all that it has to offer, as together with Divine Spirit I expand my horizons. I am grateful for the guidance that my Angels and Soul Guides bring to me, as I release fear and allow myself to think once again like a small creative child of the Universe. And so it is! Amen

My Soul's Embrace Review:

What fears would you like to overcome at this time?
Do you believe you have hidden gifts and talents?
If so what do you feel they could be?
Are you willing to take a risk and go further with these gifts?"

Chapter Nineteen

Sedona Blessings

"My dreams are manifesting with joy and ease"

For over twenty five years I wanted to make my way to Sedona, Arizona. At one point, I had felt so drawn to this part of the country that I actually put my house on the market and was going to move there. It all began when Cristina was about nine years old and I became very fond of southwestern art, clothing and the Native American culture. I wasn't quite sure why this was happening, I only knew that there was a deep yearning to be in Arizona and experience Sedona. Twenty five years ago Sedona was still expanding into the huge holistic and spiritual community it was to become. Unlike Massachusetts, old by comparison, this vast and amazing land, filled with energy vortexes and the famous red rock formations was still developing into what it is today. Perhaps it was because I was born with a pioneer spirit, always being pulled to the challenge of waking things up: I was often told that I was a born ahead of my time, and I believe now that the Sedona energies were calling me to be part of its evolution and Soul growth.

As it happened, my house didn't sell and we continued to live in Hanover, Massachusetts, where I continued to expand my work with the angels, finally opening the Angels of Light Healing and Intuitive center. So here I was again in 2013 experiencing the same pull to visit Sedona. Friends and clients that had been there to visit raved about its beauty and light. I knew that someday I would get there. In October of 2013 my cousin Suzi came to spend time in the White Mountains of New Hampshire with us and I was about to learn of an exciting opportunity. Suzi arrived and was delighted to tell me that her daughter, Jessica, had become engaged. I was thrilled to hear this and then it happened. It came out of my mouth before I could even think, "Do you think Jessica would want me to officiate the ceremony?" A big smile appeared on Suzi's face and she said "Yes!"

Apparently, Jessica had told her mother that she wished I would come to California in May and do the wedding. Shivers ran up and down my spine, as the possibilities became crystal clear. Cristina and I could fly out for the wedding and then rent a car and drive to Sedona. At that point, I really didn't know how it would unfold but my guidance was strong, and there was a pull deep within me that said, "You have to go". There were many challenges that winter before the trip, with Cristina's boyfriend getting sick and me very involved with responsibilities at the center but my Soul would not let me give up my twenty five year goal of going to Sedona. I began to save money and invited my friend, Diane, who wanted to go with us. We would spend three days at the wedding in California and then off to the desert before landing in Sedona. My cousin Suzi wanted to join us as well, so the four of us began to plan. By February it was all arranged; the flight, the hotels and the Arizona sunshine, as my Soul's desire became stronger and stronger, looking forward to what was to come.

A time to rest and rejuvenate

The day of the trip, we left for the airport at 4:30 in the morning. Our flight was at 7:20am and we wanted to make sure we had plenty of time. Cristina, Diane and I went immediately to the check-in, only to find the flight had been cancelled and that we would have to fly out eleven hours later on the 5:45 evening flight. At first my heart sank into my toes, as I wondered," Why is this happening?" and then a little angelic voice said, "This will give you all a perfect day of rest before the trip" and so we did just that.

We found a wonderful spot in the airport and sat down and had a delicious breakfast. We took our time we laughed, looked at maps of where we were going and talked about what we wanted to do when we got there. The waitress told us to take all the time we needed since it wasn't busy. Two and a half hours or more went by before we left. We began to walk through the airport and found a wonderful space with white rocking chairs, where you could see the planes coming in and taking off. We got hot drinks and relaxed in the chairs, talking more about our upcoming adventure. The day flew by rather nicely, and once again we were getting hungry so we went back to the same restaurant and had an early dinner before the flight. It was just as delicious as the last meal, so we decided that this trip would probably be filled with great food experiences. Funny how it was just that; lots of great tasting food wherever we went. Thanks food angels! Before we knew it was time to board. I had picked a particular airline that I really like and when we boarded the plane I saw the rich purple light on the ceiling. This airline is known for having the purple light on all of the planes and for me that was a true indicator that Spirit was all around us. The sun was beginning to set and the sky was majestic and beautiful. The clouds were white and puffy and shapes of all kinds began to form. I always like to picture angels on both wings holding onto the plane and guiding it perfectly with Archangel Michael beneath the plane holding it up and taking us easily over the bumps that often occur on flights.

It was a wonderful flight, and we got to see the sunset, which to me was such a gift. We landed in LAX on time, grabbed our luggage and took a bus service to the hotel where my cousin Suzi and her family were waiting. When we arrived she greeted us and was all smiles. She waited while we checked in and we were sent to a wonderful suite that offered comfortable beds, kitchenette, and a very nice bath area. The Hotel had a lovely pool, Jacuzzi, free breakfast and more, all nestled in the town of Camarillo, California. I slept like a baby, and woke to warm sunshine outside of my window. My Soul was at peace, and looking forward to the adventures that lay ahead.

The rehearsal dinner on Friday was wonderful. Filled with good people, food, and celebration, and the wedding on Saturday were beyond what I ever imagined. I was so happy to be able to marry Jessica and Travis, in a beautiful garden wedding, as many of my California relatives were there to meet me for the very first time. The exquisite reception was held at the Spanish Hills Country club and everything was elegant and amazingly beautiful, as sweet floral scents permeated the air. My heart and Soul expanded as I married this wonderful couple, ready to start their lives together, fresh and new. It was my pleasure and honor to pronounce them husband and wife. I realized that my dream had come true. By listening to my Soul's desire, I had accomplished one of my dreams and was ready to experience even more over the coming days.

The Desert was calling

On Sunday May 4th, we said our goodbyes to Jessica and the family that had stayed at the hotel and the four of us headed out for Palm Desert. We had decided to stay at my Uncle's vacation home overnight before embarking on our Sedona adventure. On the way we stopped at a little diner where I bought a cow boy hat that I wore throughout the trip. I had let go, felt relaxed and ready to enjoy. The desert was such a very interesting place. After spending most of my life in New England, Arizona felt like a whole different planet. It was beautiful in its own right and as we drove along I began to see little dirt devils moving across the land. The wind would pick up the sand and create little vortexes as it moved from one place to another. The majestic mountains were very different from what you see in New England; they were stunning in many ways. I could feel my Soul expand with wonder, like a young child who was seeing something new for the very first time.

When we arrived in Palm Desert, I could feel the light and carefree energy all around me. The town was funky and very special: the swaying palms and warmth were a welcome change. I really liked the feeling and as we arrived at my Uncle's vacation home I began to relax even more, enjoying my time away. Palm trees and cactus lined the streets and in the distance the beautiful mountain ranges of all shapes and sizes. We got settled in and changed into our swimsuits heading for the large community pool near the golf course. The water was warm and inviting and as I floated in the pool, a little voice said, "I could get used to this!" My cousin Suzi had been telling me about Palm Desert for a number of years now, and I could see why she spoke so highly of her times spent there. I actually could see myself being there in the winter, with all the beauty, warmth and light. That night we went out to dinner and watched the sunset in Palm Springs. My dream was unfolding and I knew in my heart and Soul that I would return. Upon waking, we readied ourselves to leave and packed the car for our Sedona adventure. Five hours later we could see the red rocks in the distance. My Soul expanded with delight as the beauty took my breath away.

Red Rock Heaven

On our first day in Sedona, it was cool and a bit cloudy, yet the energy of the red rocks emanated an amazing magical light. We drove into the town and headed for Cathedral Vortex Chapel that was high amongst the red rock Ledges. From the top you could see the whole city of Sedona in a panoramic view. I could feel my Soul open with wonder as I saw the many red rock shapes in the distance. Many looked like castles and fortresses and I could feel the energy moving throughout my body, as I took in the entire view. There were no words that could describe how I felt. It was as if I had landed on another planet as the energies continued to swirl into my heart and Soul. A city of pure light surrounded me that day, and through it all I felt my Soul expand with possibilities.

Bell Rock a place of great majesty and light

Sedona is known for its extraordinary energy vortexes and special spots where the twisted juniper trees emit these special energies. Bell Rock was one of these special places and as we drove up to the parking lot I could feel my Soul expand with excitement. From the moment I stepped onto the trail of pure red sand I could feel the energies. Rich and yet subtle these healing energies were everywhere. We headed up the path getting closer and closer to Bell Rock and its amazing energies. Just as a magnet will line up metal filings, a vortex will bring one's emotional and spiritual bodies into alignment with the heartbeat of the planet. A pure raw energy such as used by many of our own appliances at home, these vortex energies bring about subtle changes in our chakra system, the meridians of our body, the endocrine system, and help to unleash psychic awareness, emotional release and spiritual unfolding. Bell Rock and the four vortexes' that we visited in Sedona did just that. We were looking for special twisted Juniper trees for it is told that they harbor the highest of vortex energies.

Each day we would get up and have breakfast and head to the next vortex on the map. Some say that the stronger the vortex energy the more twisted the tree. So we walked and climbed and stood by each tree. I held a mini meditation for the four of us and we each took in the energy we needed in perfect balance. Bell Rock holds a very powerful and strengthening energy that empowers and balances the masculine side, the feminine side, and the balance of both as a whole. I could feel the left and right sides of my body, coming into balance as I stood near the twisted Juniper. It was such an amazing energy and each one of us felt it differently. It was truly one of my favorite vortexes as my Soul embraced the energies of balance and healing. We visited four in all and each one brought a special quality of healing and balance. Red Rock/Cathedral Crossing was next and brought forth the feminine side and the Goddess energy, strengthening the ability to allow others their own life path and bringing forth and enhancing the feminine qualities of kindness, compassion, and patience. Next we strolled through Buddha Beach where we found hundreds of 'Cairns' which are creative rock formations that people build and leave behind honoring Buddha and the sacred land. The rocky stream that flowed with the forest terrain felt magical and my Soul felt youthful and free.

It was a joy filled day, as each one of us experienced the amazing energy from the earth. We were being filled with specific energies for healing and movement and I knew we were being guided to each one at the right time and for our highest good. On day three of the trip we ventured back into some of the shops in Sedona and were told about a special place behind the town Library called the Stupa. We were told that it was a place which honored Buddha and the deities and so with great excitement, we took the map and headed to the Library. Buddhist Stupas were originally built to house the earthly remains of the historical Buddha and his associates and are almost invariably found at sites sacred to Buddhism. Being a student of mantras and loving the Buddhist traditions, I was very excited about experiencing the Stupa. We parked the car and headed up the trail, not quite knowing what to expect. Lanterns and prayer flags lined the rich red rock path and when we got to the top we were standing in front of a huge medicine wheel glowing in the late afternoon sunlight. In front of the wheel was a shrine and prayer altar for Buddha. We all searched for an offering which we placed on the altar as a sign of respect, honoring Buddha and his gifts to the world. I suggested we chant and so we each took a corner of the Medicine Wheel, sitting in the four directions and chanted. The energies were swirling around us and together we had become one. We chanted, walked the labyrinth silently, prayed and truly enjoyed the wonderful peace that was surrounding us. We all agreed that we would come back someday as our Souls felt nourished and at peace. My Soul was fulfilled, feeling light and free. It had been another glorious day in the Southwest and as I drifted off to sleep all I could see in my mind's eye was the rich red rock and the divine light from spirit.

The next day we were directed to the Airport Vortex shortly before sunset. The Sky Lodge was close by and we stood on the veranda watching the sunset. It was one of the most amazing sunsets I had ever seen, and as we stood at the top of the Canyon I could feel my Soul expand with wonder and delight. Once again it took my breath away and my Soul felt pure bliss. The warm rich Sedona air filled our lungs, and a soothing breeze accompanied us as we headed toward the twisted Juniper trees that overlooked the valley. The energies were subtle yet powerful and represented the masculine side in each of us, along with the strength and determination to bring forth and live life to the fullest. I seemed to resonate nicely with the energies as my Soul was empowered by the male side of my nature. We stayed until the light began to fade completely feeling nourished and renewed. On the last day in Sedona we visited Boynton Canyon where the sun shone bright and the red rock stood out in brilliant color. We walked along the path discovering special rocks and cactus that lined the land. It was all so warm and beautiful as we ventured up until we were facing the Red Rock formations once more and discovered the energies near several twisted junipers trees. They were said to balance the male and female energies with the light of the inner child, balancing all emotions to live a happier and healthier life. It was glorious, and I once again felt gratitude filling my heart and Soul.

Guidance and Light from God and the Native American Energies

After being in Sedona for close to a week, we ventured up to the Grand Canyon. I had always wanted to see this amazing place and so the day before Mothers Day we headed to the Arizona side of the Canyon. You could feel the amazing Native American energies everywhere. We pulled up to the Best Western Hotel where we had made reservations and unpacked the car. The Hotel was very plush and the beds were memory foam, which was truly a gift. Having some back issues over the years always made me leery of most hotels, but when we walked into the room it was perfect. A little voice inside of my head said, "You deserve this," and I smiled. Yes, I did, and my Soul agreed! And so we settled in and unpacked. Around 5:00 we drove into the Canyon for dinner. The views again were breathtaking as great light from the heavens expanded over the canyon. We walked along the park path and saw the sunset over the deep canyon rock formations and I remember thinking that I had never seen such majesty. With the sunset, I could feel a stirring deep within my heart center realizing that I was actually here, and that a dream had come true.

A visit from a Native American Guide

As I got ready for bed and just slipped under the covers, I remember thinking, "I'm in Heaven!" I sank deeply into the memory foam mattress and thought to myself, "I am the luckiest girl in the whole wide world." Looking forward to a good night's sleep I turned over on my side and pulled the covers up snuggling with the soft sheets. As I begin to drift off, I woke suddenly and felt spirit all around me. The room was filled with energy and light. At first I thought I might be dreaming, but then I could hear Cristina rustling in her bed next to me. She was experiencing the same thing I was. "Mom they're everywhere," "Yes I Know" "I just want to get a good night's sleep" "Me too" she replied, but the Native American Spirits had a different agenda.

I could feel the energies of the land and understood that a great American Indian tribe had once been on this location. I began to connect with their energies and felt as if a ceremony of some sort was taking place. I wondered if we might be on sacred Indian burial ground but then they began to show me their tribe and what it had looked like. They showed me a tribal ceremony that they used to do at that time of year and as I watched, I began to see a beautiful young Indian Maiden before me. She looked as if she was about to hand me a gift, and as she bowed before me she asked me to open my hand. She told me that her name was Rising Star and that she would be honored to be one of my Native American guides. She placed a huge red rock in the shape of a heart in the center of my hand, and told me that she was bringing me strength and heart healing. She told me to call upon her anytime I needed extra support and that like her I was still blossoming into my fullest potential. It was such a feeling of love that emanated from her heart to mine and I could feel the light from her heart and Soul. I thanked her and then drifted off to sleep.

When I awoke, I did feel rested and truly inspired by the vision and our meeting. I told Cristina what I had seen and she agreed that the Native Americans were partying for most of the night. I do feel in a past life, I was Native American and that the connection I had re-established with Rising Star was a gift that was meant for me. Yes, the Grand Canyon was truly filled with many gifts. The next day, as I shared my story with Diane and Suzi, they also felt that this was a special place filled with Native American Lore and beauty. I was so happy to be able to spend Mother's Day in the Grand Canyon with three of my favorite people. I am filled with gratitude for the experience and my heart and soul will carry the light from the Native American energy forever more.

One Day Left

We left the Grand Canyon on Sunday night and began our journey back to Palm Desert. We arrived very late and headed straight for bed anticipating one more day in the Southwest. The next morning was glorious with rich blue skies and the warmth of the sun. Suzi and I took a walk in the community and talked about the possibilities of me coming back during the winter. I told her that I loved it there and since it was only five hours away from Sedona it was a perfect place to hang my hat. We swam in the pool, dressed and ended our trip with a beautiful lunch at the Marriot Palm Desert. As the day came to an end, we knew that the next morning we would be headed home but somewhere deep in my heart and Soul, I knew it was only the beginning.

Home sweet home

The return from Sedona was very difficult since I felt I needed to live in the Southwest. The red rock energy had connected so deeply with my Soul, as did the Native American energy that was very present now at all times. I began to dream of the red rocks every night and built a rock garden in my kitchen near my lucky bamboo plants. It was beautiful and each morning as I came around the corner it was waiting for me. I felt rejuvenated and renewed by the energies it was emanating. The dreams were very clear and in each one I was walking amongst the red rock and the Canyons. I now know that I was still receiving energy and healing from the vortexes: much of the information was still being downloaded so that my Soul could assimilate the information with ease. At first it disturbed me to think that I was that drawn to any one place and it was then that I began to ask questions.

Where did I belong? Was I supposed to stay in Massachusetts as owner of the Angels of Light Center or was I supposed to begin anew in Sedona? I lived in that question for quite sometime and then events began to appear that answered my questions. I had to be patient and not judge, as I allowed the answers to flow to me with the help of my Soul guides and angels. Shortly after coming back from Sedona there was news of a huge wild fire. It was all over the news and really tugged at my heart. The beauty of this wonderful place was being threatened and I felt great despair. I know that the Southwest is known for their fires and that the dry land was an easy target. I watched the news and stayed informed about what was taking place. Several of the places we had visited and truly cherished were gone. The mountain side was one of the places that had succumbed to the fires and the trees were gone. My friend, Jill, and I both agreed that the fires were a cleansing and that this was part of what went on in this area. I sat and prayed, sending love and healing to the entire area. Luckily the town of Sedona was safe, and the people had built special firewalls to contain the flames and the damage. The smoke however was everywhere. I knew at that moment that it was also a sign that I could not live in a place where fire and smoke was present. I had severe issues with smoke and my lungs wouldn't be able to handle this condition. I began to feel that the information that was coming through was a sign that I was to take the knowledge and teachings from this beautiful land and bring it into the Angels of Light Center for others to experience. It had become apparent that I would of course visit Sedona again in the future, but for now my home was here.

A Grand Soul Awakening

The signs continued to unfold over the coming days. The Monday night Meditation that I had been offering for several years, was my first offering after coming back from the trip. As my clients and students entered the room they greeted me with hugs and kind comments on how much they missed me. Some expressed the fear that I would be moving away and others told me how much Monday night meant to them. I could feel their love and devotion and it truly touched my heart and Soul. Shortly after, we had scheduled an Angel/Healers Fair at the Center. The day of the fair many amazing signs began to unfold. From the moment the fair began it seemed magical. The readers, healers and vendors had an amazing day and the people just kept coming and coming. It was a grand celebration and it happened to be our four year anniversary! To both Cristina and I, it was a sign from God that we were doing a wonderful job, sharing our work with love. I could see that we were making a difference in people's lives, perhaps for the very first time and my Soul expanded with delight. The fair was an amazing success on all levels and I began to feel at home once more.

The Native American energies filled the Center

The presence of my Native American guides became very strong as many of my clients began to experience them in my Monday night Meditations.

Several told me that they began to see ceremonies and Native American energies filling the room as they journeyed and I had been drawn to play the Native American drum and use the rattle for clearings. The number of participants in the Meditations began to grow in leaps and bounds and I began to see that my work and my energy had progressed to a whole new level. As I look back now, I could see why my Soul was so determined to visit Sedona, as new doors and experiences began to open for me and all those I came in contact with. My Meditations became more and more connected to the energies of our times and profound teachings began to come each and every week. More and more people were drawn to the teachings that I was now downloading and I was called to develop the Angels, Saints and Ascended Masters Certification, as well as to plan a new Course in Miracles eight week Journey in the fall. I continued to dream of Sedona, the red rocks and the Native American energy and felt blessed to have been able to take this special journey for my Soul.

I now knew how it felt to embrace my deepest Soul stirrings and knew from that moment forward, I could trust that this pull was coming directly from God. One evening as I drifted off to sleep, I dreamed that all my past lives were in front of me. I could see glimpses of each one and especially the ones that I had taken into this life as karma and lessons. An array of square shapes surrounded each life as if they were in their own compartments and ready to be looked at in a specific order. I saw myself in the center of a large crystal cave, which I know now is the Cave of the Akashic Records, and then it happened. There before my eyes was a past life as a Native American. In this lifetime I was young girl who had seen very tragic and overwhelming pain and sorrow. She had lost both of her parents and most of her tribe had been killed in front of her very eyes. She was hungry and worn. I could see her looking up into the sky as if to say, "Why?" and then she hung her head and tears began to fall. Her life had been one of great struggle and pain, and I could feel her sadness deep within the recesses of my heart and Soul. I knew that it was something I had experienced and it began to answer many of my questions I had asked over the years. "Why was I so afraid of loss?" and "Why did I struggle through most of my life?" Now I could see that my Southwest trip had also been an activation of sorts and it was time for me to process and release that past life from my energy field. I began to use the Root Cause technique from my Emotional Freedom Technique teachings and then began to tap daily on each emotion that surfaced. Gradually, I felt lighter and lighter with each session and I know now that I am on the way to healing this past life. It amazes me how for every action there is a reaction. My Sedona and the Southwest experience continue to unfold as my Soul is ready, and I process more and more each day.

Sedona Synchronicity

Before traveling to Sedona a client and friend of mine told me about a man named Michael who was part of the Unity Church in Sedona. She told me that when she was there she had gone to the church and that I should go and listen to what he had to say. So I did just that. I had directions and we decided to go and visit. It was late afternoon when we got there and the church was about to close for the evening. They did however let us in and we explored a little inside the church. We asked about Michael and they said he wasn't there that week-end. Disappointed, we took some information, walked the grounds and headed out instead for dinner. On returning home, I was told that Michael was at the Unity Church here in Massachusetts that following weekend. I couldn't believe it. I missed him when I was in Sedona, and now he was coming here to Amesbury. My friend, Susan and I ventured out to see him.

The church was several hours away, and so we got an early start. It was a glorious day with bright blue sunny skies. We were excited and very happy to know that we were going to meet Michael and experience the Unity Church. We arrived on time and went into the church where a large group of people were coming together. It was a lovely space, and before the service we decided to explore their book store. Michael's books and CD's were everywhere and we could feel the excitement building inside the church. We found a seat as the music began to play. The joyful energies were surrounding us and then we saw Michael. As I looked at him, I could see an aura of light all around him. His presence was calm and loving and when he began to talk I knew why I was called to see him. He would become one of my many teachers and would help me to take my healing and my own teachings to another level. I hadn't been drawn to another Spiritual teacher since the Angel Ministry and now I felt blessed to meet Michael. Being a Spiritual teacher, I know how important it is to listen to my Soul's guidance. What I found so amazing is that Michael could be there at that time in my life, right after my Sedona trip. To me that is pure synchronicity in action.

The service was wonderful and his teachings felt like music to my ears. After the service we spoke and I told him of how I had been to Sedona and gone to his church. I told him that he was here when I was there and we both laughed. He took my hand and kissed me on the cheek and I could feel his warmth and his light. I felt once again that I was home. Over the next couple of weeks my friend Susan and I went to several of his workshops, and bought some of his books and tapes. We talked about his lessons and I began to use much of what he taught in my own life and work. Many of his teachings were from a Course in Miracles, which I had taken several times in the 80's and 90's and had been teaching at the center. I truly resonated with his energy and knowledge and continue to work with his teachings. My Soul has expanded even more to embrace his advanced teachings and his connection with God and the Holy Spirit. I feel my heart and Soul taking in the wisdom and light and feel better and better each day.

I started to see synchronicities around my entire trip to the Southwest especially meeting Michael and being welcomed home so warmly at the center. I realized the most important thing is that I offer my own teachings and knowledge wherever I live to those who are open and ready to heal. Would I ever go back? Of course! I have always dreamed of being a snow bird, and so Palm Desert and Sedona are first on my list of places to go. As we ask ourselves from time to time, "Where do I belong"? "What is my Soul's true purpose?" we know that as a unique and beautiful child of God, it isn't so much where we live, or what we do, it's how we open our heart and Soul to spread the love and light that is within us all. We are always connected to God and all of the Divine. We can begin to dissolve the separation, knowing that within our Soul is a pure divine light that never dies. With the help of God, I continue to learn and grow each day, as I take all that I am and all that I am becoming out into the world to share.

Embracing my Soul Prayer

As I remind myself daily to respect my Soul and its earthly journey, an abundance of possibilities begin to flow. My Angels and Soul guides help me to embrace each new adventure, as my Soul has room to stretch and grow. Great expansion takes place and a whole new chapter of my life begins to unfold. And so it is! Amen

My Soul's Embrace Review:

What distant land does your Soul feel called to visit?
What are you willing to do to make this happen?
Do you trust that this urge has a purpose for your Soul?
Where in your life have you experienced synchronicity
with a specific destination in mind?

Chapter Twenty

The Path of the Soul

"I am expansive and one with the light"

What is your Soul's magnificent plan? Are you connected to your heart and Soul in a way that guides you? Or are you feeling trapped and unaware of your Soul's purpose? Many people have this issue and feel as if they are running in circles trying to figure out who they are and what they are supposed to be doing. The mom who feels she wanted a career and instead is raising children, the career woman who never had children and feels she lost out on life, and the man who was a genius in school and works at the local supermarket bagging groceries. All of these scenarios bring us to the question who are we and why are we here?

The Path of the Soul

First and foremost I want you to know that you are a pure being of light, created as I said in the beginning from pure stardust. Your Soul is filled with this brilliant light, which emanates from the God Source. Your profession is part of what you feel called to do, and sometimes not. Sometimes we can actually end up in a job or a relationship that is farthest from what we ever imagined or dreamed of. Believe me when I tell you, your Soul has its own agenda. It's your unique essence that you bring into your relationships and all of life that truly matters. What you do as a profession is just the icing on the cake.

It all brings me back to when I was growing up. My father was an Engineer who worked for a division of NASA, in the space program. I remember thinking how my dad was such a brilliant man and how I so wanted to be like him. As you may recall, as a young adult, I had dreams of becoming a business woman, traveling the world with my briefcase filled with important papers and documents. At that time I had no desire to have children or to marry. For me it was all about freedom and accomplishment. It's funny because when I look back I could never have imagined that I would one day be the owner of a Healing and Intuitive Center helping others to find their Soul Mission. It amazes me to think that I was so off track and upon reflection I can see that my Soul was in its infancy. I believe that every experience led to the path I am on today and that my Soul was guiding this journey.

In order to run the Angels of Light Healing and Intuitive Center, I needed to have a good business sense, determination and stick-to-it-ness. I feel my father was an inspiration. I always loved the saying "You can't put the cart before the horse." This is how our Soul actually guides us. Think about it. We have a desire and we try and try again to make it happen, but no matter what we do it just doesn't manifest. Divine timing and the Soul walk hand in hand, and it is important to remember that our Souls are filled with wisdom and know exactly what is best. I remember as a child and a young adult that I was always asking questions and thinking deeply about everything. I was always very connected to the spirit world, but as I got older I began to close that down, opening up more to the material world and its offerings. As time went by, however, my deep spiritual side began to open and I could no longer deny that this was part of my life path. I remember yearning to make a difference and at one point thought about being a doctor.

Now when I look back I can see that everything that had occurred was perfect for my future path. My business skills, my desire to make a difference and my spiritual gifts were all part of my Soul's mission. I have been able to act as manager, spiritual teacher and healer for those who cross my path. I also believe that is why I love Soul coaching and decided to take my spiritual gifts and expand them in that direction. The expansion of the Soul is never ending. There is no need to place your self in a box.

So what about you? What gifts are ready to unfold? I'm sure they are many and hope that as you read this book and perhaps take the 8 Week Soul Journey that you will begin to discover that your Soul is ready to integrate all of these gifts into your mission and purpose on Earth. Please take out your Soul Journal now and answer the questions below – use the deep heart and Soul process before beginning, allowing your hand to become warm as you place them into the spot I call Deep heart and Soul.

My Soul's gifts

Where do I excel? Be loving, open and honest and your gifts will unfold.

Make a list of all of your accomplishment! Don't be shy, as you try for at least eight and let your Soul brag, you have the right!

O.K. now lets take this process one step further and bring it all into your physical and emotional body, as you anchor it within your heart and Soul.

A Great appreciation for all that you are and all you are becoming!

Please take your list of accomplishments from Chapter 15 as we transform your gifts and take them to the next level.

Take a gentle breath in and relax into your space. Another gentle breath in as your breath begins to flow down through each chakra, gently touching upon and expanding each one. Breathe deeply and allow this energy to flow through the soles of your feet into Mother Earth. One more gentle breath in now as you allow the breath to land deep within your heart space. Begin to visualize an emerald green and pink light from the center of your heart and Soul, ready to expand. See yourself standing at the threshold of a beautiful Golden Door. The door is your "Golden opportunity" to take your gifts further, and to open new doors for your Souls expansion.

With each accomplishment you read aloud you will close your eyes and see yourself walking through the Golden Door.

Your Soul has now given you permission to expand, and you have invited your angels and Soul guides in to walk with you on this new expanded path. With each accomplishment you go further and further and begin to see the possibilities that lay ahead. Breathe and allow your body to walk further and further, walking through door, after door, until you feel a fresh new energy surrounding you. Breathe in this new energy and set the intention that from this day forward you are open to receive direction through the right people, places and situations. With a little trust and faith it will all begin to unfold. Take a gentle breath in and anchor it deep into your center as a huge golden light, like a warm beautiful summer sun begins to expand out into your aura from your center. Breathe and receive. Bring your attention back to your center and take a deep grounding breath in and go about your day, filled with anticipation of what's to come.

Digging a little deeper- Astrology a mirror to for your Soul

If you look at your own astrological chart you will begin to see that your personality is multifaceted, and the gifts that you brought into this lifetime are many. A whole new arena of understanding and possibilities begins to open up for you. Each path is an awakening for the Soul, and each awakening is filled with lessons and Soul growth. All of the many people, places and situations connected to our path are there for a reason. With each astrological placement on your chart, a map of your Soul and its mission begin to unfold. Great Soul lessons are learned from each one as we continue our journey. My astrological chart and its yearly transits provide me with key information on where my path is unfolding and what's next on the agenda. I suggest that you have your chart done at least once. I know you will be fascinated by its accuracy.

Soul challenges as gifts

I believe that the bigger the challenge the greater the gift. Remember we are all here to grow into the beautiful self-expression of spirit that dwells within our Soul. The ego would of course tell you otherwise, always creating the feeling that this just isn't enough. Your Soul however knows the difference and it is the essence of your Soul that brings joy and meaning to whatever you choose to do.

All of life is important, and your Soul can experience a variety of creative self-expressions along the way. So be the very best Mom, Dad, Doctor, Lawyer or Shaman you can be. Cherish the role that you are playing in your life, knowing that there is still more to unfold. Hold onto your goals and dreams lightly because in the blink of an eye your path may change. Remember that the gentle smile, the warm and understanding touch, the kind and generous word are the things that touch the lives of others. Now invite your angels and Soul guides in daily to take your Soul's hand to show you the way.

Let the angels fill your heart and Soul affirmations:

It's all in what you say and believe so here goes:

I say "Yes to life, and life says "Yes" to me."

From the inner space in my heart and Soul I am pure love

I am cherished and loved by my angels and all of the divine

I am a unique and light filled individual, spreading my Soul's gifts to all who cross my path

I support and respect those around me, as I am supported and respected

I have all the time I need to accomplish the inner stirrings of my Soul

I delight in other peoples accomplishments for we are all in this together

I am filled with divine light and choose to spread this light out into the world

I smile each day, everyday, and let go of all else

I release the past with ease and grace, taking the lessons and leaving the rest behind

I am confident, knowing that all that is unfolding is for my highest and best

I am peace, joy, love and light, and I attract back to me peace, joy, love and light

Abundance and prosperity flows to me and through me with ease and grace

I embrace all of who I am every molecule, every cell, and every strand of DNA

I am rich, I am well, I am happy, I am healthy; I am open to receiving the blessing of the universe. For this I am grateful, and so it is!

I open my heart and Soul fully now to my true Soul Mission

Soul Balance and Joy

As the body, mind and Soul come into balance, a beautiful friendship starts to unfold. The body is the vehicle for the Soul and encases this everlasting and beautiful part of your essence lifetime after lifetime. I believe before the body and Soul meet at birth that a grand conversation takes place. The Soul has its agenda and the body is there to accommodate. This is a contract made ahead of time to experience the Souls magnificence. The body is a lifetime and loving companion who helps the Soul to experience the lessons and the incredible possibilities in each lifetime.

Opening the Doors to your heart and Soul

Do you remember the last time you opened a door? Probably not – Doors are a natural part of everyday life. We rarely notice the movement that is created as we walk through many doors each and everyday. Normally we breeze through each door we open, but sometimes we might be carrying packages, or forgot our keys and can't open a door. Doors are an instrumental part of your Soul Journey. We have all heard the saying as one door closes another opens. One of the most important doors is the one that is placed before our heart and Soul. We really never think of a door being there, but if we use it as an analogy we can see that the energy of the door is present. Doors are essential and very beneficial in our lives. We use them to keep us safe, and often as barriers to pain that we might have experienced. Doors can truly be a turning point in our lives. From the time of our birth to the present we have opened hundreds of doors, and each one has been instrumental in our Soul's movement and growth.

Special Door Expansion Journey

Begin by taking a gentle breath in as you relax and surrender to this powerful process. Begin to see a pure flowing golden energy moving through your crown and bathing your mind, clearing it to open to its fullest creative capacity. Now see your mind being drenched in this rich golden clarity light over and over again. Take another gentle breath in and relax even more, knowing you are safe and secure and surrounded by your Angels and Soul Guides. Now bring your attention to your heart and Soul area – if you like you can place your hands over your heart and begin to feel the warmth from your hands pouring into your chest. Take another gentle breath in and feel this warmth moving through all resistance as you get closer and closer to your heart and Soul center.

Next bring your attention right outside of your heart area and begin to see the door to your heart. Allow it to reveal itself to you as you take another gentle breath in and feel its thickness – is it very thick or semi thick? What is the color of your door, and how does it make you feel? Does it feel like it truly serves a purpose at this time, and if so what purpose does it serve? Now take some gentle breaths in and out of your chest area. Settle into a state of peace. Be with your door for as long as needed, as you discover the gifts it has for you.

Now bring your full attention to your door now and imagine the most beautiful Divine companion as he or she comes and opens the door. Welcome this beloved companion and remain in this peaceful state with your loving Divine companion allowing your heart and Soul to be filled with expansion and light. Now come back to visit with your Divine companion and begin to ask any questions that you might have about the door that is over your heart. Ask why it is there if you like, or just talk to your Divine Companion about what you would like to accomplish as your Soul is ready to expand and open all doors in your life fully? Give your Divine Companion full permission to work with your throughout your new found Soul Mission, as together you expand into a state of pure clarity and wisdom. Bring your attention back into the room and stretch, knowing that you have just opened the Doors to our bright and brilliant life.

What does your current door look like?

What did it have to say? Share.

6 Powerful Special steps to Opening and Closing Doors:

Intention:

Deliberately decide to close the old door daily.

Resolution:

Be determined that with Divine Spirits guidance the door can be closed.

Clearing:

Ensure that nothing blocks the door's ability to be shut. Remove what keeps the opening obstructed by bathing it with the violet flame and turning it all over to your Angels & Soul Guides.

Strength:

Remind yourself that you are strong and can move mountains – remember a time when you did just that.

Belief:

Believe with all of your heart and Soul that is it possible to move forward. Affirm daily- *I can do it I believe in me!*

Gratitude:

Be forever grateful for everything – it is the Door that opens wide to all possibilities.

As each door is about to open most people do experience a bit of apprehension or *fear – let's turn this into movement and excitement, and say it is so!*

Embracing my Soul Prayer

I embrace you my beautiful Soul, all that you are now, and have been and all that you are becoming. Together with our Angels and Soul Guides we can move mountains, attain miracles, and spread our light out into the world. We will walk hand in hand on this amazing life journey, knowing that we are always being supported and loved by the Divine. The time is right so together we will bring in the joy, the peace and the light that is part of our true Soul Essence. And so it is! Amen

My Soul's Embrace Review:

Where did your Soul take you as you read this chapter?
Did you feel a shift taking place as you went on the journeys?
If so how did this make you feel?
What new doors are you ready to open?

Chapter Twenty One

A Soul Celebration

"I give and receive from the Universe in perfect balance"

Embracing your Soul's Abundance & Gifts from the Angels

Your soul has been on this Journey lifetime after lifetime, and a pure kaleidoscope of experiences have crossed your Soul's path. Your Soul has had the opportunity to experience abundance, for this Universe waits patiently to offer you great prosperity when you realize and believe that you are indeed deserving of it. My advice is to be here now, for your Soul's power lies in the present moment; the past is over, and the future is based on what we do, think, or say now. All we have is this moment and the next moment builds on the present moment, and each moment creates our future. The beauty of this new time on the planet is that we can change our thoughts. Changing our mind, changes our reality in the twinkling of an eye. Begin by using the term, "I Desire" This term has a powerful energy and connects deeply with your inner child's magic and your second chakra!

The Power of Intention:

Remembering that intention is the divine magic that is given to us at birth, we can create what we truly desire. We are a pure energetic bubble full of ideas, as we see that where there is intention, there is movement. It's time to harness your Soul's creative power to bring forth that which is truly for the good of us and for the planet. My angels and Soul guides have given me this process to share. Believe and receive! Use the process below, and remember, expanding your thinking expands your Soul! It is time to believe in and receive the abundant powers of this amazing universe. You are a gift and the gifts of the universe are yours.

Opening your Spiritual Bank and receiving your Soul rewards

From the time we are born until we die and are reborn, we carry with us a special spiritual bank, a golden piggy bank of sorts, which collects the many good deeds that we have done lifetime after lifetime. Each kind word, helpful deed and generous outpourings of love, begin to accumulate in our bank. Most people are unaware of having this wonderful gift that continues to sit and collect the very best parts of who we are. So I am about to teach you right here, right now, how to tune in and reap the rewards of this bountiful golden piggy bank in the sky.

The Light of Source process:

Before using the Prosperity process below, begin by attuning yourself to this special Source energy. This special energy is filled with unconditional love that helps us to see that we are truly worthy.

Bring your attention to your crown chakra and begin to see a pure golden crown being placed upon your head. Take a gentle breath in and allow the energies to flow from the top of your head to beneath the soles of your feet. Allow the energies to flow even further into the beautiful pulsating crystal in the center of Mother Earth. Feel yourself being held in pure grace, as you are supported by her generous grounding gift. One more gentle breath in and relax. Bring your attention back to the top of your head where you connect once more with your crown. In your mind's eye, look up into the heavens and begin to see a rich pillar of Source light flowing down until it begins to circulate through your crown chakra. It moves easily through the 12 petal crown that sits at the top of your head as it awakens your gift of receptivity. Allow it to flow for several moments and then see it moving directly down through our third eye, throat, heart and landing in the center of your Solar Plexus in the center of your stomach area. The golden light expands even more as it moves deep beneath your 3rd chakra into the twelve crystals that lay deep beneath the surface. Each crystal comes alive as the rich golden Source light pours through each one.

Now say, *I am one with Source and worthy of all good things.* You will begin to feel a sense of accomplishment and worthiness as it expands to fill your aura. Breathe in several times to expand this rich golden light until it reaches the tip of your aura and extend it out like a warm ray of sunshine towards everyone and everything. You have now harnessed this magical vehicle and will go about your day, drawing in the abundance of this giving and loving Universe.

As we ask, so shall we receive! Wonderful beliefs to embrace as you allow the universe to bless you with its many gifts!" I suggest you practice this every morning as you open your arms wide, feeling the rich golden light of abundance pouring down upon you. Try this for thirty days and begin to see that you are a light filled, lucky individual who is now ready to expand and receive the gifts of the universe. Remember you are a true creative being of light – and your thoughts create your world.

Creating a new story:

Imagine what you would like to see unfold and write it down. Write it out as if you already have it. Example:

I am now receiving more love and nurturing from those around me. I feel safe, happy and secure. I am able to express my emotions with ease, and I am going with the flow of energies that are now supporting these emotions. And so it is!

Using your Soul Journal, write down your deepest hearts desires as if they have manifested. *Beginning with I now have-*

Embracing my Soul affirmation

I am the Peace, I am the Power, I am the Light, I am the Love, I am the Joy, I am the energy that can now flow with ease and grace, and I give myself full permission to allow my Soul to soar into its perfection. I claim who I am in each moment of everyday, knowing that I am being held in the light of God, and the love of all of the Divine.

Know that you are on the right path, and that gifts will come if you continue to follow the path of grace that has been laid out before you. Each hunch, each intuitive stirring is connected to your Soul's deepest knowing, and when followed keeps you on this amazing path, free from worry or fear. Miracles flow along with the path of synchronicity, and with ease open us to our true mission and Soul contracts on the earth. Celebrate when you notice them and they will continue to unfold. Acknowledge them and smile, and the energies will keep flowing, as everything you could ever truly want or need, will be provided for your highest and best.

Remember that allowing doubt to creep in only takes you off the path, so tune in and begin to see yourself each morning stepping on the path of grace. Remember to ask for what you need, acknowledging it with gratitude when it shows up, and be grateful for the many gifts that are unfolding. Expect miracles and they will come. Begin to see that that there is a divine reason behind each miracle, and look deep into the lessons and gifts that are unfolding. Take each lesson and leave the rest behind, as you have faith in your Soul, and your divine plan, for as you do, your angels and guides can show you the way!

A loving reminder

Remember that you are a beautiful child of the Universe and deserve to be happy – So spread your wings and fly and embrace more of life's gifts, remembering to open your heart and Soul and say "Yes" as you continue to expand your horizons fearlessly. Know that that age is just a number -enjoy more fun, more love, more joy - be willing to tell others about your dreams for the now and the future - expand each dream to include that which is for your highest and best - and hold on lightly, knowing that something even better could be coming your way - embrace and acknowledge yourself, and all of your beauty and light, as your Angels and all of the Divine Smile.... remember that you are a blessing to the world, and that you are truly cherished and loved.

May you receive the blessings of this abundant universe! And so it is.

Embracing my Soul Prayer

As I reach up into the Heavens the answers pour down upon me with ease and grace. I affirm that I am one with God and worthy of all that is good, and my aura shimmers and shines with possibilities. Saying "Yes" to life and all its gifts is all I need to do, as the Universe begins to pour it blessings to me and through me from this day forward.
And so it is! Amen

My Soul's Embrace Review

After reading this book, how are you beginning to embrace your Soul? In the last chapter of My Soul's Embrace you will find and array 44 Special Channeled Messages, which are a gift from me to you. Each one is there to inspire, as you embrace your Soul's beauty and light.

Chapter Twenty Two

Daily Soul Affirmations

"I embrace the love and guidance from my Angels and Guides"

44 -Messages of Light from your Angels and
Soul Guides- given to me through special"

As My Souls Embrace comes to an end, I wanted to share extra special sprinkles of love and guidance from the Angels, Archangels, and Soul Guides, for they are with us always and will be working with you as you affirm your deepest hearts desires each day. Begin with day one, and continue to day forty four as your heart and Soul connects with the highest and most divine. Remember that you are created in the image of God and deserve all that is good!

Day One – Patience is the key today, trust that the highest and most divine sources are working with you for your highest and best. Stop for a moment or two and tune into their whispers and their light. Relax and listen, allowing your Angels and Guides to show you the way. Ask for a special sign as you go about your day, and when you see it smile. Know that you are going in the right direction for your highest and best. Enjoy your day! Enjoy your life!

I am patient as I embrace life and all its beauty

Day Two – To have Faith today is the greatest gift you can give to yourself and others. Embracing faith will help to strengthen you today, tomorrow and the day after that. Place your faith in the highest and the most divine, as your Soul and its many Guides help you to feel calm and safe. See and feel your faith growing each day, like a beautiful spring flower emerging from the ground. You are never alone, and faith will help you to move mountains, as your Soul expands with delight.

I am filled with faith, knowing all is unfolding perfectly in my world

Day Three – Thank you, Thank you, Thank you, for all that I have and all that is coming my way. I have so much to be grateful for today, and as I count each blessing my Soul smiles, knowing that I am opening the doors to greater abundance and light.

The abundance of the universe is mine

Day Four – I am aware of everything that surrounds me in this new day, and I have full acceptance of what is unfolding before me. My Soul knows that the lessons that are being learned today are monumental to its expansion and growth, and with acceptance I share my light with all who cross my path.

My life unfolds before me with ease and grace

Day Five – I choose to acknowledge my beauty and light in this new day. I acknowledge my desires, and that which makes me happy. I nurture myself as I reach out to others and acknowledge their light and their gifts. I stop for a moment and recognize who I truly am, a pure being of light, spreading my wisdom and knowledge out into the world.

My divine light shines out into the world for all to see

Day Six – Great wisdom is coming to me with ease and grace today, as I tune into my Soul Guides and all of the Divine. I call upon them today to show me that wisdom runs deep within me, and that I have all the wisdom I will ever need to move forward on my Souls path and Mission.

Wisdom flows through me and I am one with the light

Day Seven – Creativity blossoms within me and around me in this new day. My creative powers expand, as the doors to my Soul's deepest desires begin to manifest. My imagination flows freely, as my Angels and Soul Guides remind me that I am a co-creator with Source, and have the power to create with all of the Divine.

Creative power is a gift that I harbor within me
I choose to spread my creative power out into the world

Day Eight – I am free and flexible today as I explore the options that surround me. I embrace everything that comes my way with joy, as I freely and easily move through each situation with clarity and light.

I am a vehicle for great wisdom as I spread this
wisdom out into the world with joy

Day Nine – Love flows to me and through me in this new day. All hurt and anger are dissolved, connecting my heart and Soul with the purest and most divine love. I stop throughout my day and feel the gold rose ray of love flowing deep into my heart and Soul, and know that I am truly cherished and loved.

Pure love is who I am, as I delight in spreading
this love out into the world today

Day Ten – Rich luminous light shines down upon me today. My heart and Soul open wide to receive the light of the Universe, as I see that I am pure light. I share this light with all who cross my path, as it returns to me ten fold.

Light shines from within me out into the world as I feel my Soul smile

Day Eleven – I open my heart and Soul, as I allow vulnerability to be part of my day. I see that as I reach out and allow myself to give and receive love it returns to me ten fold. My Angels and Soul Guides help me today to dispel all fears, as I see that I am always protected and safe.

Glorious love surrounds me; I am safe, nurtured and loved

Day Twelve – I am a beautiful being of light. My Soul shines bright, and my heart begins to sing. My radiance shines upon others, and shines back to me again, as I see that I am so much more than I ever imagined. Today I choose to walk with my Soul's true beauty and light.

Radiant light flows from my heart and Soul out into the world

Day Thirteen – As I give out I receive back, I am filled with generosity today and everyday, as I give to those around me, and share the light and gifts of my Soul. I give freely, in an open and loving way, as my heart and Soul sing.

I rejoice in the beauty and the light that surrounds me in this new day

Day Fourteen – I breathe deeply throughout my day, as greater clarity flows up from my heart and Soul. My Angels and Soul Guides, communicate with me today with ease, as I open the channels of pure clarity and light.

Clarity is mine, as I see with eyes of love, and share my love with the world

Day Fifteen – I am rich in divine power, as knowledge flows from my heart and Soul today. I embrace the gift of knowledge and feel compelled to share it with those who cross my path in a loving and light filled way. Great confidence flows through me, as I see that I am a teacher, and that my knowledge is valuable and ready to be shared.

I love to share my wisdom and knowledge with others, I am confident in all things

Day Sixteen – Everything is unfolding perfectly today in my life. A pure path of synchronicity and grace surround me. I invite my Angels and Soul

Guides in to keep me on this light filled path, as I see that the Universe always provides.

*The Universe always provides, I am connected
on the path of synchronicity and grace*

Day Seventeen – Life flows to me and through me today, as I surrender over everything that is connected to my ego based thinking. My Soul comes alive, empowered and ready to guide me today on a path of pure understanding and faith. I relax and surrender all that is in my way, knowing that the answers are flowing to me with ease.

I honor all that I am and all that I am becoming, my Soul is alive and well

Day Eighteen – The truth will set my Soul free today, as I work from the place within myself of pure honesty and light. Love is the key as I am honest and loving in my communications, radiating pure honesty and light upon each situation.

I speak my truth and delight in the outcome

Day Nineteen – My Soul is open today and everyday to the healing that is abundant in my Universe. Rich healing light brings forth balance, and enhances the healer within me. I am healed, the world is healed and so it is!

I claim my healing now, I am whole, I am healthy, and I am healed

Day Twenty – My Soul is on a glorious adventure today, as I am open to all the possibilities that lay ahead. I delight in the energy of this adventure, as doors and opportunities begin to open, and grace flows into my life, filling my heart and Soul with joy.

Life is an amazing journey; I am free from all limitations

Day Twenty One – Wisdom surrounds me in this new day; it flows to me and through me with ease and with grace. My Angels and Soul Guides take my hand and together we walk the path of wisdom and light. My

Soul smiles, as it is nourished, knowing that its wisdom and knowledge are being shared with all whom cross my path.

I am nourished as great wisdom and knowledge are gifted to me today

Day Twenty Two – Humor fills the air today, as my Soul expands with great laughter and delight. I release all drama, as I see that I am at the helm of the ship, and can see humor in all situations. I laugh today and experience the pure delight and healing grace of humor.

Life is a joyful experience, filled with opportunities to laugh and sing

Day Twenty Three – I am strong, confident and positive today, as I look at each Divine happening in my life as just that! Divine! I forge forward on my path, knowing that I can accomplish anything I put my mind to, as my Angels and Soul guides walk hand in hand with me today and always.

Positive energies flow through me with every beat of my heart and Soul

Day Twenty Four – I value all that I am and all that I am becoming, as my Soul expands to receive. I am confident that all that is unfolding is for my highest and best, and I value myself as a being of light, love and peace.

My heart and Soul expand today to receive the highest and best

Day Twenty Five – Hand in Hand with my Angels and Soul Guides I walk in pure cooperation and light in this new day. I spread harmony to those who cross my path, and see both sides of the coin, as rich and lasting connections are made, and my heart and Soul sing.

*I am connected to the divine within me, as my
heart and Soul spreads harmony to all*

Day Twenty Six – New Beginnings are on the horizon today, as the energies around me shift and my Soul is about to expand. New ideas, people, places and situations surround me now, and I delight in the fresh ideas and faces that are coming my way. Fear dissolves, and I am confident that all is unfolding for my highest and best.

I welcome the New Beginnings that are on the
horizon today, I am fearless and free

Day Twenty Seven – I am filled with mercy today, as I look at each situation in my life with forgiveness and compassion. My heart and Soul open wide to receive this special gifts that comes from mercy, as great freedom flows throughout my being. I am released from all that has held me back, as I allow the gift of freedom into my life.

I am cleansed, I am clear, I am free

Day Twenty Eight – Kindness is the key in this new day. My heart and Soul are filled with compassion and light, as I spread kindness to all who cross my path. A simple smile, kind word and gentle hug, accompany me today, as I reach out with kindness and love, and my Soul expands to receive all the blessings of this abundant universe.

I am a kind and loving Soul, who is filled with compassion and love

Day Twenty Nine – My Soul is ready to explore all the many possibilities today. I am free to explore and expand my energies, as each gift expands my spirit, and enriches my life. I delight in all that I find, and know that everything has been put in front of me to enrich the depths of my Soul.

I am an explorer on the path of life, and I delight as each gift unfolds

Day Thirty – I am reminded today of how much I am loved and protected, knowing that Archangel Michael walks hand in hand with my Soul. I see that I am never alone and that Michael is filling me with courage and strength. I call upon him often and feel his blue ray of protection shining all around me. I am protected and safe.

I am safe, nurtured and loved

Day Thirty One – It's time to release the old to welcome the new, as my heart and Soul open freely to connect with the gifts of order and clarity in my life. Hand in hand with my Soul I walk together into my bright and brilliant future.

My bright and brilliant life is unfolding perfectly as my heart and Soul sing

Day Thirty Two – I give myself full permission today to imagine the life that I truly desire. My heart and Soul expand to accommodate each goal, each dream and each hearts desire, as I see and feel my beautiful life unfolding. I hold the vision of what I truly want; releasing all that no longer serves me, as my path of grace opens wide.

My imagination directs me towards my goals
and dreams with ease and grace

Day Thirty Three – My thoughts are directed today towards that which is for my highest and best. I ask my Angels and Soul guides to support and guide me on the way. Pure light shines down upon me, as each thought turns into the manifestation of my dreams.

I am always supported by my Angels, and Guides
as divine light shines down upon me

Day Thirty Four – With determination I know that all is possible. I align today with my strength, my willpower, and my purpose. My Soul and its mission are activated with ease. I am ready to succeed and so it is!

With great determination I align to my Soul and its
mission for I am ready and willing to succeed

Day Thirty Five – The essence of hope is surrounding me today. I see beauty and light as it shines down upon me. I know that in the right time and for my highest good, all is unfolding perfectly, and that as I engage in hope, it activates faith in all areas of my life.

I am filled with faith, as I see the beauty and the light that surround me

Day Thirty Six – My intuition is strong today, and I tune into it with ease. I am connected to my heart and Soul, and all of my intuitive centers, as I stop throughout my day to listen and receive the signs that surround me. I act only on my inner stirrings, and see that I am truly an intuitive being of light.

I am an intuitive being of light, acknowledging each sign that comes my way

Day Thirty Seven – As I stop throughout my day, I look within for the answers. With great introspection I can see that my Soul is guiding me, and that all is unfolding perfectly as I give myself the space to just be and receive.

I reflect on my life today, knowing that my Soul is guiding me, as I relax and receive

Day Thirty Eight – Pure peace and serenity surround me in this new day, as I am blanketed in rich golden light, and I feel nurtured, loved and safe. My Soul expands to receive these divine gifts, and I am at peace, as the light of God surrounds me.

I am in a blanket of pure peace and serenity today, surrounded by the light of God

Day Thirty Nine – My decisions are made from the deep well of knowledge, wisdom and power that lies deep within the resources of my Soul. I choose wisely as I tune into the guidance from my Angels, as they connect to my Soul with ease.

Great knowledge and wisdom come to the surface today with ease

Day Forty – My Soul is free, as all attachments that no longer serve me are released. Cords are cut, and all lower energies are released, as I feel the new and fresh and light filled energies flowing throughout my body, mind and Soul. I feel and see my aura expand with delight, as freedom reigns.

My Soul's Embrace

*My aura expands, my Soul is free, and I move
forward on my path of freedom*

Day Forty One – The riches of the universe are mine. Great prosperity and abundance flow down upon me, as I open my heart and Soul to receive. I release all that holds me back, as my spiritual bank opens wide. I allow these gifts, knowing that I am loved and deserve the very best.

*My spiritual bank opens wide, pouring down upon
me all the blessings of this abundant universe*

Day Forty Two – I am here today to celebrate, all that I am and all that I am becoming. My heart and Soul sing, as I celebrate the unique and light filled being that I am. I give back to myself in loving ways today, as I see that I am a gift, and loved in the eyes of my Angels and all of the Divine.

I celebrate the love that resides deep within my heart and Soul

Day Forty Three – The spirit of joy expands within my heart and Soul today as I see a rich liquid golden light flowing into my being. My heart sings as joy fills every nook and cranny, and I expand the gifts of joy out into the world to all who cross my path.

The power of Joy flows to me and through me today and always

Day Forty Four – I am light and carefree today, as I allow the energy of fun and play to energize my life. I dance, I sing, I romp and play, as my inner child comes alive. I give myself full permission to add fun back into my life from this day forward, as my inner Soul child spreads joy throughout my body, mind and spirit.

I spread my wings and fly, as fun and play are part of my day

Give your Soul full permission to be all that it was meant to be! Allow your Soul to expand and accumulate the knowledge and wisdom of the ages, and love your self for all of its uniqueness, beauty and light.

Your Soul is on an amazing adventure; remember to embrace its many gifts, knowing that you are truly cherished and loved.

Many Blessings

Rev. Cathi Burke, Angel of Light

Resources to expand your Horizons

The Angels of Light Healing & Intuitive Center
320 Washington Street, Norwell MA
www.angeloflightministry.com

Cristina Burke
Divine Healing Light
www.divinehealinglight.net

Divine Resources also include:
Books and Teachings by:

Americo Michael "Surrounded by Angels" by Cathi Burke
The Foundation for Inner Peace – A Course in Miracles

Author James Redfield - Celestine Prophecy

Authors Jerry & Ester Hicks

Rev. Kimberly Marooney, Author and Creator of the Angel Ministry

Author and Channel Lee Carroll – Kryon

Index of Divine Process's & Energy Tools for transformation

Printed in the United States
By Bookmasters